praise for america's test kitchen titles

"This 'very' Chinese cookbook from a father-son duo is a keeper. The book—ATK's first devoted to Chinese cooking—proves that you can teach and entertain in the same volume . . . All in all, it's one of the most charming works I've seen in years, and I already want to get a second copy."

Washington Post on *A Very Chinese Cookbook*

A Best Cookbook of 2023

New York Times on *A Very Chinese Cookbook*

"This comprehensive guide is packed with delicious recipes and fun menu ideas but its unique draw is the personal narrative and knowledge-sharing of each ATK chef, which will make this a hit."

Booklist on *Gatherings*

"An exhaustive but approachable primer for those looking for a 'flexible' diet. Chock-full of tips, you can dive into the science of plant-based cooking or just sit back and enjoy the 500 recipes."

Minneapolis Star Tribune on *The Complete Plant-Based Cookbook*

Best Overall Mediterranean Cookbook 2022

Runner's World on *The Complete Mediterranean Cookbook*

"Here are the words just about any vegan would be happy to read: 'Why This Recipe Works.' Fans of America's Test Kitchen are used to seeing the phrase, and now it applies to the growing collection of plant-based creations in *Vegan for Everybody*."

Washington Post on *Vegan for Everybody*

"True to its name, this smart and endlessly enlightening cookbook is about as definitive as it's possible to get in the modern vegetarian realm."

Men's Journal on *The Complete Vegetarian Cookbook*

"A mood board for one's food board is served up in this excellent guide . . . This has instant classic written all over it."

Publishers Weekly (starred review) on *Boards: Stylish Spreads for Casual Gatherings*

"Reassuringly hefty and comprehensive, *The Complete Autumn and Winter Cookbook* by America's Test Kitchen has you covered with a seemingly endless array of seasonal fare . . . This overstuffed compendium is guaranteed to warm you from the inside out."

NPR on *The Complete Autumn and Winter Cookbook*

"If you're one of the 30 million Americans with diabetes, *The Complete Diabetes Cookbook* by America's Test Kitchen belongs on your kitchen shelf."

Parade.com on *The Complete Diabetes Cookbook*

"Another flawless entry in the America's Test Kitchen canon, *Bowls* guides readers of all culinary skill levels in composing one-bowl meals from a variety of cuisines."

BuzzFeed Books on *Bowls*

Cookbook Award Winner of 2021 in the Single Subject category

International Association of Culinary Professionals (IACP) on *Foolproof Fish*

"The book's depth, breadth, and practicality makes it a must-have for seafood lovers."

Publishers Weekly (starred review) on *Foolproof Fish*

"*The Perfect Cookie* . . . is, in a word, perfect. This is an important and substantial cookbook . . . If you love cookies, but have been a tad shy to bake on your own, all your fears will be dissipated. This is one book you can use for years with magnificently happy results."

HuffPost on *The Perfect Cookie*

"The book offers an impressive education for curious cake makers, new and experienced alike. A summation of 25 years of cake making at ATK, there are cakes for every taste."

Wall Street Journal on *The Perfect Cake*

"In this latest offering from the fertile minds at America's Test Kitchen the recipes focus on savory baked goods. Pizzas, flatbreads, crackers, and stuffed breads all shine here . . . Introductory essays for each recipe give background information and tips for making things come out perfectly."

Booklist (starred review) on *The Savory Baker*

"The go-to gift book for newlyweds, small families, or empty nesters."

Orlando Sentinel on *The Complete Cooking for Two Cookbook*

Cookbook Award Winner of 2021 in the General category

International Association of Culinary Professionals (IACP) on *Meat Illustrated*

"*Five-Ingredient Dinners* is as close to a sure thing to an easy meal as you'll find . . . If you want to get cooking, cut down on takeout, and deliver a ton of flavor, you can't lose with these recipes."

Providence Journal on *Five-Ingredient Dinners*

baking *for* two

200+ Small-Batch Recipes, from Lazy Bakes to Layer Cakes

America's Test Kitchen

Library of Congress Cataloging-in-Publication Data has been applied for.

ISBN 978-1-954210-99-8

America's Test Kitchen
21 Drydock Avenue, Boston, MA 02210

Printed in China
10 9 8 7 6 5 4 3 2 1

Distributed by
Penguin Random House Publisher Services
Tel: 800.733.3000

Pictured on front cover From-the-Freezer Cinnamon Buns (page 298)

Pictured on back cover Chocolate-Raspberry Torte (page 130), Pound Cakes (page 114), Chocolate Crinkle Cookies (page 34), Pear and Bacon Flatbread (page 325)

Editorial Director, Books Adam Kowit

Executive Food Editor Dan Zuccarello

Deputy Food Editor Stephanie Pixley

Executive Managing Editor Debra Hudak

Senior Editors Camila Chaparro, Joe Gitter, Sacha Madadian, and Sara Mayer

Test Cooks Olivia Counter, Carmen Dongo, Laila Ibrahim, José Maldonado, Stephanie Winter, and David Yu

Kitchen Interns Brooke Calhoun and Eva Mehr

Additional Kitchen Support Lee Tan

Contributing Editor Cheryl Redmond

Assistant Editor Julia Arwine

Design Director Lindsey Timko Chandler

Associate Art Director Kylie Alexander

Photography Director Julie Bozzo Cote

Senior Photography Producer Meredith Mulcahy

Senior Staff Photographers Steve Klise and Daniel J. van Ackere

Staff Photographers Kritsada Panichgul and Kevin White

Additional Photography Beth Fuller, Joseph Keller, and Carl Tremblay

Food Styling Joy Howard, Sheila Jarnes, Catrine Kelty, Chantal Lambeth, Gina McCreadie, Kendra McNight, Ashley Moore, Christie Morrison, Marie Piraino, Elle Simone Scott, and Kendra Smith

Senior Print Production Specialist Lauren Robbins

Production and Imaging Coordinator Amanda Yong

Production and Imaging Specialist Tricia Neumyer

Production and Imaging Assistant Chloe Petraske

Copy Editor Deri Reed

Proofreader Ann-Marie Imbornoni

Indexer Elizabeth Parson

Chief Executive Officer Dan Suratt

Chief Content Officer Dan Souza

Executive Editorial Directors Julia Collin Davison and Bridget Lancaster

Senior Director, Book Sales Emily Logan

contents

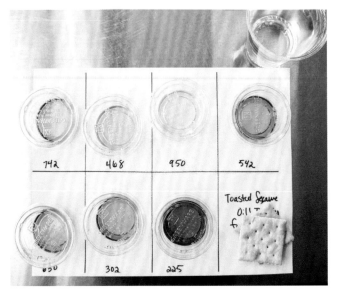

welcome to america's test kitchen

This book has been tested, written, and edited by the folks at America's Test Kitchen, where curious home cooks become confident cooks. Located in Boston's Seaport District in the historic Innovation and Design Building, it features 15,000 square feet of kitchen space including multiple photography and video studios. It is the home of *Cook's Illustrated* magazine and *Cook's Country* magazine and is the workday destination for more than 60 test cooks, editors, and cookware specialists. Our mission is to empower and inspire confidence, community, and creativity in the kitchen.

We start the process of testing a recipe with a complete lack of preconceptions, which means that we accept no claim, no technique, and no recipe at face value. We simply assemble as many variations as possible, test a half dozen of the most promising, and taste the results blind. We then construct our own recipe and continue to test it, varying ingredients, techniques, and cooking times until we reach a consensus. As we like to say in the test kitchen, "We make the mistakes so you don't have to." The result is our best version of every recipe. We use the same rigorous approach when we test equipment and taste ingredients.

All of this would not be possible without a belief that good cooking, much like good music, is based on a foundation of objective technique. Some people like spicy foods and others don't, but there is a right way to sauté, there is a best way to cook a pot roast, and there are measurable scientific principles involved in producing perfectly beaten, stable egg whites. Our ultimate goal is to investigate the fundamental principles of cooking to give you the techniques, tools, and ingredients you need to become a better cook. It is as simple as that.

To see what goes on behind the scenes at America's Test Kitchen, check out our social media channels for kitchen snapshots, exclusive content, video tips, and much more. You can watch us work (in our actual test kitchen) by tuning in to *America's Test Kitchen* or *Cook's Country* on public television or on our websites.

Listen to *Proof* (AmericasTestKitchen.com/podcasts) to hear engaging, complex stories about people and food. Want to hone your cooking skills or finally learn how to bake—with an America's Test Kitchen test cook? Enroll in one of our online cooking classes.

However you choose to visit us, we welcome you into our kitchen, where you can stand by our side as we test our way to the best recipes in America.

 facebook.com/AmericasTestKitchen
 instagram.com/TestKitchen
 youtube.com/AmericasTestKitchen
 tiktok.com/@TestKitchen
 x.com/TestKitchen
 pinterest.com/TestKitchen

AmericasTestKitchen.com
OnlineCookingSchool.com

join our community of recipe testers
Our recipe testers provide valuable feedback on recipes under development by ensuring that they are foolproof in home kitchens. Help the America's Test Kitchen book team investigate the how and why behind successful recipes from your home kitchen.

baking smaller, better, and more often

Baking isn't essential. And that's why it's wonderful. You don't need a chocolate chip cookie after dinner; but biting into one, with its crisp edges, chewy center, and warm, gooey pockets of chocolate, creates a comfort you can get from little else. When there are only two people indulging, however, baking a batch of cookies, or anything else, is more likely to fall off the schedule, reserved for when you might justify (or hand off) all the extra brownies, or mark a holiday with a 12-inch cake. But you shouldn't have to live with days of leftovers to bake some brownies, or invite over a crowd of guests to rip into chewy rolls at dinner, or throw a big birthday party to celebrate with a festive cake. And that's why America's Test Kitchen has tackled our next for-two project, to encourage you to make something wonderful, whenever.

A good small-batch recipe can be hard to find. We don't recommend you scale down your favorite recipe. If you've tried, you know what it's like to divide that one egg in half, hoping you capture the perfect amount of white and yolk and, hands shaking, pile a third of a teaspoon of baking soda into your spoon. And that's before you play Goldilocks with your baking pans to find something that seems right—and hope your baked good turns out.

We stopped halving eggs and measuring out odd amounts of ingredients years ago, and we have created countless tricks to bake smaller batches of sweet and savory goods in the perfect amount. Sometimes that's two microwave mug cakes, two monkey breads (formed with store-bought biscuit dough), or a bubbly fruit crisp baked in a 10-inch skillet to satisfy cravings—all without fuss or even a trip to the store. Other times that's four cupcakes or apple turnovers—because two dozen are too many, but having a couple extra to be enjoyed later can make the next day just as sweet. Or that's six buttermilk biscuits that you can freeze before baking so you can pull out two or a few at a time to bake.

The freezer, in fact, will become your best friend, one that makes it easy to bake even on your busiest days. You can turn your freezer into a treat factory, storing individual cookies, rolls, biscuits, croissants, Danish, and more. Take our From-the-Freezer Cinnamon Buns: You make them, shape them, portion them, and freeze them so you can bake as many as you like—one or all six—for a no-effort brunch. Do the same with muffin batter to start any day of the week with a warm treat. Reach into a bag of frozen cookie dough disks to bake a single-serve sweet. Or put two frozen sun-dried tomato Danish in the oven for 15 minutes— the time it takes to make a salad—and you have dinner. We've engineered all the recipes to withstand the cold, drying environ- ment of the freezer—whether that's by adjusting the moisture content or adding more leavener—so frozen baked goods taste just as good as those baked fresh. The freezer is also the place for workhorse doughs (both homemade and store-bought) that jump-start future baked projects—pizza dough, pie and tart crust, puff pastry, and phyllo. With these, you have a leg up on garlicky breadsticks, a 6-inch cherry pie, turnovers like pastelitos, and a savory phyllo pie filled with summer vegetables.

Our hope is that you will bake small-batch recipes often and at whim, so we've designed them to be flexible. Many of our recipes offer the option to swap one baking pan for another based on what you own or love. You can bake just two muffins in a 12-cup muffin tin if that's what you have. Small springform pans are recommended and convenient, but we'll show you how to make a special foil sling to extract delicate cakes from a regular cake pan instead. Bake bar cookies in a loaf pan, small skillet, cake pan, or ramekins—you're likely to find one of those in your cabinet. Portion pound cake batter into mini Bundt pans—well, just because. And if heating the oven on a summer day to make two blueberry crumbles is a source of hesitation, you can bake nearly all of the recipes in the book in the toaster oven. Or select one of the 35 recipes that come with full air-fryer instructions (you can even make cheesecake in there!).

The barriers to baking for two have been lifted when you have a freezer stash of disks of buttery tart dough ready to be filled with fresh summer fruit; an easy recipe for a couple maple-glazed scones you can bake in your air fryer; easy pizzas that keep delivery (and its cold morning leftovers) away; and a slew of other craving-ready recipes like chocolaty banana bread and dreamy tahini parfaits to satisfy your sweet tooth. And we think that's wonderful.

equipment corner

While you likely already have the standard tools for baking—bowls for mixing, spatulas for folding, whisks for whipping—here are a few items that make it easier to work with smaller amounts of batter and dough.

food processor

For small-scale kitchen prep, you don't need a mini processor: The cup capacity of a food processor is less important than the gap between the blade and the bottom of the bowl, which should be small. Our winning processor, the **Cuisinart Custom 14 Cup Food Processor**, fits the bill with a compact, streamlined design that takes up less space than most food processors despite its large capacity. Look for a processor that has a powerful motor and is easy to use and clean. A basic set of blades is enough for most tasks. Certainly, if you have a 9- or 11-cup processor it will also work well for our recipes.

mini offset spatula

A small angled spatula offers great control when you're spreading batter in tight spaces like a mini-loaf pan or 6-inch cake pan, or when icing a tiny layer cake. Look for a sturdy spatula with a comfortable grip and a blade that's about 4½ inches long. Our favorite is the **Wilton 9-Inch Angled Spatula**.

small wire rack

In addition to its obvious function as a cooling rack, a wire rack set in a rimmed baking sheet becomes the perfect surface for glazing and decorating cakes and cookies. Look for a strong rack with wires in a grid pattern. Our favorite is the **Checkered Chef Quarter Sheet Cooling/Baking Rack**. The rack provides enough space to cool a dozen cookies yet still fits inside a quarter sheet pan (with a little wiggle room), which we find ourselves reaching for often (see page 4).

oven mitts

For reaching into tight spaces and grabbing hot small pans, you want a combination of protection and dexterity; fabric-lined silicone mitts, such as our favorite **OXO Silicone Oven Mitts**, give you the best of both worlds. The silicone is heavily textured for better grip, and the flexibility of the material lets you easily pinch thin cookie sheets and small handles or knobs.

essential pans for small-batch baking

You don't need a new collection of pans to bake on a small scale. You might already own a 10-inch skillet, standard loaf pan, or muffin tin. Here are the basics we turn to most often; stock your kitchen with them so you can bake whenever the mood strikes.

loaf pans

A standard 8½ by 4½-inch loaf pan is the right size for baking just six brownies or bars, a snack cake, or a scaled-down fruit crisp or cobbler. For small-batch quick breads, a 5½ by 3-inch mini-loaf pan produces loaves with a nice crust and a sliceable shape. We like the **USA Pan Loaf Pan, 1 lb Volume** and the **Chicago Metallic Set of 4 Mini Loaf Pans**.

10-inch skillet

Not only can a skillet simmer and sauté, it can also act as a baking dish: Fruit desserts such as Apple Crisp (page 52) call for cooking the filling in a skillet (traditional, nonstick, or cast-iron) and then topping and baking. You can make a cast-iron pizza with cheesy edges or bar cookies with nice browning in skillets as well.

muffin tin

In addition to muffins, you can use a muffin tin for individual pastries and mini quick breads. We've found that it doesn't affect the quality of your baked goods if you don't fill all the cups in a muffin tin, so a standard 12-cup tin is fine for small-batch baking. You can also use a smaller one. Our favorites are the **OXO Good Grips Non-Stick Pro 12 Cup Muffin Pan** and the **Williams Sonoma Goldtouch Pro Muffin Pan, 6-Well**. That said, if you bake in an air fryer, you will need a 4-cup tin so it fits in the machine.

ramekins

We use ramekins in several sizes and in a multitude of ways. They're ideal for custards, of course, but also for fruit desserts and bread pudding. The smallest one we use, a 4-ounce ramekin, makes a handy baking vessel for muffins and brownies, especially in the air fryer. The largest, a 16-ounce ramekin, bakes a cake sized for two that rises high, perfect for cutting into layers.

6-inch cake pan

A small round cake pan works well for both single- and double-layer cakes and is also good for brownies and bars. We prefer the **Williams Sonoma Goldtouch Pro Nonstick Round Cake Pan**.

6-inch pie plate

It's a necessity for pies, but this pan is also handy when rolling cookies in sugar or pressing dough for empanadas. Ceramic and glass plates work equally well when baking pies of this size.

digital scale

Weighing is not only the most accurate way of measuring ingredients, it's also the easiest—especially when you're measuring small amounts. Using a digital scale with a tare function, you can measure ingredients directly into your mixing bowl and reset the displayed weight to zero between each addition—no need to fuss with measuring cups. Our favorite is the **OXO Good Grips 11 lb Food Scale with Pull Out Display**.

13 inches
9 inches
quarter

6 inches
9 inches
eighth

half

18 inches
13 inches

there's no baking without a baking sheet

A baking sheet is one of our most reached-for pieces of kitchen equipment no matter what we're making. In our full-scale recipes, when we call for a rimmed baking sheet, we mean standard half sheet pans, the most common size used in the home kitchen. But small-batch baking increases the opportunities for employing smaller pans. It's convenient to store and use eighth and quarter sheet pans so we love those too. For many baked goods, the size of the baking sheet doesn't have any effect on the outcome: It's fine to bake off one biscuit on an expansive half sheet pan, for example.

In some cases, though, size does matter—like when you need to stretch dough or spread batter to the edges of the pan. For mini cakes (see page 120) and slab pies (see pages 162 and 164), you'll want an eighth sheet pan (9 by 6 inches) with a rim. This pan is also convenient for using in your toaster oven. A quarter sheet pan, which is 13 by 9 inches, is the right size for focaccia and sheet-pan pizza. Our favorite rimmed baking sheets of all sizes are made by **Nordic Ware Naturals**.

mixing things up

If you have a hand mixer, there are plenty of recipes in this book where you can use it—it's particularly good at mixing recipes that have a very small volume of batter, such as our Olive Oil Cake (page 105). But while you could get away with owning just a hand mixer for baking sweet treats and quick breads, the mixer doesn't have the power to knead bread dough. We recommend owning a 4.5- or 5-quart stand mixer if you're baking for a small household (we developed the recipes in this book in a 4.5-quart stand mixer). They handle most small quantities of batter and knead small amounts of dough perfectly for proper gluten development.

What if you own a 6-quart stand mixer? Many people do, as it's a market standard. In this roomier mixer, it takes longer for the attachments to engage low-volume batters or doughs and for them to achieve the expected visual cues, so use your intuition; you will encounter longer mixing and kneading times.

specialty pans we love

If you love to bake, these pans will earn their space in your kitchen. Whether it's for their fun shapes or their handy features, they'll expand the range of what you can make.

6-inch springform pan

This pan isn't just for cheesecake (but you'll love our Basque Cheesecake on page 145). We use it for cake that can't be inverted from a standard cake pan; for example, we use a springform pan for our Olive Oil Cake on page 105, to preserve its crackly top. (You can also seek out 4½-inch springform pans for our Individual New York Cheesecakes on page 142.)

4-inch tart pans

These fluted pans with removable bottoms make it simple to turn out perfectly formed personal-size tarts, like our Walnut Tartlets (page 184). They make elegance easy.

mini bundt pans

Using a Bundt pan is an automatic path to an impressive-looking cake, and that effect is magnified when you go small. A mini Bundt pan turns out cakes with crisply patterned shapes, ready for a simple dusting of sugar or drizzle of icing to take them to the next level. We like the **Nordic Ware Platinum Anniversary Bundtlette Pan** which looks like a muffin tin. You can also buy individual baby Bundts, but we find the tray-style pan easier to use. While the pans are mostly interchangeable, the size can vary across brands, so you may get more or fewer cakes out of the same amount of batter depending on the model you have. Check cakes early and often and adjust bake times accordingly. Also note that darker pans will affect the browning of your cakes.

popover pan

You can make decent popovers in a muffin tin, but the open design of a popover pan allows more hot air to surround each cup, helping to produce tall, bronzed, airy popovers. Our winning pan is the **Chicago Metallic 6-Cup Popover Pan, Non-Stick**.

madeleine pan

Madeleines (page 40), those moist and light shell-shaped cake-cookie hybrids, can be made in a multitude of flavors and enjoyed any time. With its signature indentations, a madeleine pan is a single-use pan you'll find yourself reaching for on multiple occasions.

The **KitchenAid Classic Series 4.5 Quart Tilt-Head Stand Mixer** is our favorite mid-priced mixer, and it is ideal for any recipe in this book that calls for a stand mixer. This basic, compact, heavy machine can produce billowy egg whites as capably as a batch of pizza dough, and its beater height is adjustable. Note: If you own the **KitchenAid Artisan Mini 3.5 Quart Tilt-Head Stand Mixer**, we like it and it handles batters well. It can knead the doughs in this book but isn't the best at larger batches.

Our favorite hand mixer is the **Breville Handy Mix Scraper**. It's powerful (it can handle stiff cookie dough) and works quickly, with wide beater heads that make for efficient mixing and zero clogging. It's designed with features that make mixing more convenient, including a timer and a light that shines into the mixing bowl.

the best mixers for small-batch baking

Hand mixer: Good for cake batters and cookie doughs

4.5-Quart Stand Mixer*: Good for batters and bread doughs (and most everything else)

*A 6-quart stand mixer can also be used but will take longer to mix batters and knead doughs.

choose your pan adventure

You'll find all kinds of sized-down vessels for small-batch baking on the market. Some work better than others for certain baked goods or when baking in a toaster oven or air fryer (see pages 18 and 20). But you can often choose what pan to use based on what you own (or how cute you want your baked goods to look). Recipes that can be baked in more than one kind of vessel include a **Pan Swap** that lists your options and any recipe modifications. Here's a roundup of what you can use to make various baked goods, and how each pan affects the finished result.

layer cakes

Choose your pan for our Vanilla and Chocolate Cakes (pages 119–120) based on the look and number of layers you're going for. For information on assembling different shaped mini layer cakes, see pages 122–124.

option 1	option 2	option 3
6-inch round cake pan	16-ounce ramekin	6 by 9-inch pan (eighth sheet pan)
Cakes baked in this pan can be frosted as is, or split into two layers before frosting for the classic birthday-cake look.	*Slightly taller and narrower than a 6-inch cake pan, this dish produces a high-rise cake that can be sliced into three elegant layers. The longer baking time means that the crust becomes nicely golden. Sometimes the ramekin produces a domed top, which you can slice off if desired.*	*This pan creates a thin, quick-baking cake that can be sliced and stacked for a sleek rectangular look.*

snack cakes and pound cake

Snack cakes are a casual affair so don't panic about pans. Our snack cakes (see pages 107–108) and coffee cake (see page 112) can be either round or rectangular. And pound cake (see page 114) is flexible too: It can be dressed up or down based on the pan you use.

option 1	option 2	option 3
6-inch round cake pan	8½ by 4½-inch loaf pan	mini bundt pans *(pound cake only)*
This pan allows you to cut wedge-shaped slices of cake.	*The standard loaf pan yields square pieces of cut cake that have proportionately more crust than those baked in a round pan–good for snack cakes.*	*Our pound cake gives you an additional option: You can bake it as two elegant individual Bundt cakes (gorgeous with a filling of fruit or whipped cream in the center).*

Four different ways to bake bars

brownies and bars

While a standard-size loaf pan is perfect for baking small-batch brownies and bars, these swaps each provide different textures and shapes.

option 1	*option 2*	*option 3*	*option 4* (brownies and blondies only)
8½ by 4½-inch loaf pan	**6-inch cake pan**	**8-inch cast-iron skillet**	**muffin tin or ramekins**
With a perimeter of 38 inches, this is the pan of choice if you're a brownie edge aficionado. It's also the one if you're after the traditional square slice.	*A smaller surface area than the loaf pan means cake-pan bars are thicker, with a higher proportion of the soft interior. You can slice them into squares (with rounded pieces around the perimeter) or wedges.*	*The heat-retaining property of cast iron means a more pronounced crust on our bars, if you're into that. Cut the bars in wedges for great crisp-chewy texture contrast.*	*Use these for personal brownies and blondies that are chunky, superportable—and supercute.*

Three different ways to bake quick breads

quick breads

You probably think of a quick bread as a single loaf, but the batter for any of our quick breads on pages 276–281 can be distributed among individual-size vessels as well.

option 1	option 2	option 3
5½ by 3-inch loaf pan	**muffin tin**	**4-ounce ramekins**
A loaf is the iconic shape for these moist, sturdy baked goods. Choose this petite pan for nice flat slices encircled with a golden crust—great for toasting, spreading with cream cheese, and/or topping with fruit.	The smaller size of a muffin cup means each item has a high ratio of crust to crumb and is also perfect for popping into a lunch bag.	Ramekins are the vessel of choice for baking quick bread in an air fryer or toaster oven, or if you want to serve right out of the vessel.

muffins and cupcakes

Many people own a muffin tin, and you can use any size in the oven, no matter the number of muffins you're making. But ramekins support muffin batter all the same and give similarly great results.

option 1	option 2
4-cup, 6-cup, or 12-cup muffin tin	4-ounce ceramic ramekins
A nonstick muffin tin (any size that will fit in the appliance you use for baking) yields muffins with lightly domed tops, golden-brown crusts, and a moist crumb, and the muffins easily release once baked.	Ramekins have straighter sides so muffins will be a slightly different shape and may have less doming on top. Within their thick walls, muffins bake gently and evenly and turn out nicely browned. Ramekins are also handy when using air fryers and toaster ovens.

muffin-tin myth buster

It's commonly taught that if you're making a small batch of muffins, you should fill the empty cups with water. Proponents of this practice contend that it prevents the pan from warping and acts as a "heat sink" to ensure that cupcakes next to empty cups heat evenly. We tested this theory by baking one muffin tin completely filled with batter, one tin in which six of the cups were filled with batter and the remaining six with water, and one tin in which six of the cups were filled with batter and the remaining six left empty. The results? All the muffins had the same height, texture, and color and none of the tins warped. This actually makes sense: In a full 12-cup muffin tin, all but the two center cupcakes are directly exposed to the oven's heat on at least one side to no ill effect.

crisps, crumbles, and cobblers

A skillet is often the most streamlined choice, but if you're baking a fruit dessert in a toaster oven, you'll need to make a switch.

option 1	option 2	option 3
10-inch ovensafe skillet	2½- to 3½-cup casserole dish	8½ by 4½-inch loaf pan
With an ovensafe skillet (stainless, cast-iron, or nonstick), you can parcook the fruit filling on the stovetop, add your topping, and bake the dessert all in the same pan.	Use this if you want to bake in a toaster oven rather than the oven. You'll need to transfer the filling from the skillet to the casserole dish before topping and baking. Any shape of dish is fine, and it makes for a nice presentation if you want to serve dessert at the table.	This option is less fancy than a casserole dish but just as practical, good when you plan to bake off a fruit cobbler, crumble, or crisp in the toaster oven.

the impromptu baker's pantry

Baking isn't just about having a fancy dessert—it's about satisfying a late-night chocolate craving, keeping something easy on hand for breakfast before a busy day, or making a weeknight dessert on a whim. For times like these, small-batch baking often proves ideal. For baking on any scale, you probably know to have eggs, sugar, flour, butter, and a dairy product on hand. Here are some non-perishable and longer-life items we recommend you always keep to enjoy last-minute baking anytime.

flour and grains

Chances are if you're baking you're using some kind of flour. But packages are large (and grains are more affordable in bulk), and you may work slowly through one if your household is small.

store them

Store whole-wheat and other whole-grain flours, and grains such as cornmeal and oats, in airtight containers or zipper-lock bags in the freezer. If you use all-purpose flour especially slowly, you can store that in the freezer as well. To ensure that baked goods rise properly, let flour come to room temperature before using.

use them

Flaky Whole-Wheat Buttermilk Biscuits (page 246), Blue Cheese–Apple Rye Scones (page 254), Corn Muffins (page 263), No-Knead Mini Country Boule (page 284), Apple Crisp (page 52), Whole-Wheat Carrot Snack Cake (page 108), Mini Cider-Glazed Apple-Spelt Bundt Cakes (page 116)

buttermilk and sour cream

Buttermilk and sour cream are common additions to our batters and doughs for flavor (tang) and texture (tenderness).

store them

These dairy products last up to three weeks in the fridge. Buttermilk can lose its flavor over time; to keep it longer, pour or spoon excess into ice cube trays and pop them in the freezer. Once the cubes are solid, transfer to zipper-lock bags and store in the freezer for up to a month. To use, either microwave cubes at medium power or defrost in the refrigerator overnight. Whisk if separated.

use them

Easiest-Ever Drop Biscuits (page 240), Brown Soda Bread (page 283), Vanilla Cupcakes (page 102), Individual New York Cheesecakes (page 142), Cheese Bread with Feta and Nigella (page 276)

chocolate, chocolate chips, and cocoa powder

We think many impromptu bakers turn to desserts that require one (or more) of these. (Sometimes you need that fix!)

store them

Because cocoa butter easily picks up off-flavors, don't store chocolate in the refrigerator or freezer. Store it tightly wrapped in a cool, dry place. Also: Don't throw away any cocoa powder that's past its expiration date, even by a couple of years. The compounds that give cocoa powder its flavor can last for several years without a decrease in quality.

use them

Chocolate Crinkle Cookies (page 34), Molten Chocolate Microwave Mug Cakes (page 100), Chocolate Cake (page 120), Chocolate Chunk Financiers (page 129), Chocolate Banana Bread (page 279)

cream cheese

Cream cheese is used in cake frosting and to make its namesake (cheese) cake, but the spread is surprisingly useful beyond those applications, often the perfect ingredient to bring together a creamy filling without opening a large package of perishable cheese.

store it

Always keep cream cheese refrigerated, unless you need to soften it (at room temperature) for a recipe, and be mindful of the expiration date. Wrap an opened package of cream cheese in its foil

wrapper, and then enclose it in plastic wrap; stored carefully, it should last up to 10 days.

use it
Basque Cheesecake (page 145), Icebox Strawberry Pie (page 154), Guava and Cheese Pastelitos (page 195), Everything Bagel Danish (page 196)

dried fruit
We fold dried fruit into cookies, scones, and breads for pops of flavor, and use it to boost the flavor in fresh fruit desserts without adding more moisture.

store it
Stored in airtight containers in the pantry, packaged dried fruit will keep for about a year unopened. Once opened, it will continue to dry out over time. You can re-plump dried fruit by soaking it for a few minutes in boiling water and then draining.

use it
British-Style Currant Scones (page 250), Cherry-Pecan Crumble (page 58), Apple Strudel (page 207), Oatmeal Raisin Cookies (page 30), Brown Soda Bread with Currants and Caraway (page 283)

frozen fruit
When you turn to frozen fruit, you can have a fresh, bright dessert no matter what season it is.

store it
In addition to buying bags of already-frozen fruit, you can easily freeze fresh fruit such as bagged cranberries. As long as it's well wrapped, frozen fruit will last up to a year.

use it
Lemon Blueberry Muffins (page 257), Cherry Streusel Bars (page 48), Strawberry-Rhubarb Crumble (page 61), Cranberry Upside-Down Cake (page 138)

maple syrup
Maple syrup is a favorite condiment to have on hand and it also adds complex sweetness to baked goods.

store it
Unopened containers of maple syrup can be stored in the pantry. Once you open the container, transfer the syrup to the refrigerator where it should last for about a year, or repack it in smaller glass vessels such as Mason jars to store in the freezer. If the syrup crystallizes, a zap in the microwave will restore it.

use it
Maple-Pecan Scones with Maple Glaze (page 253)

nuts and nut flour
Nuts add richness or texture to all kinds of baked goods as a mix-in, topping, or the main ingredient. They're great to buy in bulk, but they're high in fat, so they spoil easily.

store them

Place nuts in a zipper-lock bag, press out the air, and seal. Keep in the freezer for up to one year. There's no need to defrost them before chopping and using.

use them

Lemon, Blueberry, and Almond Parfaits (page 88), Chocolate-Pecan Slab Pie (page 162), Walnut Tartlets (page 184), Zucchini Bread (page 280), Chocolate-Raspberry Torte (page 130), Ultranutty Pecan Bars (page 46), Pear-Walnut Upside-Down Cake (page 141)

instant espresso powder

Sometimes we call for espresso powder in chocolate recipes even when coffee flavor isn't the goal. Just a pinch amplifies chocolate flavor considerably without imparting a noticeable coffee presence. Or use more to create a mocha flavoring. Either way, it's one of the most convenient flavor-boosters in your small-batch baking arsenal.

store it

Kept in the original jar, espresso powder will keep in your pantry for up to one year.

use it

Chocolate Crinkle Cookies (page 34) Individual Mocha Soufflés (page 78), Chocolate Ermine Frosting (page 126), Molten Mocha Microwave Mug Cakes (page 101), Chocolate-Raspberry Torte (page 130)

pie, tart, and pizza doughs

Recipes that require dough don't have a reputation for being the simplest to put together whenever. They absolutely can be if you make the dough ahead of time, when you have the time, and then store in your freezer. (Or buy balls of pizza dough and pie dough rounds.) The hard part will already be done for you.

store them

Wrapped individually in plastic and stored in zipper-lock bags, disks of homemade pie and tart dough and 8-ounce balls of pizza dough can be kept in the freezer for up to two weeks.

use them

Sweet Cherry Pie (page 150), Lemon Ricotta Pie (page 152), Classic Cheese Quiche (page 160), Rustic Berry Tart (page 172), Ham and Cheddar Hand Pies (page 218), Easy Skillet Cheese Pizza (page 328), Caprese Sheet-Pan Pizza (page 340), Buffalo Chicken Calzones (page 225), Pear and Bacon Flatbread (page 325)

puff pastry and phyllo dough

We think every cook should always have a box or two of each of these in their freezer—if they want the fastest route to sweet or savory, buttery, flaky pastries at their fingertips. And who doesn't?

store them

Both of these freezer items come with expiration dates and package directions for thawing. If you thaw more puff pastry than you need, simply wrap the extra

dough well and pop it back in the freezer. Leftover phyllo sheets cannot be refrozen, but they can be rerolled, wrapped in plastic wrap, and stored in the refrigerator for up to five days.

use them

Apple Galette (page 171), Everything Bagel Danish (page 196), Eggplant and Tomato Phyllo Pie (page 204), Guava and Cheese Pastelitos (page 195), Apple Strudel (page 207), Pear and Chestnut Tarts (page 176)

spices

A robust spice pantry elevates cooking and baking with a dash. In addition to sweet baking spices, savory spices and blends such as za'atar, nigella, and curry powder support the savory side of baking. And flake sea salt works wonders on both savory and sweet treats.

store them

Kept away from light and heat in airtight jars, whole spices are good for up to two years and ground spices for up to one year. To keep track of their freshness, mark the jar with the date of purchase. If possible, shop in the bulk aisle so you can buy just the amount that you'll use in a reasonable amount of time.

use them

Soft and Chewy Molasses Spice Cookies (page 32), Cheese Bread with Feta and Nigella (page 276), Mana'eesh Za'atar (page 315), Whole-Wheat Apple-Spice Muffins (page 258)

bake and store

While many of the recipes in this book are likely to be devoured the day they're baked, others yield enough for a couple of people to enjoy over a few days; these include a 6-inch snack cake or pie, four scones, or a pan of six brownies. But letting baked treats sit for even a day means you'll want to store them properly to preserve their freshness. Here's how to do that.

cookies

Most kinds of cookies will keep for about three days in an airtight container at room temperature. To prevent chewy cookies from turning dry and brittle, place them in a zipper-lock bag along with a small piece of bread (no more than half of a slice). The cookies will absorb moisture from the bread and hold on to that moisture to stay at their peak chewy softness for longer.

bar cookies

Brownies and bars keep for about five days in an airtight container at room temperature. Uncut bars will last longer than cut ones.

muffins, quick breads, and snack cakes

Wrapped in plastic wrap or stored in an airtight container at room temperature, these moist baked goods keep for up to four days, depending on the recipe. For longer-term storage, the freezer sometimes works better than the refrigerator, which can make some cakes stale. Wrap well in plastic wrap, then in aluminum foil, and freeze for up to 1 month. To serve, thaw completely at room temperature, about 4 hours. (To ensure a nice, firm crust, do not unwrap cake until thawed.)

pies

Pies containing fillings with perishable ingredients, such as eggs or dairy, must be refrigerated once cool and should be eaten within two days. Fruit pies are food-safe at room temperature for up to two days. Keep the pie in an airtight container or set it on a plate and cover with an inverted bowl.

breads

Enriched rolls and buns taste good after being stored in a zipper-lock bag at room temperature for up to two days. Lean bread and rolls are really best the day they're made, but you could go as long as the next day if stored in a zipper-lock bag and then reheated. All rolls can be wrapped in foil, placed in a bag, and frozen for up to one month. To reheat rolls stored either way, wrap them (thawed if frozen) in aluminum foil, place on a rimmed baking sheet, and heat in a 350-degree oven for 10 minutes.

puff pastries

Buttery, flaky pastries made with puff pastry can be stored in an airtight container for up to four days. Rewarm them in a 300-degree oven for about 10 minutes.

make the most of your freezer

The benefits of a freezer are many: It preserves perishable ingredients like fruit and nuts. It stores doughs that offer a head-start on baking pizzas and pies, along with flaky pastries made with phyllo and puff pastry. But perhaps our favorite use, one tackled by many of the recipes in this book, is for small-serving baking.

While developing many of the recipes in this book—from chewy cookies to buttery biscuits to flaky Danish—in addition to devising methods for baking the recipes right away, we tested second methods that would allow you to freeze items to bake later (or do both: bake some treats right away and freeze a couple to bake another time). Many of these baked goods can be shaped and frozen for a month or so, then baked directly from the freezer—usually without thawing and just a few extra minutes in the oven.

When this is possible, you'll see **Freeze and Bake** variations alongside the recipe. These show you exactly where in the recipe you should break—whether right after shaping yeasted treats like Cardamom-Orange Morning Buns (page 226) or after stuffing pastries with filling like Everything Bagel Danish (page 196)—and how you should bake the frozen items when you're ready.

While some recipes can be stored in the freezer as they are, other batters and doughs need a little extra help to withstand the dry environment of a freezer so they bake up fluffy and tall. In these cases, we took our testing a step further and came up with a few **From-the-Freezer** recipes formulated specifically for success. We altered hydration levels in yeasted doughs (like From-the-Freezer Dinner Rolls on page 288), increased leaveners (as in From-the-Freezer Cranberry-Cardamom Muffins on page 260), and made other adjustments to ensure the results tasted as good as their freshly made counterparts.

Whether you want to prepare cinnamon buns ahead of a small brunch (rather than waking at dawn to prepare them), or you like having pastries on hand to bake off for yourself whenever a craving strikes, the freezer will allow you to enjoy baked goods often.

freezer storage best practices

We chill most baked goods as individual units on a parchment paper–lined baking sheet just long enough for them to solidify before we package them for their longer stay in the freezer; this prevents the items from fusing together. For food that's baked from frozen, we sometimes need to increase the baking time by about 5 minutes (cookies are an exception and bake in the same time from frozen as they do when baked fresh), but you'll find those times listed with recipes. Here are our techniques for transforming different doughs (and batters) into frozen assets.

cookies - *freeze for up to 1 month*
A cookie is the ultimate treat of convenience—handheld and neat enough to pack for lunch, but indulgent enough to satisfy a craving for something warm and gooey. We think you should have cookies in your freezer at all times.

We form cookie dough into balls, roll them in sugar (when applicable), and then press the balls to ½-inch thickness. We freeze these disks until solid before storing them together in a zipper-lock bag or airtight container. When you're ready to bake—one or the whole batch—they go straight from freezer to oven or air fryer (for more information, see page 20). By flattening them before freezing, we ensure that the cookies spread and bake through in the same amount of time that they properly brown.

biscuits - *freeze for up to 1 month*
We think fresh-baked biscuits should become part of anyone's routine—they're handy for breakfast, lunch, and dinner.

Our easy Cream Biscuits (page 243) and Flaky Whole-Wheat Buttermilk Biscuits (page 246) can be frozen before baking. To stock up, we freeze portioned dough until firm, then transfer the frozen biscuits to a zipper-lock bag and store in the freezer. To boot, these buttery, flaky breads benefit from their freezer stay: When the frozen pieces of butter among the layers of dough melt and turn to stream, they propel the biscuit's rise and leave tender pockets in their wake. Don't thaw the biscuits before baking.

Typical muffin recipe, baked from frozen
Stunted, misshapen

Our muffin recipe
Evenly lofty, golden brown

Parbaked roll
Pale exterior, fully set interior

Fully baked roll
Crisp, browned exterior, warm interior

muffins - *freeze for up to 2 months*

Never thought to freeze muffins before baking? You'll love being able to bake our from-the-freezer muffins (page 260)—flavored with berries, spices, or chocolate and ginger—to enjoy on the go (they take about 35 minutes, enough time to get ready for the day). The aroma, tender crumb, and crisp edges are so much nicer than what you get by warming up baked frozen ones.

We engineered the batter specifically for the freezer because conventional muffin batter doesn't freeze well: The cold, dry air and freeze-thaw cycle negatively impact the batter's leavening and wick away moisture, leading to stunted muffins with dry exteriors and cold or raw centers. We use plenty of leaveners: A hefty amount of double-acting baking powder lightens the batter immediately, making it easy to add mix-ins while withholding its heat-activated leavening power until the muffins bake. Baking soda helps leaven the batter and enhance browning. To boost moisture, we switch from butter to vegetable oil. We also add more sugar because it's hygroscopic and so helps the batter retain moisture. We portion our reworked batter into a tin fitted with paper liners, freeze the batter in portions, and transfer them to a zipper-lock bag until it's time to bake.

dinner rolls - *freeze for up to 6 weeks*

Our From-the-Freezer Dinner Rolls (page 288) save the day (or night) by ensuring you're never more than 15 minutes away from the warm comforts of fresh, homemade bread.

To design a dinner roll that could be baked from the freezer, we make, shape, and proof our rolls, parbake them in a low oven to set their shape, then move them to the freezer to await a brief final bake. To compensate for the moisture loss that comes from twice-baking the rolls, we incorporate a flour and water paste known as tangzhong, which adds extra moisture to the dough without making it difficult to handle.

Baking the rolls at 300 degrees keeps the heat low enough to avoid browning but hot enough to increase yeast activity so the rolls expand. We remove the rolls when their interiors are fully set and their exteriors are still pale. Then we let them cool and freeze them directly on their baking sheet to avoid compromising their still-delicate structure before moving them to a zipper-lock bag to stash in the freezer. These rolls may look wrinkly and wan, but they need just 8 to 10 minutes in a 425-degree oven to heat up and expand slightly as the crust turns a rich brown and develops lots of flavor compounds. This last step is easy enough that you can place a roll or two in a toaster oven just before dinner is ready. Let them cool for just 5 minutes and slather with butter.

pastries - *freeze for up to 1 month*

A fancy pastry is precious. Flaky laminated pastry, whether made from homemade dough or store-bought frozen puff pastry, is at its most shatteringly crisp before humidity can get to it. For that reason, it's nice to bake these kinds of pastries on the day you want to eat them and in the quantity you want.

Unleavened pastries that start with frozen puff pastry, such as Goat Cheese, Sun-Dried Tomato, and Basil Danish (page 199) and Guava and Cheese Pastelitos (page 195), bake up well directly from frozen, achieving good browning and puff. (Baked goods with a modest amount of filling that's not too wet are best for this.) You could bake two pastries fresh and then freeze the other two individually, so they're ready to be popped into a toaster oven for a morning of easy indulgence.

croissants and morning buns - *freeze for up to 2 months*

We think each and every one of these labors of love deserves to be savored at its fresh-baked best; no day-olds for us. To enjoy them that way, freeze shaped croissants and morning buns just before their final proofing stage. Then remove them from the freezer to thaw and proof overnight at room temperature, 7 to 10 hours for croissants and 10 to 12 hours for morning buns. If your kitchen's ambient temperature is cooler than 70 degrees, you'll likely need the longer end of that proof time.

cinnamon buns - *freeze for up to 1 month*

Homemade cinnamon buns are often reserved for a holiday morning, but our proprietary freezer method turns any day into a holiday. And there's no more waking up at dawn to prepare. We make the dough, let it rise, fill it, spiral it, portion it, and then put it to bed in the freezer.

Usually buns are baked in a dish together. To bake off only as many as we want at a time, we fashion aluminum foil cups to place the buns in and bake—these cups contain all the gooey sweetness and encourage a beautiful blooming rise in the oven. Place portions of rolled dough cut side down on parchment paper–lined rimmed baking sheet; cover with plastic; and freeze until solid, at least 1 hour.

Morning buns, thawed and baked

bake it in your toaster oven

Nearly every recipe in this book can be made without turning on an oven—well, a full-size oven. Luckily for the small-batch baker, toaster ovens can be used for much more than just toast. A good toaster oven is incredibly versatile—able to toast, broil, and bake—so you can turn your countertop oven into a treat incubator, perfectly sized for making just a few servings.

Our favorite toaster oven, the **Breville Smart Oven**, is extremely accurate. In testing, it held a target temperature within 2 degrees for a 2-hour period—and gave consistently good results across toasting, broiling, roasting, and baking. Its larger size also means that it can accommodate a 3½-quart casserole dish for a fruit cobbler, an 8½ by 4½-inch loaf pan for brownies, or a 6-inch springform pan for cheesecake while still taking less time to preheat, and less energy overall, than a full-size oven.

During recipe development, we found that the toaster oven could stand in for a regular full-size oven in almost all cases, but with a few exceptions such as skillet pizzas and certain pastries (headnotes identify when a recipe cannot be baked in a toaster oven or needs to be modified by using a different pan). Here are a few tips for ensuring a successful toaster oven bake.

use the lowest rack

Different toaster ovens have different rack configurations, usually allowing for two or three different placements. For baking, we place the rack in the lowest position in order to accommodate the height of baking vessels as well as the potential rise of baked goods.

use the "bake/roast" function

While it varies by manufacturer, this function operates the same as it would in your main oven, and often means the most heat is generated from the bottom heating element with the top element at a reduced wattage. We used this setting as our default function for all recipes in this book.

keep an eye on browning

During testing, we found that some items browned much more quickly in the toaster oven than in a conventional oven. Fortunately, the eye-level placement of the toaster oven makes it easy to check on baked goods, but you may want to check items before the lower end of the time range given. For some items, like slab pies with a parbaked crust, you may need to tent the pie with foil toward the end of baking to make sure the crust doesn't get too dark before the filling is cooked through.

pay attention to hot spots

Generally, the outer edge of items will get hotter and the middle will stay cooler, but this can also be affected by your toaster oven's hot spots. We account for potential hot spots by rotating the pan or vessel midway through baking for longer recipes, similar to our recommendation for recipes baked in a conventional oven.

keep the heat in

Be sure not to leave the toaster oven door open too long when moving things in and out or rotating items—you will lose heat more dramatically because of the smaller and less insulated space of the toaster oven compared to a full-size oven.

While most recipes in this book can be translated to the toaster oven without modification to the temperature or bake time, there are a few exceptions, which are called out in recipe headnotes. For example, recipes that require a very hot oven (toaster ovens often don't go above 450 degrees) and recipes that involve a change in oven temperature (starting out hotter and then turning the temperature down, as with our Individual New York Cheesecakes on page 142) may require a significantly different bake time due to the inferior heat retention of a toaster oven compared with a full-size oven.

Will these recipes work in any toaster oven?

Your baked goods are likely to succeed if your toaster oven's temperature is accurate and consistent. We found that lower-end models averaged as much as 60 degrees lower than the target temperature, and this greatly impacted cook time. Test your toaster oven's accuracy by using a freestanding oven thermometer in the middle of the oven to gauge its effectiveness. Our favorite analog thermometer is the **CDN DOT2 ProAccurate Oven Thermometer**; our winning digital oven thermometer is the **ThermoWorks Square DOT**.

In addition, older or lower-end toaster ovens may be smaller and thus not fit all baking vessels used in this book. Measure your toaster oven's interior so you know what will fit.

The smallest oven we tested that worked for most recipes was 12½ inches (inside wall to inside wall) by 9½ inches (back wall to door) by 4½ inches (from lowest rack position to top heating element). This is fine for baking items in a 6-inch cake pan or an eighth sheet pan.

bake it in your air fryer

Air fryers in a baking book? Yes! Despite their name, air fryers don't actually fry your food: These small convection ovens with powerful fans circulate hot air around food, distributing heat more quickly and evenly, which can lead to increased browning. So with a few adaptations—and exceptions—air fryers can be used for baking many kinds of baked goods. After all, many professional bakeries use convection ovens to achieve more even browning of baked goods and faster bake times.

The smaller size of air fryers makes them particularly convenient for small-batch baking. There's no need to heat up the whole kitchen to preheat the oven to bake one or two pastries you pulled from the freezer, for example. Air fryers also fit conveniently on your counter—they're at the ready for a spur-of-the-moment baking project. Some models even have clear windows that make monitoring browning and baking progress easy at eye level.

Since we began testing air fryers in 2018, we have consistently preferred machines with drawer-style frying baskets, a wide cooking surface, and larger drawer capacity. Our winning model, the **Instant Vortex Plus 6-Quart Air Fryer** (and its upgrade, the **Instant Vortex Plus ClearCook + OdorErase 6-Quart**, with a clear cooking drawer and odor filtering technology) has a wide drawer-style basket that is not only easy to remove and insert, but also wide enough to accommodate a 4-cup muffin tin, as well as deep enough for a 6-inch springform pan or mini-loaf pan. We also like this air fryer's relatively compact footprint and found the nonstick basket made cleanup a breeze.

Recipes that are good candidates for making in your air fryer have **Bake in Your Air Fryer** instructions on the page. Here are some best practices when using your air fryer for baking.

no need to preheat

Some air fryer models—including our winner—recommend preheating and may have automatic preheating times. We found preheating unnecessary as the small air-fryer basket heats up quickly. To allow for differences across models, the bake times for air-fryer instructions in our recipes are meant to be counted as soon as you press "start."

avoid pre-set cooking options

Many air-fryer models have preprogrammed cooking options (like Bake, Broil, or Dehydrate). To account for differences across models, all air-fryer instructions in this book use the standard Air Fry setting.

no need to rotate

Some air fryers have automatic presets indicating when to turn food. While we do recommend rotating some foods in the air fryer for more even cooking (meat, for example), we found that for baked goods, rotating was unnecessary; moreover, moving delicate baked items in the tight space of the hot air fryer was challenging. Some baked items—quick breads and muffins, for example—got slightly uneven tops due to the air fryer's intense fan, but we didn't find that it affected the overall quality of the baked goods.

turn down the heat

Food in an air fryer cooks more quickly on the outside because of the circulating hot air created by the air fryer's fans. When translating a baking recipe from a conventional oven to the air fryer, we sometimes found we needed to reduce the temperature by anywhere from 50 degrees (for cookies) to 125 degrees (for biscuits), and increase the bake time—sometimes by a significant amount—in order for food to bake through in the same time that it cooks on the outside.

account for the rise

When determining whether you can bake something in an air fryer, make sure there is sufficient headspace between the top of the item and the air fryer's heating elements: 2 inches of space above the top of your baking vessel is good. Note that the closer your baked good is to the heating element, the faster it will brown. Take into account the potential rise on baked goods like quick breads and muffins as well as items like cheesecake, which can puff slightly when baked.

fold down foil or parchment paper to prevent flapping

Lining the air-fryer basket, as we instruct in many of our recipes, creates a surface to bake on in lieu of a baking sheet. You can also then use the sling to help lift items out of the air fryer if needed. This step minimizes cleanup. Make sure any loose edges are folded down or crimped to prevent them from flapping in the air fryer or potentially falling into your food.

What can't you do in an air fryer?

As much as we love our air fryers—and we definitely pushed the limits of what we tried to bake in them—they can't do everything. For a few baked goods, we either couldn't bake them in the air fryer due to size or shape constraints (anything baked on a baking sheet, in skillet, or on a pizza stone, to name a few), or the results in the air fryer fell short. For example, we found that store-bought puff pastry got gorgeous golden-brown color on the top, but the underside stayed pale and doughy. Pizza dough suffered a similar fate when we tried to bake calzones in the air fryer. Cakes were also hit-or-miss, with some developing a tough skin on the outside or staying extremely pale or dense. We also skipped using the air fryer for delicate bakes that would be adversely affected by the air fryer's intense convection, like soufflés.

However, for many other baked goods—from muffins to biscuits, scones, cookies, quick breads, and even morning buns and cheesecake!—the air fryer worked well. In addition, the appliance is particularly well suited for baking from-the-freezer items when you want just one or two servings, like dinner rolls. These small items cooked through evenly.

just for two

Whether you live in a two-person household, are looking for something to serve with tea for two, or want to make something for yourself without many leftovers, here is a list of the recipes in this book that yield just two servings—no freezing or storing needed, just eating. Savory flatbreads are a great solution for dinner (or breakfast), fruit desserts are perfect for using small amounts of produce, and individual-size cakes are so functional (and just so cute).

crisps, crumbles, custards, and more

lazy bakes

Even if you enjoy being in the kitchen, there are times when you want a fresh homemade treat without investing much time or effort. We call these lazy bakes: They're quick or easy, or both; and they often have a nonbaked component or call for ingredients that are already prepared, like frozen puff pastry. Sometimes they're deceptive, like elegant Pear and Chestnut Tarts, which appear like they take a lot of skill. Sometimes they're just made for tucking into on the couch in front of a movie, like Molten Chocolate Microwave Mug Cakes.

breads and rolls

Banana Bread, 278

Chocolate Banana Bread, 279

Cheese Bread with Feta and Nigella, 276

Date Banana Bread, 279

Fennel–Black Pepper Breadsticks, 268

Garlic and Herb Breadsticks, 268

Individual Honey-Thyme Monkey Breads, 270

Individual Onion, Poppy Seed, and Parmesan Monkey Breads, 271

Individual Pumpkin Spice Monkey Breads, 271

Spicy Parmesan Breadsticks, 268

Zucchini Bread, 280

flatbread and pizzas

Caprese Sheet-Pan Pizza, 340

Easy Skillet Cheese Pizza, 328

special-occasion bakes

Three's company—and a party. When you're having a small gathering or holiday party, you might not need a 16-serving layer cake, but you'll also need more than a two-person cake. These baked goods serve your needs when you're sharing, and they're also a little dressed up for the occasion. For the most success when hosting a gathering, we recommend turning to some surprisingly lazy bakes (think: puff pastry treats or stir-together cakes) in addition to more involved items.

cookies and bars

Lemon Bars, 44

Madeleines, 40

cakes

Basque Cheesecake, 145

Chocolate Chunk Financiers, 129

Chocolate-Raspberry Torte, 130

Cranberry Upside-Down Cake, 138

Financiers, 129

French Apple Cake, 134

Pear-Walnut Upside-Down Cake, 141

Plum Financiers, 129

Raspberry Financiers, 129

Semolina and Ricotta Cake, 136

pies and tarts

Chocolate-Pecan Slab Pie, 162

Quiche Lorraine, 160

Lemon Ricotta Pie, 152

Triple-Berry Slab Pie with Ginger-Lemon Streusel, 164

pastries and pockets

Cardamom-Orange Morning Buns, 226

Croissants, 228

Goat Cheese, Sun-Dried Tomato, and Basil Danish, 199

Pain au Chocolat, 233

Prosciutto and Gruyère Croissants, 236

biscuits and muffins

British-Style Currant Scones, 250

Flaky Whole-Wheat Buttermilk Biscuits, 246

bread and rolls

Brioche Hamburger Buns, 294

From-the-Freezer Cinnamon Buns, 298

No-Knead Spelt, Olive, and Herb Dinner Rolls, 293

No-Knead Whole-Wheat Dinner Rolls, 292

No-Knead Whole-Wheat Fruit and Nut Rolls, 293

flatbreads and pizzas

Anchovy and Chive Focaccia, 323

Focaccia, 321

Fontina, Arugula, and Prosciutto Pizza, 333

Grape, Fennel, and Charred Shallot Focaccia, 323

Goat Cheese, Olive, and Garlic Pizza, 333

Ricotta, Bacon, and Scallion Pizza, 333

Thin-Crust Pizza, 332

chapter one
cookies and bars

chewy chocolate chip cookies

makes 12 cookies • **total time** 50 minutes

1 cup (5 ounces) all-purpose flour

½ teaspoon baking soda

¼ teaspoon table salt

½ cup packed (3½ ounces) light brown sugar

¼ cup (1¾ ounces) granulated sugar

5 tablespoons unsalted butter, melted and cooled

1 large egg

1½ teaspoons vanilla extract

1 cup (6 ounces) semisweet chocolate chips

---

freeze and bake

At end of step 3, freeze dough rounds on parchment-lined plate until very firm, at least 1 hour; transfer frozen dough rounds to zipper-lock bag and store in freezer for up to 1 month. Do not thaw before baking.

---

bake in your air fryer

Line air-fryer basket with aluminum foil, crimping edges. Space desired number of cookies at least ½ inch apart in prepared basket. Place basket in air fryer, set temperature to 300 degrees, and bake for 13 to 16 minutes.

why this recipe works Few treats satisfy like a homemade chocolate chip cookie. But for a household of two, getting through an entire full-size batch of them before they lose that chewy-crispy sweet spot can feel like a race against time. Our recipe solves that dilemma: It yields a batch of 12 perfectly chewy chocolate chip cookies that you can eat whenever you like. Bake all the cookies at once or freeze and bake any amount on demand. Rather than pull out a mixer for these cookies, you melt the butter and simply stir everything together in one bowl, gently folding the dry ingredients into the wet ingredients for tender and chewy cookies. Plenty of brown sugar adds a subtle caramelized flavor and bolsters the chewy texture. To avoid overbaking, pull the cookies out of the oven when they are still slightly underbaked in the center; they will finish cooking on the baking sheet.

1 Adjust oven rack to middle position and heat oven to 350 degrees. Line rimmed baking sheet with parchment paper. Whisk flour, baking soda, and salt together in bowl.

2 Whisk brown sugar and granulated sugar together in medium bowl. Whisk in melted butter until combined. Whisk in egg and vanilla until smooth. Using wooden spoon or rubber spatula, gently stir in flour mixture until soft dough forms. Fold in chocolate chips.

3 Working with 2 tablespoons dough at a time, roll into balls. Evenly space dough balls on prepared sheet. Using bottom of greased drinking glass, flatten dough balls to ½-inch thickness.

4 Bake cookies until edges are set but centers are still soft and puffy, about 13 to 16 minutes, rotating sheet halfway through baking. Let cookies cool on sheet for 5 minutes, then transfer to wire rack. Serve warm or at room temperature.

oatmeal raisin cookies

makes 12 cookies • **total time** 50 minutes

- 1¼ cups (3¾ ounces) old-fashioned rolled oats
- ½ cup (2½ ounces) plus 2 tablespoons all-purpose flour
- ¼ teaspoon baking powder
- ¼ teaspoon table salt
- ⅛ teaspoon ground cinnamon
- ½ cup packed (3½ ounces) brown sugar
- ¼ cup (1¾ ounces) granulated sugar
- 6 tablespoons unsalted butter, melted and cooled
- 1 large egg yolk
- 2 tablespoons milk
- ¾ teaspoon vanilla extract
- ⅓ cup raisins

---

freeze and bake

At end of step 3, freeze dough rounds on parchment-lined plate until very firm, at least 1 hour; transfer frozen dough rounds to zipper-lock bag and store in freezer for up to 1 month. Do not thaw before baking.

---

bake in your air fryer

Line air-fryer basket with aluminum foil, crimping edges. Space desired number of cookies at least ½ inch apart in prepared basket. Place basket in air fryer, set temperature to 300 degrees, and bake for 13 to 16 minutes.

why this recipe works These cookies are crisp around the edges, chewy in the middle, and packed throughout with satisfying old-fashioned oats. A couple tablespoons of milk lighten the batter, which helps the cookies spread correctly, and ensures that they aren't dry or crumbly. An oatmeal cookie is a common afternoon sweet snack break; like all of our cookies, you can pull one from the freezer and bake when the 3 p.m. slump hits. We freeze most of our cookies as flattened rounds rather than balls so the frozen dough bakes through at the same rate that it browns. Do not substitute quick or instant oats in this recipe; they're less flavorful than old-fashioned oats and will make the cookies dry.

1 Adjust oven rack to middle position and heat oven to 350 degrees. Line rimmed baking sheet with parchment paper. Whisk oats, flour, baking powder, salt, and cinnamon together in bowl.

2 Whisk brown sugar and granulated sugar together in medium bowl. Whisk in melted butter until combined. Whisk in egg yolk, milk, and vanilla until smooth. Using wooden spoon or rubber spatula, gently stir in oat mixture until soft dough forms. Fold in raisins.

3 Working with heaping 1½ tablespoons dough at a time, roll into balls. Evenly space dough balls on prepared sheet. Using bottom of greased drinking glass, flatten dough balls to ½-inch thickness.

4 Bake cookies until edges are set and beginning to brown, 13 to 16 minutes, rotating sheet halfway through baking. Let cookies cool on sheet for 5 minutes, then transfer to wire rack. Serve warm or at room temperature.

soft and chewy molasses spice cookies

makes 12 cookies • **total time** 45 minutes

¼ cup (1¾ ounces) granulated sugar, plus ¼ cup for rolling

1⅓ cups (6⅔ ounces) all-purpose flour

¾ teaspoon ground cinnamon

¾ teaspoon ground ginger

½ teaspoon baking soda

¼ teaspoon ground cloves

⅛ teaspoon ground allspice

⅛ teaspoon table salt

⅛ teaspoon pepper

¼ cup (1¾ ounces) packed brown sugar

6 tablespoons unsalted butter, melted and cooled

¼ cup molasses

1 large egg yolk

½ teaspoon vanilla extract

---

freeze and bake

At end of step 3, freeze dough rounds on parchment-lined plate until very firm, at least 1 hour; transfer frozen dough rounds to zipper-lock bag and store in freezer for up to 1 month. Do not thaw before baking.

---

bake in your air fryer

Line air-fryer basket with aluminum foil, crimping edges. Space desired number of cookies at least ½ inch apart in prepared basket. Place basket in air fryer, set temperature to 325 degrees, and bake for 9 to 12 minutes.

why this recipe works Whether for a small holiday celebration or an everyday treat, these warm-spiced cookies can be made in the time it takes to heat the oven, thanks to a simple stir-together dough that uses melted butter. Halving an egg—or in this case, egg yolk—can be one of the quirkiest parts of scaling down recipes. We don't do it. To avoid using half an egg yolk when we cut our popular molasses cookie recipe in half, we add extra flour and increase the sugar just enough to get the right consistency without bumping up the yield too much. Cinnamon, ginger, cloves, allspice, and black pepper provide warmth and just enough bite, and a spoonful of vanilla smoothes out any rough edges. We like these made with dark brown sugar but you can use light brown sugar if that's what you have on hand.

1 Adjust oven rack to middle position and heat oven to 375 degrees. Line rimmed baking sheet with parchment paper. Place ¼ cup sugar for rolling in small bowl.

2 Whisk flour, cinnamon, ginger, baking soda, cloves, allspice, salt, and pepper in bowl until thoroughly combined. Combine brown sugar and remaining ¼ cup granulated sugar in medium bowl. Add butter and whisk until smooth. Add molasses, egg yolk, and vanilla and whisk until smooth. Using wooden spoon or rubber spatula, gently stir in flour mixture until soft dough forms.

3 Working with heaping 1½ tablespoons dough at a time, roll into balls. Drop dough balls directly into sugar and roll to coat. Evenly space dough balls on prepared sheet. Using bottom of greased drinking glass, flatten dough balls to ½-inch thickness.

4 Bake cookies until browned, still puffy, and edges have begun to set but centers are still soft (cookies will look raw between cracks and seem underdone), 9 to 12 minutes, rotating baking sheet halfway through baking. Let cookies cool on sheet for 5 minutes, then transfer to wire rack. Let cookies cool completely before serving.

chocolate crinkle cookies

makes 12 cookies • **total time** 1¼ hours

½ cup (2½ ounces) all-purpose flour

¼ cup (¾ ounce) unsweetened cocoa powder

½ teaspoon baking powder

⅛ teaspoon baking soda

¼ teaspoon table salt

¾ cups packed (5¼ ounces) brown sugar

1 large egg plus 1 large yolk

2 teaspoons instant espresso powder (optional)

½ teaspoon vanilla extract

2 ounces unsweetened chocolate, chopped

2 tablespoons unsalted butter

¼ cup (1¾ ounces) granulated sugar for rolling

¼ cup (1 ounce) confectioners' sugar for rolling

why this recipe works This small batch of crinkle cookies packs a big chocolate punch from both unsweetened chocolate and cocoa, underscored by espresso powder. Rolling the balls of dough in granulated sugar first helps the hallmark powdered sugar set, for a dramatic-looking fissured appearance. The rolling process happens before you freeze any unbaked cookies, so when it's time to bake, you simply set them on the baking sheet or place in your air-fryer basket and bake your way to chocolate bliss. Both natural and Dutch-processed cocoa will work in this recipe.

1 Adjust oven rack to middle position and heat oven to 325 degrees. Line rimmed baking sheet with parchment paper. Whisk flour, cocoa, baking powder, baking soda, and salt together in bowl.

2 Whisk brown sugar, egg and yolk, espresso powder, if using, and vanilla together in medium bowl. Combine chocolate and butter in separate bowl and microwave at 50 percent power, stirring occasionally, until melted, about 2 minutes.

3 Whisk chocolate mixture into egg mixture until combined. Using wooden spoon or rubber spatula, gently stir in flour mixture until soft dough forms. Let dough sit at room temperature for 10 minutes.

4 Place granulated sugar and confectioners' sugar in separate small bowls. Working with 1½ tablespoons dough at a time, roll into balls. Drop dough balls directly into granulated sugar and roll to coat. Transfer dough balls to confectioners' sugar and roll to coat. Evenly space dough balls on prepared sheet. Using bottom of greased drinking glass, flatten dough balls to ½-inch thickness.

5 Bake cookies until puffed and cracked and edges have begun to set but centers are still soft (cookies will look raw between cracks and seem underdone), 9 to 12 minutes, rotating sheet halfway through baking. Let cookies cool completely on sheet before serving.

freeze and bake

At end of step 4, freeze dough rounds on parchment-lined plate until very firm, at least 1 hour; transfer frozen dough rounds to zipper-lock bag and store in freezer for up to 1 month. Do not thaw before baking.

bake in your air fryer

Line air-fryer basket with aluminum foil, crimping edges. Space desired number of cookies at least ½ inch apart in prepared basket. Place basket in air fryer, set temperature to 275 degrees, and bake for 9 to 12 minutes.

coffee toffee cookies

makes 12 cookies • **total time** 50 minutes

1 cup (5 ounces) all-purpose flour

¼ teaspoon baking soda

¼ teaspoon table salt

4 teaspoons instant espresso powder

1½ teaspoons warm tap water

½ cup (3½ ounces) plus 2 tablespoons sugar

5 tablespoons unsalted butter, melted and cooled

1 large egg

½ teaspoon vanilla extract

¼ cup Heath Toffee Bits

---

freeze and bake

At end of step 3, freeze dough rounds on parchment-lined plate until very firm, at least 1 hour; transfer frozen dough rounds to zipper-lock bag and store in freezer for up to 1 month. Do not thaw before baking.

---

bake in your air fryer

Line air-fryer basket with aluminum foil, crimping edges. Space desired number of cookies at least ½ inch apart in prepared basket. Place basket in air fryer, set temperature to 300 degrees, and bake for 13 minutes.

why this recipe works The flavor combination of rich coffee and buttery, nutty toffee gives these cookies sophisticated allure. Instant espresso powder, with its concentrated flavor and fine texture, is a quick and easy way to add bold coffee flavor. Since instant espresso is water soluble, we dissolve it in a bit of water (rather than adding it directly to the melted butter in the recipe). We then add the butter and sugar directly to the "brewed" espresso. A little vanilla extract balances and softens the espresso's bite. Plenty of toffee pieces add texture and rich caramel flavor.

1 Adjust oven rack to middle position and heat oven to 350 degrees. Line rimmed baking sheet with parchment paper. Whisk flour, baking soda, and salt together in bowl.

2 Whisk espresso powder and warm water together in medium bowl until espresso powder has dissolved, then whisk in sugar and melted butter until combined. Whisk in egg and vanilla until smooth. Using wooden spoon or rubber spatula, gently stir in flour mixture until soft dough forms. Fold in toffee bits.

3 Working with 2 tablespoons dough at a time, roll into balls. Evenly space dough balls on prepared sheet. Using bottom of greased drinking glass, flatten dough balls to ½-inch thickness.

4 Bake cookies until edges are set but centers are still soft and puffy, about 13 minutes, rotating sheet halfway through baking. Let cookies cool on sheet for 5 minutes, then transfer to wire rack. Serve warm or at room temperature.

peanut butter sandwich cookies

makes 6 cookies • **total time** 50 minutes, plus 1½ hours cooling and setting

cookies

¼ cup (1¼ ounces) all-purpose flour

¼ teaspoon baking soda

⅛ teaspoon table salt

2 tablespoons creamy peanut butter

2 tablespoons granulated sugar

2 tablespoons packed brown sugar

1 tablespoon unsalted butter, melted

1 tablespoon milk

⅓ cup unsalted dry-roasted peanuts, toasted and chopped fine

filling

3 tablespoons creamy peanut butter

1 tablespoon unsalted butter

¼ cup (1 ounce) confectioners' sugar

why this recipe works Our original Peanut Butter Sandwich Cookies are a fan favorite, but if you find the prospect of forming two dozen sandwich cookies tedious— or you just don't need that many—this smaller version is for you. One tablespoon of milk and a small amount of baking soda give the cookies the thin, flat dimensions and sturdy crunch, respectively, that are vital to a sandwich cookie. Our easy peanut butter filling beautifully solves the baking puzzle of how to maximize peanut flavor in a cookie without compromising texture. If using natural peanut butter, be sure to stir it well before measuring. Do not use unsalted peanut butter for these cookies.

1 For the cookies: Adjust oven rack to middle position and heat oven to 350 degrees. Line rimmed baking sheet with parchment paper. Whisk flour, baking soda, and salt together in medium bowl. Add peanut butter, granulated sugar, brown sugar, melted butter, and milk and stir with wooden spoon or rubber spatula until combined. Stir in peanuts until evenly distributed.

2 Use ⅓-cup dry measuring cup to divide dough into 3 equal portions and place portions on cutting board. Using knife, cut each portion into 4 pieces. Roll each quadrant into ball and space evenly on prepared sheet. Dampen your hand and flatten dough balls until 2 inches in diameter.

3 Bake until deep golden brown and firm to touch, 15 to 18 minutes, rotating sheet halfway through baking. Let cookies cool on sheet for 5 minutes, then transfer to wire rack. Let cookies cool completely before filling.

4 For the filling: Microwave peanut butter and butter in bowl until butter is melted and warm, 30 to 50 seconds. Using wooden spoon or rubber spatula, stir in confectioners' sugar until mixture is smooth.

5 To assemble, place 6 cookies upside down on cutting board. Place scant tablespoon warm filling in center of each cookie. Place second cookie on top of filling, right side up, pressing gently until filling spreads to edges. Allow filling to set for 1 hour before serving. (Assembled cookies can be stored at room temperature for up to 3 days.)

madeleines

makes 6 madeleines • **total time** 40 minutes, plus 30 minutes chilling

3 tablespoons all-purpose flour

¼ teaspoon baking powder

⅛ teaspoon table salt

2 tablespoons granulated sugar

1 large egg yolk, room temperature

1 tablespoon whole milk, room temperature

½ teaspoon vanilla extract

2 tablespoons unsalted butter, melted and cooled

Confectioners' sugar, for dusting

why this recipe works These light, airy treats are sponge cakes in cookie form, with a beautiful ridged exterior formed by the shell-shaped tins in which they are baked. Easy to prepare at home, our elegant madeleine recipe is just right when you want a small batch of something lightly sweet to go with coffee or tea. A quarter teaspoon of baking powder lifts the madeleines and creates the signature hump in the center of each cookie. An egg yolk imparts a nice custardy flavor, and using almost as much sugar as flour produces golden-brown, lightly caramelized edges. The batter emulsifies best with room temperature ingredients. To cool the baked madeleines without ruining their ridged exteriors, let them sit in the molds for 10 minutes after baking before transferring them to a wire rack. There is no need to spread the batter out in the molds as it will spread during baking. We had the best success using a noncoated aluminum madeleine pan. If using a nonstick madeleine pan, reduce the baking time to about 6 minutes; the cookies will be slightly darker.

1 Whisk flour, baking powder, and salt together in bowl. In separate medium bowl, whisk granulated sugar, egg yolk, milk, and vanilla until smooth. Using wooden spoon or rubber spatula, stir flour mixture into egg mixture until thoroughly combined, then fold in melted butter until batter is homogeneous. Cover and refrigerate for at least 30 minutes or up to 12 hours.

2 Adjust oven rack to lowest position and heat oven to 375 degrees. Spray 6 cups of 12-cup madeleine pan with baking spray with flour. Divide batter evenly among prepared cups (about 1 tablespoon per cup). Bake until madeleines are golden and spring back when pressed lightly, 7 to 9 minutes, rotating pan halfway through baking.

3 Let madeleines cool in pan for 10 minutes. Using offset spatula or butter knife, loosen edges of madeleines, then transfer to wire rack, shell pattern down. Let madeleines cool completely, then dust with confectioners' sugar. Serve immediately.

variations

browned butter–cardamom madeleines

Melt 2 tablespoons unsalted butter in 8-inch skillet over medium-high heat. Continue to cook, swirling skillet and stirring constantly with rubber spatula, until butter is dark golden brown and has nutty aroma, 1 to 3 minutes. Off heat, transfer browned butter to small heat-proof bowl. Substitute browned butter for melted butter. Increase milk to 1½ tablespoons and add ⅛ teaspoon ground cardamom to flour mixture.

chocolate-hazelnut madeleines

Substitute ¾ teaspoon hazelnut or almond extract for vanilla extract. Once madeleines have cooled completely, microwave 1 ounce bittersweet or semi-sweet chocolate in bowl at 50 percent power, stirring frequently, until melted, 1 to 2 minutes. Using small spoon, drizzle chocolate evenly over shell-pattern side of madeleines. Let sit until chocolate is set, about 15 minutes.

lemon madeleines

Substitute ¾ teaspoon grated lemon zest for vanilla extract.

brownies and blondies

Brownie and blondie batters are some of the most versatile shape-shifters in the book. Our recipes are simple stir-together affairs, and they call for a common loaf pan, but they can bake in a number of pans, depending on what you have on hand. If you have options to choose from, you can bake brownies and blondies according to your preferred bar shape and texture; the pan can dictate that outcome (for more information, see page 7). The test kitchen's preferred loaf pan measures 8½ by 4½ inches; if you use a 9 by 5-inch loaf pan, start checking for doneness 5 minutes earlier than advised in the recipe. Do not use a glass pan.

fudgy brownies

makes *6 brownies*
total time *1¼ hours, plus 1 hour cooling*

why this recipe works A full pan of brownies is way too much for even the most ardent pair of brownie lovers. To scale back our batch of fudgy brownies, we employ a loaf pan, which makes just six brownies—perfect for two people to enjoy over a couple days. The deep sides of the loaf pan make it hard to cut the brownies neatly, so we line the pan with a sling that allows us to lift the brownies out in one piece before cutting. A whole egg plus an extra yolk make our ultrachocolaty brownies rich, moist, and chewy; be careful not to overbake these brownies or their texture will become dry and cakey.

3½	ounces semisweet chocolate, chopped
4	tablespoons unsalted butter, cut into 4 pieces
1	tablespoon unsweetened cocoa powder
½	cup (3½ ounces) plus 2 tablespoons sugar
1	large egg plus 1 large yolk
1	teaspoon vanilla extract
¼	teaspoon table salt
½	cup (2½ ounces) all-purpose flour

1 Adjust oven rack to middle position and heat oven to 350 degrees. Make foil sling for 8½ by 4½-inch loaf pan by folding 2 long sheets of aluminum foil; first sheet should be 8½ inches wide and second sheet should be 4½ inches wide. Lay sheets of foil in pan perpendicular to each other, with extra foil hanging over edges of pan. Push foil into corners and up sides of pan, smoothing foil flush to pan. Grease foil.

2 Microwave chocolate, butter, and cocoa in bowl at 50 percent power, stirring occasionally, until melted and smooth, 1 to 3 minutes; let cool slightly. Whisk sugar, egg and yolk, vanilla, and salt together in medium bowl until combined. Whisk in melted chocolate mixture until combined. Using wooden spoon or rubber spatula stir in flour until just combined.

3 Transfer batter to prepared pan. Using spatula, spread batter into corners of pan and smooth surface. Bake until toothpick inserted in center comes out with few moist crumbs attached, 35 to 40 minutes, rotating pan halfway through baking. Let brownies cool completely in pan on wire rack, about 1 hour. Using foil overhang, lift brownies out of pan, loosening sides with paring knife, if needed. Cut into 6 bars and serve.

browned butter blondies

makes *6 blondies*
total time *1¼ hours, plus 1 hour cooling*

why this recipe works These blondies have nutty complexity from browned butter. Melting (rather than creaming) the butter is also beneficial because it creates a dense and chewy blondie. To tone down the sweetness, we replace a portion of the sugar with corn syrup. A generous amount of salt in the batter and sprinkled on top brings all the flavors into focus. Due to the greater depth of batter and the high sides of the loaf pan, our small batches of brownies and blondies bake for just as long as standard full batches, but what's the wait when rich, chewy bars are on the way?

¾ cup (3¾ ounces) all-purpose flour

½ teaspoon table salt

¼ teaspoon baking powder

4 tablespoons unsalted butter

½ cup packed (3½ ounces) plus 2 tablespoons packed light brown sugar

1 large egg

2 tablespoons corn syrup

2 teaspoons vanilla extract

⅓ cup pecans, toasted and chopped coarse

2 tablespoons milk chocolate chips

⅛ teaspoon flake sea salt, crumbled (optional)

1 Adjust oven rack to middle position and heat oven to 350 degrees. Make foil sling for 8½ by 4½-inch loaf pan by folding 2 long sheets of aluminum foil; first sheet should be 8½ inches wide and second sheet should be 4½ inches wide. Lay sheets of foil in pan perpendicular to each other, with extra foil hanging over edges of pan. Push foil into corners and up sides of pan, smoothing foil flush to pan. Grease foil.

2 Whisk flour, table salt, and baking powder together in bowl. Melt butter in 8-inch skillet over medium-high heat, 1 to 2 minutes. Continue to cook, swirling skillet and stirring constantly with rubber spatula, until butter is dark golden brown and has nutty aroma, 1 to 3 minutes. Transfer to medium bowl.

3 Add sugar to hot browned butter and whisk until combined. Whisk in egg, corn syrup, and vanilla until smooth. Using wooden spoon or rubber spatula, stir in flour mixture until fully incorporated. Stir in pecans and chocolate chips. Transfer batter to prepared pan. Using spatula, spread batter into corners of pan and smooth surface. Sprinkle with sea salt, if using. Bake until top is deep golden brown and toothpick inserted in center comes out clean, 35 to 40 minutes.

4 Let blondies cool completely in pan on wire rack, about 1 hour. Using foil overhang, lift blondies out of pan, loosening sides with paring knife, if needed. Cut into 6 bars and serve.

---

pan swap

6-inch cake pan: Make foil sling for pan and line with parchment following instructions on page 125. Increase baking time to about 45 minutes.

8-inch cast-iron skillet: Omit sling and grease skillet. Reduce baking time to 25 minutes for brownies and 30 minutes for blondies; bars will have a more pronounced crust.

muffin tin or ramekins: Omit sling. Divide batter evenly among six greased cups of muffin tin or six 4-ounce ramekins. Reduce baking time to about 25 minutes. Remove bars from muffin cups or ramekins when still warm (but not hot) to prevent overbaking.

---

bake in your air fryer

Use 6-inch cake pan. Place pan in air-fryer basket, set temperature to 275 degrees, and bake, 35 to 40 minutes for brownies and 50 to 55 minutes for blondies.

lemon bars

makes 6 bars • **total time** 1 hour, plus 1½ hours cooling

crust

- ½ cup (2½ ounces) all-purpose flour
- 2 tablespoons granulated sugar
- ¼ teaspoon table salt
- 4 tablespoons unsalted butter, melted

filling

- ½ cup (3½ ounces) granulated sugar
- 1 tablespoon all-purpose flour
- 1 teaspoon cream of tartar
- ⅛ teaspoon table salt
- 1 large egg plus 2 large yolks
- 1 teaspoon grated lemon zest plus ⅓ cup juice (2 lemons)
- 2 tablespoons unsalted butter, cut into 4 pieces
- Confectioners' sugar (optional)

pan swap

To make recipe in a 6-inch cake pan, make foil sling and line with parchment paper following instructions on page 125. In step 4, bake bars for 13 to 15 minutes. To make recipe in an 8-inch cast-iron skillet, omit sling, bake crust in step 2 for 16 minutes, and bake bars in step 4 for 7 minutes; bars will have a more pronounced crust.

why this recipe works Lemon bars are at their citrusy-bright best when freshly baked, so a small batch makes sense for a small household. The easy stir-together crust for these bars uses granulated sugar and bakes up golden brown and crisp. A combination of lemon juice and zest plus cream of tartar gives the filling multifaceted lemon flavor with extra tang. Cooking the lemon filling on the stovetop shortens the oven time. One shortcut not to take: bottled lemon juice—it can't compare to fresh. The test kitchen's preferred loaf pan measures 8½ by 4½ inches; if you use a 9 by 5-inch loaf pan, start checking for doneness 5 minutes earlier than advised in the recipe. Avoid using a glass loaf pan, which will cause the bars to overbake.

1 **For the crust:** Adjust oven rack to middle position and heat oven to 350 degrees. Make foil sling for 8½ by 4½-inch loaf pan by folding 2 long sheets of aluminum foil; first sheet should be 8½ inches wide and second sheet should be 4½ inches wide. Lay sheets of foil in pan perpendicular to each other, with extra foil hanging over edges of pan. Push foil into corners and up sides of pan, smoothing foil flush to pan.

2 Whisk flour, sugar, and salt together in medium bowl. Add melted butter and stir until combined. Transfer mixture to prepared pan and press into even layer over entire bottom of pan. Bake crust until light golden brown, 19 to 24 minutes, rotating pan halfway through baking.

3 **For the filling:** Set fine-mesh strainer into 4-cup liquid measuring cup, pitcher, or clean medium bowl. While crust bakes, whisk sugar, flour, cream of tartar, and salt together in medium bowl. Whisk in egg and yolks until no streaks of egg remain. Whisk in lemon zest and juice. Transfer mixture to medium saucepan and cook over medium-low heat, stirring constantly with rubber spatula, until mixture thickens and registers 160 degrees, about 4 minutes. Off heat, stir in butter until melted. Immediately pour custard through prepared strainer; discard solids.

4 Pour filling over hot crust and tilt pan to spread evenly. Bake until filling is set and barely jiggles when pan is shaken, about 10 minutes. (Filling around perimeter may be slightly raised.) Let bars cool completely in pan on wire rack, about 1½ hours. Using foil overhang, lift bars out of pan, loosening sides with paring knife, if needed. Cut into 6 bars, wiping knife clean between cuts as necessary. Dust bars with confectioners' sugar, if using, and serve.

ultranutty pecan bars

makes 6 bars • **total time** 50 minutes, plus 1½ hours cooling

crust

- ¼ cup (1¼ ounces) plus 3 tablespoons all-purpose flour
- 1½ tablespoons granulated sugar
- ⅛ teaspoon table salt
- 2 tablespoons unsalted butter, melted

topping

- ¼ cup packed (1¾ ounces) light brown sugar
- 3 tablespoons light corn syrup
- 2 tablespoons unsalted butter, melted and hot
- ¼ teaspoon vanilla extract
- ⅛ teaspoon table salt
- 1½ cups pecans, toasted
- ⅛ teaspoon flake sea salt (optional)

---

pan swap

To make recipe in a 6-inch cake pan, make foil sling and line with parchment paper following instructions on page 125. In step 4, bake bars for 35 to 40 minutes. To make recipe in an 8-inch cast-iron skillet, omit sling and bake as directed; bars will have a more pronounced crust.

---

bake in your air fryer

Use a 6-inch cake pan. Place pan in air-fryer basket, set temperature to 275 degrees, and bake for 45 to 50 minutes.

why this recipe works For a pecan bar that's all about the pecans, we use a generous 1½ cups in the topping, and toss them in a thick mixture of brown sugar, corn syrup, and melted butter. This easy dump-and-stir filling spreads itself evenly in the oven and bakes up with varying textures, some parts chewy and some crunchy. An easy press-in crust made with melted butter needs no parbaking. A final sprinkling of flaky sea salt elevates the flavor and appearance of the treat. It is important to use pecan halves, not pieces. The edges of the bars will be slightly firmer than the center. If desired, trim ¼ inch from the edges before cutting into bars. Toast the pecans on a rimmed baking sheet in a 350-degree oven until fragrant, 8 to 12 minutes, shaking the sheet halfway through. The test kitchen's preferred loaf pan measures 8½ by 4½ inches; if you use a 9 by 5-inch loaf pan, start checking for doneness 5 minutes earlier than advised in the recipe. Avoid using a glass loaf pan, which will cause the bars to overbake.

1 **For the crust:** Adjust oven rack to lowest position and heat oven to 350 degrees. Make foil sling for 8½ by 4½-inch loaf pan by folding 2 long sheets of aluminum foil; first sheet should be 8½ inches wide and second sheet should be 4½ inches wide. Lay sheets of foil in pan perpendicular to each other, with extra foil hanging over edges of pan. Push foil into corners and up sides of pan, smoothing foil flush to pan. Grease foil.

2 Whisk flour, sugar, and salt together in medium bowl. Using wooden spoon or rubber spatula, stir in melted butter until dough begins to form. Using your hands, continue to combine until no dry flour remains and small portion of dough holds together when squeezed in palm of your hand. Evenly scatter tablespoon-size pieces of dough over surface of prepared pan. Using your fingertips and palm of your hand, press and smooth dough into even thickness in bottom of pan.

3 **For the topping:** Whisk sugar, corn syrup, melted butter, vanilla, and table salt in medium bowl until smooth (mixture will look separated at first but will become homogeneous). Fold in pecans until evenly coated.

4 Pour topping over crust. Using spatula, spread topping over crust, pushing to edges and into corners (there will be bare patches). Bake until topping is evenly distributed and rapidly bubbling across entire surface, about 20 minutes.

5 Transfer pan to wire rack and lightly sprinkle with flake sea salt, if using. Let bars cool completely in pan on rack, about 1½ hours. Using foil overhang, lift bars out of pan, loosening sides with paring knife, if needed. Cut into 6 bars and serve.

cherry streusel bars

makes 6 bars • **total time** 1½ hours, plus 1 hour cooling

crust

⅔ cup (3⅓ ounces) all-purpose flour

2 tablespoons plus 2 teaspoons granulated sugar

Pinch table salt

4 tablespoons unsalted butter, cut into ½-inch pieces and chilled

cherry filling

½ cup (2¼ ounces) frozen sweet cherries, thawed

¼ cup cherry preserves

½ teaspoon lemon juice

⅛ teaspoon almond extract

Pinch table salt

streusel

2 tablespoons old-fashioned rolled oats

2 tablespoons slivered almonds, chopped

2 tablespoons packed brown sugar

1 tablespoon unsalted butter, cut into ½-inch pieces and softened

why this recipe works For these three-layer bars, you make one dough and use it for both the base and the streusel topping (with a couple of crunchy additions). The bottom layer may look dry and powdery as you press it in the pan, but baking transforms it into a crisp yet tender base for the cherry filling. A mixture of frozen cherries and jarred cherry preserves is a winning combination that requires no stovetop cooking time. Measure the cherries while they are still frozen, and then transfer them to a paper towel–lined baking sheet to thaw. The test kitchen's preferred loaf pan measures 8½ x 4½ inches; if you use a 9 by 5-inch loaf pan, start checking for doneness 5 minutes earlier than advised in the recipe. Avoid using a glass loaf pan, which will cause the bars to overbake.

1 **For the crust:** Adjust oven rack to middle position and heat oven to 375 degrees. Make foil sling for 8½ by 4½-inch loaf pan by folding 2 long sheets of aluminum foil; first sheet should be 8½ inches wide and second sheet should be 4½ inches wide. Lay sheets of foil in pan perpendicular to each other, with extra foil hanging over edges of pan. Push foil into corners and up sides of pan, smoothing foil flush to pan. Grease foil.

2 Process flour, sugar, and salt in food processor until combined, about 5 seconds. Add butter and pulse until mixture resembles wet sand, about 15 pulses.

3 Transfer ⅓ cup dough to medium bowl and set aside. Transfer remaining dough to prepared pan and use your hands to evenly distribute it over bottom of pan (dough will be slightly dry). Using your fingertips and palm of your hand, firmly press dough into even layer. Bake until light golden brown, 15 to 18 minutes, rotating pan halfway through baking.

4 **For the cherry filling:** Meanwhile, wipe processor bowl clean with paper towels. Pulse all ingredients in food processor until finely chopped, about 7 pulses; set aside.

5 **For the streusel:** Add oats, almonds, and sugar to reserved dough and toss to combine. Add butter and rub mixture between your fingers until butter is fully incorporated and mixture forms small clumps.

6 Transfer filling to pan and spread evenly over crust (crust needn't be cool). Sprinkle streusel evenly over filling (do not press streusel into filling). Bake until filling is bubbling and streusel is deep golden brown, 24 to 27 minutes, rotating pan halfway through baking. Transfer pan to wire rack and let bars cool completely, about 1 hour. Using foil overhang, lift bars out of pan, loosening sides with paring knife, if needed. Cut into 6 bars and serve. (Bars can be refrigerated for up to 2 days; crust and streusel will soften.)

---

pan swap
To make recipe in a 6-inch cake pan, make foil sling and line with parchment paper following instructions on page 125. In step 6, bake for 27 to 30 minutes. To make recipe in an 8-inch cast-iron skillet, omit sling and bake in step 6 for 18 to 21 minutes; bars will have a more pronounced crust.

chapter two
crisps, crumbles, custards, and more

apple crisp

serves 2 • **total time** 1¼ hours

topping

- ¼ cup (1¼ ounces) all-purpose flour
- ¼ cup pecans, toasted and chopped fine
- ¼ cup (¾ ounce) old-fashioned rolled oats
- 3 tablespoons packed light brown sugar
- 1 tablespoon granulated sugar
- ¼ teaspoon ground cinnamon
- ¼ teaspoon table salt
- 3 tablespoons unsalted butter, melted

filling

- 1½ pounds Fuji, Gala, or Golden Delicious apples, peeled, cored, halved, and cut into ½-inch-thick wedges
- 2 tablespoons granulated sugar
- ¼ teaspoon ground cinnamon (optional)
- ½ cup apple cider
- 1 teaspoon lemon juice
- 1 tablespoon unsalted butter

pan swap

Recipe can be prepared through step 3 then transferred to a 2½- to 3½-cup casserole dish or 8½ by 4½-inch loaf pan.

why this recipe works Casual and cozy, apple crisp is just right as a dessert for two, something you can make whenever the fall apples look good at the market. The key to a successful small-scale crisp is bringing the textures and proportions of the two components into harmony: a juicy yet cohesive filling of tender fruit under a judicious layer of buttery, golden-brown topping. Sautéing the apples before baking the crisp softens and lightly caramelizes them; a reduction of apple cider intensifies their fruitiness. Rolled oats and pecans make a topping that is satisfyingly crunchy. Do not use instant or quick oats in this recipe. If you want to bake the crisp in a toaster oven, follow the directions for making the recipe in a casserole dish or loaf pan.

1 **For the topping:** Adjust oven rack to middle position and heat oven to 450 degrees. Combine flour, pecans, oats, brown sugar, granulated sugar, cinnamon, and salt in medium bowl. Stir in melted butter until mixture resembles wet sand and no dry flour remains. Refrigerate until ready to use.

2 **For the filling:** In separate bowl, toss together apples, granulated sugar, and cinnamon, if using; set aside. Bring cider to simmer in 10-inch ovensafe skillet over medium heat and cook until reduced to ⅓ cup, about 3 minutes. Transfer reduced cider to small bowl and stir in lemon juice.

3 Melt butter in now-empty skillet over medium heat. Add apple mixture and cook, stirring frequently, until apples begin to soften and become translucent, 12 to 14 minutes. (Do not fully cook apples.) Off heat, gently stir in cider mixture until apples are coated.

4 Sprinkle topping evenly over fruit, breaking up any large pieces. Place skillet on baking sheet and bake until fruit is tender and topping is deep golden brown, 15 to 20 minutes. Let cool on wire rack for 15 minutes before serving.

individual blueberry crumbles with cornmeal and lavender

serves 2 • **total time** 1¼ hours

filling

- ¼ cup (1¾ ounces) granulated sugar, plus extra as needed
- 1½ teaspoons cornstarch
  Pinch table salt
- 10 ounces (2 cups) blueberries

topping

- ½ cup (2½ ounces) all-purpose flour
- ⅓ cup (1⅔ ounces) fine cornmeal
- ¼ cup packed (1¾ ounces) light brown sugar
- ¼ teaspoon dried lavender flowers, crumbled
- ¼ teaspoon vanilla extract
  Pinch table salt
- 4 tablespoons unsalted butter, melted

---

pan swap

A single crumble can be made in a 2½- to 3½-cup casserole dish.

---

bake in your air fryer

Place ramekins, spaced evenly apart, or casserole dish in air-fryer basket. Place basket in air fryer, set temperature to 300 degrees, and bake for 35 to 45 minutes.

why this recipe works Crisps and crumbles are rustic desserts, but put either in two ramekins and they instantly feel extra-special and personalized. To make these summery blueberry crumbles even more special, we feature cornmeal in our streusel—corn and blueberry is a lovely combination. The cornmeal gives the topping nutty flavor, while dried lavender provides a hint of floral essence. We do not recommend using frozen berries or stone-ground cornmeal in this recipe. Avoid pressing the topping into the berry mixture in step 2 or it may sink and become soggy. The lavender can be omitted.

1   For the filling: Adjust oven rack to lower-middle position and heat oven to 375 degrees. Line rimmed baking sheet with aluminum foil. Combine ¼ cup granulated sugar, cornstarch, and salt in medium bowl. Gently toss blueberries in sugar mixture. (If blueberries taste tart, add up to 4 teaspoons more sugar.) Divide blueberries evenly between two 12-ounce ramekins.

2   For the topping: Mix flour, cornmeal, brown sugar, lavender, vanilla, and salt together in clean medium bowl. Stir in melted butter until mixture resembles wet sand and no dry flour remains. Sprinkle topping evenly over blueberries, breaking up any large pieces.

3   Place ramekins on prepared sheet and bake until filling is bubbling around edges and topping is deep golden brown, about 30 minutes, rotating sheet halfway through baking. Let cool on wire rack for 15 minutes before serving.

pear crumble with miso and almonds

serves 2 • **total time** 1¼ hours

topping

- 6 tablespoons (1¾ ounces) all-purpose flour
- ¼ cup panko bread crumbs
- 2 tablespoons coarsely chopped toasted sliced almonds
- 2 tablespoons packed light brown sugar
- ½ teaspoon grated lemon zest
- ⅛ teaspoon ground cinnamon
- 2 tablespoons unsalted butter, melted
- 1 tablespoon white miso
- ⅛ teaspoon almond extract

filling

- 1 pound slightly underripe Bosc or Bartlett pears, peeled, quartered lengthwise, cored, and sliced crosswise ½ inch thick
- ¼ cup dried cherries or cranberries
- ¼ cup packed (1¾ ounces) light brown sugar
- ¼ cup heavy cream
- 2 tablespoons water
- 1½ teaspoons lemon juice
- ⅛ teaspoon table salt
- 1 tablespoon unsalted butter

why this recipe works Crumbles are a great way to turn juicy seasonal fruit into dessert for two with ease. This recipe ensures that they never get boring. We cook fragrant pears and sweet-tart dried cherries with cream, brown sugar, and butter to drape the fruit in rich caramel. The topping is luxurious, too—a salty-sweet miso-almond crumble. Adding a surprising tablespoon of miso to the crumble animates all the other ingredients. Be sure to use white (shiro) miso—which is relatively mellow and sweet. If it's unavailable, you can substitute ¼ teaspoon table salt. If you want to bake the crumble in a toaster oven, follow the directions for making the recipe in a casserole dish or loaf pan.

1 **For the topping:** Adjust oven rack to middle position and heat oven to 375 degrees. Whisk flour, panko, almonds, sugar, lemon zest, and cinnamon together in bowl. Whisk melted butter, miso, and almond extract in second bowl until miso has dissolved. Stir butter mixture into flour mixture until no dry spots of flour remain and mixture forms clumps. Refrigerate until ready to use.

2 **For the filling:** Toss pears, cherries, sugar, cream, water, lemon juice, and salt in bowl until thoroughly combined. Melt butter in 10-inch ovensafe skillet over medium-high heat. Add pear mixture and cook, stirring frequently, until pears are just beginning to soften and juices have thickened and caramelized slightly, 6 to 9 minutes. Off heat, stir to ensure cherries are evenly distributed throughout filling.

3 Squeeze topping into large clumps with your hands. Crumble topping over filling, breaking up any large pieces. Bake until topping is browned and filling is bubbling around edges of skillet, 20 to 25 minutes. Let cool on wire rack for 15 minutes before serving.

---

pan swap
Recipe can be prepared through step 2, then transferred to a 2½- to 3½-cup casserole dish or 8½ by 4½-inch loaf pan.

cherry-pecan crumble

serves 2 • **total time** 1 hour

topping

- ⅓ cup (1⅔ ounces) all-purpose flour
- 1 tablespoon packed light brown sugar
- 1 tablespoon granulated sugar
- ¼ teaspoon vanilla extract
- Pinch ground cinnamon
- Pinch table salt
- 2 tablespoons unsalted butter, melted
- ¼ cup pecans, chopped

filling

- 1½ tablespoons granulated sugar, divided
- ½ teaspoon cornstarch
- 10 ounces frozen sweet cherries
- ¼ cup water
- 2 teaspoons lemon juice
- ¼ teaspoon vanilla extract
- ⅛ teaspoon table salt
- ¼ cup dried cherries

why this recipe works From nuts to topping to fruit, this pantry dessert is cooked completely in one skillet on the stovetop: We toast the pecans and brown the crumble in the skillet, then use the same pan to cook the filling before the two parts are briefly heated together. A combination of frozen sweet cherries and dried cherries gives us the big flavor we want from the fruit—and lets us make the crisp anytime. Waiting for this dessert to cool is the hardest part of the recipe. There's no need to thaw the cherries.

1 **For the topping:** Combine flour, brown sugar, granulated sugar, vanilla, cinnamon, and salt in bowl. Stir in melted butter until mixture resembles wet sand and no dry flour remains. Refrigerate until ready to use.

2 Toast pecans in 10-inch ovensafe skillet over medium-low heat until fragrant, about 4 minutes. Add flour mixture and cook, stirring constantly, until lightly browned, about 4 minutes; transfer to plate to cool. Wipe skillet clean with paper towels.

3 **For the filling:** Combine 1½ teaspoons granulated sugar and cornstarch in small bowl; set aside. Combine sweet cherries, water, lemon juice, vanilla, salt, and remaining 1 table-spoon sugar in now-empty skillet. Cook, covered, over medium heat until cherries thaw and release their juice and mixture starts to simmer, about 5 minutes, stirring halfway through cooking. Stir in dried cherries and simmer, uncovered, until plumped and tender, about 2 minutes. Stir in cornstarch mixture and cook, stirring constantly, until mixture is thickened, about 30 seconds.

4 Off heat, sprinkle topping evenly over filling. Return skillet to medium-low heat and cook until filling is bubbling around edges, about 1 minute. Let cool on wire rack for 15 minutes before serving.

strawberry-rhubarb crumble

serves 2 • **total time** 1¼ hours

topping

- 6 tablespoons (1¾ ounces) all-purpose flour
- ¼ cup panko bread crumbs
- 2 tablespoons packed light brown sugar
- ¼ teaspoon table salt
- ⅛ teaspoon ground cinnamon
- 3 tablespoons unsalted butter, melted

filling

- 8 ounces fresh rhubarb, trimmed and cut into ½-inch pieces (1¾ cups)
- 6 ounces fresh strawberries, hulled and chopped coarse (1 cup)
- ½ cup plus 2 tablespoons packed (4⅓ ounces) light brown sugar
- 1 tablespoon cornstarch
- Pinch table salt

pan swap

Recipe can be prepared through step 2, then transferred to a 2½- to 3½-cup casserole dish or 8½ by 4½-inch loaf pan.

why this recipe works The pairing of sweet strawberries and tart rhubarb is a classic for good reason, but it can be hard for two people to tackle a whole strawberry-rhubarb pie. A crumble can cut the dessert to size and take care of a common early summer problem: When strawberry and rhubarb are cooked, they are juicy to a fault. Sautéing them on the stovetop with some brown sugar and cornstarch coaxes out excess liquid and creates a jammy consistency. Light panko crumbs amp up the crispness (even as they absorb moisture) in an easy stir-together topping that bakes up golden brown. Frozen rhubarb and strawberries can be substituted for fresh. If using frozen strawberries, there's no need to thaw them completely; you can chop them as soon as they're soft enough. Depending on the amount of trimming required, you may need to buy more than 8 ounces of rhubarb to ensure that you end up with 1¾ cups. If you want to bake the crumble in a toaster oven, follow the directions for making the recipe in a casserole dish or loaf pan.

1 **For the topping:** Adjust oven rack to middle position and heat oven to 375 degrees. Whisk flour, panko, sugar, salt, and cinnamon together in bowl. Stir in melted butter until mixture resembles wet sand and no dry flour remains. Refrigerate until ready to use.

2 **For the filling:** Toss all ingredients in bowl until thoroughly combined. Transfer to 10-inch ovensafe skillet. Cook over medium-high heat, stirring frequently, until fruit has released enough liquid to be mostly submerged, rhubarb is just beginning to break down, and juices have thickened, 5 to 7 minutes. Remove skillet from heat.

3 Squeeze topping into large clumps with your hands. Crumble topping over filling, breaking up any large pieces. Bake until topping is browned and filling is bubbling around sides of skillet, 15 to 20 minutes. Let cool on wire rack for 15 minutes before serving.

apple-blackberry betty

serves 2 • **total time** 1½ hours, plus 20 minutes cooling

4   slices hearty white sandwich
     bread, cut into 1-inch pieces

⅓   cup packed (2⅓ ounces) light
     brown sugar, divided

¼   teaspoon table salt, divided

3   tablespoons unsalted butter,
     melted

8   ounces Fuji, Gala, or Golden
     Delicious apples, peeled, cored,
     and cut into ½-inch pieces

2   tablespoons water

½   teaspoon vanilla extract

     Pinch ground nutmeg

4   ounces fresh or frozen
     blackberries, berries halved if
     larger than ¾ inch

pan swap
Recipe can be made in an 8-inch square baking pan or 8½ by 4½-inch loaf pan.

why this recipe works If you've got a couple apples and you're looking for fall's unfussiest dessert for two, look no further than an apple Betty. The baked dessert features lightly sweetened bread crumbs both above and below the apples. But the bread crumbs do more than simplify the dish; those on the bottom absorb excess moisture from the apples, while those on the top crisp and brown to an almost caramelized topping. We like adding fresh blackberries to the mix (you can also use frozen or simply omit them) for pops of contrasting flavor. Along with hearty white bread, soft enriched breads such as challah or brioche also work well here.

1 Adjust oven racks to upper-middle and lower-middle positions and heat oven to 375 degrees. Pulse bread in food processor until coarsely ground, about 10 pulses. Add ¼ cup sugar and ⅛ teaspoon salt and pulse to combine, about 5 pulses. Drizzle with melted butter and pulse until evenly distributed, about 5 pulses. Scatter 1 cup bread crumb mixture in 3½-cup casserole dish. Press gently to create even layer.

2 Combine apples, water, vanilla, nutmeg, remaining 4 teaspoons sugar, and remaining ⅛ teaspoon salt in bowl. Pile apple mixture atop bread crumb mixture in dish and spread and press into even layer. Sprinkle blackberries over apples. Distribute remaining bread crumb mixture evenly over blackberries and press lightly to form uniform layer. Cover tightly with aluminum foil. Place on rimmed baking sheet and bake on lower rack until apples are soft, about 45 minutes.

3 Remove foil and transfer dish to upper rack. Bake until crumbs on top are crisp and well browned, about 10 minutes. Transfer to wire rack and let cool for at least 20 minutes before serving.

peach cobbler

serves 2 • **total time** 55 minutes, plus 20 minutes cooling

topping

- ½ cup (2½ ounces) all-purpose flour
- 2 tablespoons granulated sugar
- ½ teaspoon baking powder
- ⅛ teaspoon baking soda
- ⅛ teaspoon table salt
- ¼ cup buttermilk, chilled
- 2 tablespoons unsalted butter, melted
- 1 teaspoon turbinado sugar

filling

- 3 tablespoons packed brown sugar
- 1 tablespoon unsalted butter
- ⅛ teaspoon table salt
- ⅛ teaspoon ground cinnamon
- 1¼ pounds fresh peaches, peeled, halved, pitted, and cut into ½-inch wedges
- 1 tablespoon water
- 1½ teaspoons lemon juice
- 1 teaspoon all-purpose flour
- ½ teaspoon vanilla extract

pan swap

Recipe can be prepared through step 2, then transferred to a 2½- to 3½-cup casserole dish or 8½ by 4½-inch loaf pan.

why this recipe works If you're making cobbler for two, chances are you don't want to spend time rolling and cutting out perfect biscuits. Quickly stirring together and dropping buttermilk biscuit dough onto a hot filling is an easy shortcut that also helps jump-start the biscuits' cooking. For the filling, parcooking the peaches with butter and brown sugar in a skillet beforehand concentrates their luscious juices into a syrup. The whole skillet goes into the oven and the cobbler emerges looking comforting and homey, with its bubbling filling and crispy, craggy, golden-brown top—ready for two spoons to crack through. You can substitute 1 pound frozen sliced peaches for fresh. If using frozen peaches, don't thaw them, but do increase their cooking time in step 2 to about 7 minutes. A serrated peeler makes quick work of peeling fresh peaches. We prefer the crunchy texture of turbinado sugar sprinkled over the biscuits before baking, but granulated sugar can be substituted. If you want to bake the cobbler in a toaster oven, follow the directions for making the recipe in a casserole dish or loaf pan.

1 **For the topping:** Adjust oven rack to middle position and heat oven to 400 degrees. Whisk flour, granulated sugar, baking powder, baking soda, and salt together in medium bowl. In separate bowl, stir buttermilk and melted butter together until butter forms small clumps. Using wooden spoon or rubber spatula, stir buttermilk mixture into flour mixture until just incorporated. Cover and set aside.

2 **For the filling:** Combine brown sugar, butter, salt, and cinnamon in 10-inch ovensafe skillet. Bring mixture to simmer over medium-high heat and cook until sugar is dissolved, about 2 minutes. Add peaches, cover, and cook until peaches release their juice, about 5 minutes. Whisk water, lemon juice, and flour together in bowl, then stir into peaches. Off heat, stir in vanilla.

3 Using large spoon, scoop and drop 1-inch pieces of dough, spaced about ½ inch apart, over hot peach mixture in skillet, then sprinkle with turbinado sugar. Bake until biscuits are golden brown and filling is thick, 20 to 25 minutes. Let cool on wire rack for 20 minutes before serving.

cherry cobbler with spiced wine

serves 2 • **total time** 45 minutes, plus 20 minutes cooling

topping

- ½ cup (2½ ounces) all-purpose flour
- 3 tablespoons granulated sugar
- ½ teaspoon baking powder
- ⅛ teaspoon baking soda
- ⅛ teaspoon table salt
- ¼ cup buttermilk, chilled
- 2 tablespoons unsalted butter, melted
- 1 teaspoon turbinado sugar

filling

- ¼ cup (1¾ ounces) granulated sugar
- 1 tablespoon cornstarch
- Pinch table salt
- 1⅓ cups jarred sour cherries in light syrup, drained with ¼ cup syrup reserved
- ½ cup dry red wine
- ¼ teaspoon vanilla extract
- 1 small cinnamon stick

pan swap

Recipe can be prepared through step 2, then transferred to a 2½- to 3½-cup casserole dish or 8½ by 4½-inch loaf pan.

why this recipe works Cobblers are simple topping-and-filling affairs, but their flavor can be as complex as you want. Here we rely on jarred sour cherries, which are plump, tart, already pitted, and available year-round. We combine them with complementary cinnamon-spiked red wine, sugar, and cornstarch. A bit of the cherry syrup from the jar reduces on the stovetop to a silky consistency that clings to the cherries. We prefer the crunchy texture of turbinado sugar sprinkled over the biscuits before baking, but granulated sugar can be substituted. If you want to bake the cobbler in a toaster oven, follow the directions for making the recipe in a casserole dish or loaf pan.

1 **For the topping:** Adjust oven rack to middle position and heat oven to 400 degrees. Whisk flour, granulated sugar, baking powder, baking soda, and salt together in medium bowl. In separate bowl, stir buttermilk and melted butter together until butter forms small clumps. Using wooden spoon or rubber spatula, stir buttermilk mixture into flour mixture until just incorporated. Cover and set aside.

2 **For the filling:** Whisk granulated sugar, cornstarch, and salt together in 10-inch ovensafe skillet. Whisk in reserved ¼ cup cherry syrup, wine, and vanilla, then add cinnamon stick. Bring mixture to simmer over medium-high heat and cook, whisking frequently, until slightly thickened, 1 to 3 minutes. Off heat, remove cinnamon stick and stir in cherries.

3 Using large spoon, scoop and drop 1-inch pieces of dough, spaced about ½ inch apart, over cherry filling, then sprinkle with turbinado sugar. Bake until biscuits are golden brown and filling is thick and glossy, 20 to 25 minutes. Let cool on wire rack for 20 minutes before serving.

griddled corn cakes with berry compote and cream

serves 2 • **total time** 55 minutes

berry compote

5	ounces blackberries, raspberries, and/or strawberries
1½	tablespoons sugar, plus extra to taste
1	teaspoon cornstarch
	Pinch table salt

corn cakes

⅓	cup fresh or thawed frozen corn
5	tablespoons whole milk
¼	cup (2 ounces) whole-milk ricotta cheese
¼	cup (1¼ ounces) all-purpose flour
¼	cup (1¼ ounces) fine cornmeal
2	tablespoons unsalted butter, melted
1	tablespoon sugar
½	teaspoon vanilla extract
½	teaspoon baking powder
¼	teaspoon table salt
2	teaspoons vegetable oil
1	recipe Whipped Cream (page 85)

why this recipe works Think outside the dessert box with these hot-off-the-griddle corn cakes, soaked through with juicy berries and topped with whipped cream, that feel uniquely sophisticated while requiring no more work than making pancakes. Ricotta gives the cakes creaminess, and butter and whole milk make them rich and dessert-worthy. Do not use stone-ground cornmeal in this recipe.

1 **For the compote:** Hull strawberries, if using, and halve if small or quarter if large. Halve blackberries larger than ¾ inch, if using. Combine berries, 1½ tablespoons sugar, cornstarch, and salt in medium bowl and microwave until berries begin to break down and sauce is thickened, about 2 minutes, stirring once halfway through microwaving. Let compote cool completely and season with extra sugar to taste. (Compote can be refrigerated for up to 4 days.)

2 **For the corn cakes:** Whisk corn, milk, ricotta, flour, cornmeal, melted butter, sugar, vanilla, baking powder, and salt in bowl until fully incorporated. Cover and let sit for 15 minutes.

3 Line rimmed baking sheet with double layer of paper towels and place near stovetop. Heat oil in 12-inch nonstick skillet over medium-low heat until shimmering.

4 Using greased ¼-cup dry measuring cup, portion batter into skillet in 4 places, leaving ½ inch between portions. If necessary, gently spread batter into 4-inch rounds. Cook until edges are set, first sides are golden brown, and bubbles on surface are just beginning to break, about 3 minutes. Using thin, wide spatula, carefully flip cakes and continue to cook until second sides are golden brown, about 3 minutes. Transfer cakes to paper towel–lined baking sheet.

5 Transfer corn cakes to individual plates, top with compote and whipped cream, and serve.

clafouti

serves 2 • **total time** 1 hour, plus 25 minutes cooling

8 ounces fresh sweet cherries, pitted and halved

½ teaspoon lemon juice

1 teaspoon plus 3 tablespoons all-purpose flour, divided

Pinch ground cinnamon

1 large egg

¼ cup (1¾ ounces) plus 1 teaspoon sugar, divided

1 teaspoon vanilla extract

Pinch table salt

½ cup half-and-half

1 tablespoon unsalted butter

why this recipe works When fleeting cherry season arrives, clafouti, the custardy baked dessert created in and beloved across the French countryside, is a sweet, simple, and less expected way to use the fruit. All you need are those cherries, some half-and-half, and a few ingredients you should always have in your pantry. We pit and halve the cherries in no time (since we need only enough for two) and then roast them in the oven, which concentrates their flavor and drives off some of their moisture. A pinch of cinnamon recovers the slightly spicy, floral flavor that cherry pits traditionally contribute. Rather than bake the clafouti in a small casserole dish, we found that a 10-inch skillet imparted better browning and made the custard easy to slice and serve. Do not substitute frozen cherries.

1 Adjust oven racks to upper-middle and lowest positions. Place 10-inch ovensafe skillet on lower rack and heat oven to 425 degrees. Line rimmed baking sheet with aluminum foil and place cherries cut side up on sheet. Roast cherries on upper rack until just tender and cut sides look dry, about 10 minutes. Transfer cherries to small bowl, toss with lemon juice, and let cool for 5 minutes. Combine 1 teaspoon flour and cinnamon in small bowl. Dust flour mixture evenly over cherries and toss to coat thoroughly.

2 Whisk egg, ¼ cup sugar, vanilla, and salt in medium bowl until smooth and pale yellow, about 1 minute. Whisk in remaining 3 tablespoons flour until smooth. Whisk in half-and-half until incorporated.

3 Using oven mitts, remove skillet from oven and set on wire rack. Being careful of hot skillet handle, add butter and swirl to coat bottom and sides of skillet (butter will melt and brown quickly). Pour batter into skillet and arrange cherries evenly on top (some will sink). Transfer skillet to lower rack and bake until clafouti puffs and turns golden brown (edges will be dark brown), 18 to 22 minutes, rotating skillet halfway through baking. Transfer skillet to wire rack and let cool for 25 minutes. Sprinkle evenly with remaining 1 teaspoon sugar. Slice into wedges and serve.

german pancake

serves 2 • **total time** 45 minutes

1¼ cups (6¼ ounces) all-purpose flour

3 tablespoons sugar, divided

2 teaspoons grated lemon zest plus 1 tablespoon juice

¼ teaspoon table salt

Pinch ground nutmeg

1 cup milk

4 large eggs

1 teaspoon vanilla extract

2 tablespoons unsalted butter

---

pan swap
Recipe can be made in a 10-inch stainless-steel skillet or well-seasoned cast-iron skillet; coat lightly with vegetable oil spray before using.

why this recipe works You might be used to a sprawling German pancake made at a certain breakfast joint, but this appealing puffed pancake can be prepared at home and for just two. To ensure a dramatic puff (without a dramatic procedure) as well as a delicate texture, rather than incorporate the fruit into the batter, we use it in optional brown sugar–boosted apple or banana toppings.

1 Whisk flour, 2 tablespoons sugar, lemon zest, salt, and nutmeg together in medium bowl. Whisk milk, eggs, and vanilla together in second bowl. Whisk two-thirds of milk mixture into flour mixture until no lumps remain, then slowly whisk in remaining milk mixture until smooth.

2 Adjust oven rack to lower-middle position. Melt butter in 10-inch ovensafe nonstick skillet over medium-low heat. Add batter to skillet, immediately transfer to oven, and set oven to 375 degrees. Bake until edges are deep golden brown and center is beginning to brown, 25 to 30 minutes.

3 Transfer skillet to wire rack and sprinkle pancake with lemon juice and remaining 1 tablespoon sugar. Gently transfer pancake to cutting board, cut into wedges, and serve.

apple topping
makes 1 cup
total time 20 minutes

1 tablespoon unsalted butter

3 tablespoons water

2 tablespoons packed brown sugar

⅛ teaspoon ground cinnamon

Pinch table salt

10 ounces Braeburn, Honeycrisp, or Fuji apples (1 to 2 apples), peeled, cored, and cut into ½-inch-thick wedges, wedges halved crosswise

Melt butter in 10-inch skillet over medium heat. Add water, sugar, cinnamon, and salt; whisk until sugar dissolves. Add apples, increase heat to medium-high, and bring to simmer. Cover and cook, stirring occasionally, for 5 minutes. Uncover and continue to cook until apples are translucent and just tender and sauce is thickened, 5 to 7 minutes. (Topping can be refrigerated for up to 2 days.)

banana topping

makes *1 cup*
total time *15 minutes*

- 1 tablespoon unsalted butter
- 2 tablespoons packed brown sugar
- 1 tablespoon water
- ½ teaspoon lemon juice
- ⅛ teaspoon ground cardamom
- Pinch table salt
- 2 small ripe bananas, peeled and sliced on bias ½ inch thick

Melt butter in 10-inch skillet over medium heat. Add sugar, water, lemon juice, cardamom, and salt and whisk until sugar dissolves. Add bananas and cook, stirring frequently, until bananas have softened at edges, 2 to 3 minutes.

crepes with sugar and lemon

yield 4 crepes • **total time** 45 minutes

½ teaspoon vegetable oil

½ cup (2½ ounces) all-purpose flour

1½ tablespoons sugar, divided

⅛ teaspoon table salt

¾ cup whole milk

1 large egg

1 tablespoon unsalted butter, melted and cooled

Lemon wedges

why this recipe works Crepe batter is simple, so it's worth it to prepare a short stack any time you want a refined sweet treat. Our technique ensures foolproof results: We heat an oiled skillet over low heat for a full 10 minutes to get the pan to the ideal temperature for crepe success. Tilting and gently shaking the pan while adding the batter guarantees even distribution. And flipping each crepe when the top surface is dry and the edges are starting to brown ensures golden-brown perfection for this French classic à deux. Crepes will give off steam as they cook, but if at any point the skillet begins to smoke, remove it from the heat immediately and turn down the heat. Stacking the crepes on a wire rack allows excess steam to escape so they won't stick together. To allow for practice, the recipe yields five crepes; only four are needed for the dessert.

1 Heat oil in 12-inch nonstick skillet over low heat for at least 10 minutes.

2 While skillet is heating, whisk flour, ½ teaspoon sugar, and salt together in medium bowl. In separate bowl, whisk milk and egg together. Add half of milk mixture to flour mixture and whisk until smooth. Add melted butter and whisk until incorporated. Whisk in remaining milk mixture until smooth.

3 Wipe out skillet with paper towel, leaving thin film of oil on bottom and sides of skillet. Increase heat to medium and let skillet heat for 1 minute. After 1 minute, test heat of skillet by placing 1 teaspoon batter in center and cook for 20 seconds. If mini crepe is golden brown on bottom, skillet is properly heated; if it is too light or too dark, adjust heat accordingly and retest.

4 Pour ¼ cup batter into far side of skillet and tilt and shake gently until batter evenly covers bottom of skillet. Cook crepe without moving it until top surface is dry and edges are starting to brown, loosening crepe from side of skillet with heat-resistant rubber spatula, about 25 seconds.

5 Gently slide spatula underneath edge of crepe, grasp edge with your fingertips, and flip crepe. Cook until second side is lightly spotted, about 20 seconds. Transfer cooked crepe to wire rack, inverting so spotted side is facing up. Return skillet to heat and heat for 10 seconds before repeating with remaining batter to make 3 more crepes. As crepes are done, stack on wire rack.

6 If crepes have cooled, transfer stack to large plate and invert second plate over crepes. Microwave until crepes are warm, 30 to 45 seconds (45 to 60 seconds if crepes have cooled completely). Remove top plate and wipe dry with paper towel. Sprinkle half of top crepe with 1 teaspoon sugar. Fold unsugared half over sugared half, then fold into quarters. Transfer sugared crepe to second plate. Continue with remaining crepes and remaining 1 tablespoon sugar. Serve immediately with lemon wedges.

variations

crepes with chocolate and orange

Omit 4 teaspoons sugar used for sprinkling in step 6 and lemon wedges. Using your fingertips, rub ½ teaspoon finely grated orange zest into 2 tablespoons sugar, then stir in 1 ounce finely grated bittersweet chocolate. In step 6, sprinkle 1½ tablespoons chocolate-orange mixture over half of each crepe. Fold crepes into quarters.

crepes with honey and toasted almonds

Omit 4 teaspoons sugar used for sprinkling in step 6 and lemon wedges. In step 6, drizzle 1 teaspoon honey over half of each crepe and sprinkle with 2 teaspoons finely chopped toasted sliced almonds and small pinch salt. Fold crepes into quarters.

making a crepe

1 Pour ¼ cup batter into far side of skillet. Tilt and shake skillet gently until batter evenly covers bottom of skillet.

2 Gently slide spatula underneath edge of crepe, grasp edge with your fingertips, and flip crepe.

3 Cook until second side is lightly spotted, about 20 seconds. Transfer cooked crepe to wire rack, inverting so spotted side is facing up.

classic bread pudding

serves 2 • **total time** 1¾ hours, plus 15 minutes cooling

6 ounces baguette, torn into 1-inch pieces (4 cups)

1 cup half-and-half

⅓ cup packed (2⅓ ounces) light brown sugar

2 large egg yolks

1 teaspoon vanilla extract

½ teaspoon ground cinnamon, divided

⅛ teaspoon table salt

Pinch ground nutmeg

¼ cup raisins

2 tablespoons unsalted butter, cut into ¼-inch pieces

1 tablespoon granulated sugar

---

pan swap

Recipe can be made in 12- or 16-ounce ramekins. Single bread pudding can be made in a 2½- to 3½-cup casserole dish or 8½ by 4½-inch loaf pan; increase covered baking time to 40 minutes.

---

bake in your air fryer

Line air-fryer basket with aluminum foil, crimping edges. Arrange bread directly in prepared basket. Place basket in air fryer, set temperature to 300 degrees, and bake for 10 to 20 minutes. Assemble bread puddings and place ramekins in air-fryer basket. Set temperature to 300 degrees and bake, covered, for 30 minutes; uncover ramekins and bake for 10 to 15 minutes.

why this recipe works Bread pudding is so rich and indulgent, you probably don't want to eat through a large casserole of it all week. For a one-time special, we scale down the pudding to bake in two ramekins (or one mini casserole). Swapping out whole eggs for yolks and covering the ramekins with foil keeps the pudding from curdling. We remove the foil for the last 10 minutes of baking to form a crisp, golden crust. We also include two variations that up the comfort even more on bread pudding: dirty chai, with the flavor of a chai tea latte with a shot of espresso, and the well-loved flavor combination of peanut butter and banana.

1 Adjust oven rack to middle position and heat oven to 375 degrees. Spread bread in single layer on rimmed baking sheet and bake until golden brown and crisp, 10 to 20 minutes, tossing halfway through baking. Let bread cool completely. Do not turn off oven.

2 Whisk half-and-half, brown sugar, yolks, vanilla, ¼ teaspoon cinnamon, salt, and nutmeg together in large bowl. Add bread and raisins and toss until evenly coated. Let mixture sit, tossing occasionally, until bread begins to absorb custard and is softened, about 20 minutes.

3 Grease two 12-ounce ramekins. Divide bread mixture evenly between prepared ramekins, dot with butter, and sprinkle with granulated sugar and remaining ¼ teaspoon cinnamon. Cover each ramekin with aluminum foil, place on rimmed baking sheet, and bake for 30 minutes.

4 Remove foil and continue to bake until tops are crisp and golden brown, 10 to 15 minutes. Transfer to wire rack and let cool for 15 minutes before serving.

variations

banana–peanut butter bread pudding

Omit raisins and nutmeg. Whisk 2 tablespoons creamy or chunky peanut butter into half-and-half mixture until fully combined. Stir 1 small banana, cut into ¼-inch pieces, and ¼ cup toasted, unsalted peanuts into custard with bread.

dirty chai bread pudding

Omit raisins and cinnamon for sprinkling. Substitute 1 teaspoon chai spice blend and 1 teaspoon espresso powder for cinnamon and nutmeg in custard.

individual chocolate soufflés

serves 2 • **total time** 35 minutes

1 tablespoon unsalted butter, cut into 2 pieces, plus softened butter for ramekins

2 tablespoons granulated sugar, plus extra for ramekins

3 ounces bittersweet chocolate, chopped

1 teaspoon orange-flavored liqueur

¼ teaspoon vanilla extract

Pinch table salt

2 large eggs, separated, plus 1 large white

⅛ teaspoon cream of tartar

Confectioners' sugar (optional)

---

pan swap

Recipe can be made in 8-ounce or 10-ounce ramekins. A single soufflé can be made in a 16-ounce ramekin; bake for 18 to 20 minutes.

variation

individual mocha soufflés

Add 1 teaspoon instant espresso powder dissolved in 1 teaspoon hot water to chocolate mixture along with liqueur in step 2.

why this recipe works The romance of receiving your own tall, airy but decadently chocolate soufflé may be unmatched by any other dessert. These perfect soufflés rise to any occasion. The base consists of egg yolks beaten with sugar until thick, giving each soufflé plenty of volume without the flavor-muting milk that's found in many recipes. A touch of orange liqueur emphasizes the adult sophistication. Grand Marnier is our preferred orange-flavored liqueur in this recipe. Your thermometer will not come out clean when temping the soufflé in step 5. It can be a little hard to gauge when the soufflé is fully risen; if you're unsure, keep the soufflé in the oven for a few extra minutes and watch to see if it continues to rise. If not, your soufflé is likely done. If you bake the soufflés in a toaster oven, you should reduce the toaster oven temperature to 350 degrees.

1 Adjust oven rack to lower-middle position and heat oven to 375 degrees. Grease two 8-ounce ramekins with straight sides with softened butter, then coat dishes evenly with granulated sugar; refrigerate until ready to use.

2 Microwave butter and chocolate in medium bowl at 50 percent power, stirring occasionally, until melted and smooth, 2 to 4 minutes. Stir in liqueur, vanilla, and salt; set aside.

3 Using stand mixer fitted with paddle, beat granulated sugar and egg yolks on medium speed until thick and pale yellow, about 3 minutes. Fold into reserved chocolate mixture.

4 Using clean, dry mixer bowl and whisk attachment, whip egg whites and cream of tartar on medium-low speed until foamy, about 1 minute. Increase speed to medium-high and whip until stiff peaks form, 3 to 4 minutes.

5 Using rubber spatula, stir one-quarter whipped whites into chocolate mixture until combined. Gently fold remaining whipped whites into chocolate mixture in 2 additions, until no white streaks remain. Carefully spoon mixture into prepared dishes and smooth tops. Gently tap each dish once against counter and set on rimmed baking sheet. Bake until fully risen above rim of dish and edge is set, soufflé barely jiggles, and center of soufflé registers 165 degrees, 10 to 15 minutes.

6 Dust with confectioners' sugar, if using, and serve immediately.

individual pavlovas with berries, lime, and basil topping

serves 2 • **total time** 2 hours, plus 1½ hours resting

meringue

⅔ cup (4⅔ ounces) sugar

2 large egg whites

½ teaspoon distilled white vinegar

½ teaspoon cornstarch

¼ teaspoon vanilla extract

topping

8 ounces blackberries, blueberries, raspberries, and/or strawberries

1¼ teaspoons sugar

⅛ teaspoon grated lime zest plus ¼ teaspoon juice

Pinch table salt

1 recipe Whipped Cream (page 85)

1 tablespoon chopped fresh basil, plus 2 small leaves, divided

why this recipe works With its contrasting colors, textures, and flavors, a pavlova is a special occasion–worthy dessert. Luckily, it's one that is easily served as a dessert for two and can even be made ahead. We like to make individual meringues instead of one big one; they develop extra-crisp exteriors (and may even crack, which is perfectly OK), while the insides remain soft. Choose whatever berries you like—as long as they're fresh, not frozen—and let them sit with a little sugar and lime zest until they're bright and juicy. Spoon them onto the cooled meringues along with whipped cream, top with fresh basil, and let the pavlovas sit for a few minutes to meld—then enjoy a taste of summer. Open the oven door as infrequently as possible while the meringue is inside. The baked, cooled meringue can be stored for up to a week, so all you need to do before serving is prepare the fruit topping and whip the cream. You will need a 3½- to 5-quart stand mixer for this recipe; larger stand mixers or hand mixers will not adequately whip the meringue. If baking the pavlovas in a toaster oven, reduce the oven temperature to 225 degrees.

1 **For the meringue:** Adjust oven rack to middle position and heat oven to 250 degrees. Combine sugar and egg whites in bowl of stand mixer; place bowl over saucepan filled with 1 inch simmering water, making sure that water does not touch bottom of bowl. Whisking gently but constantly, heat until sugar is dissolved and mixture registers 160 degrees, 4 to 6 minutes.

2 Fit stand mixer with whisk attachment and whip mixture on high speed until meringue forms stiff peaks, is smooth and creamy, and is bright white with sheen, about 5 minutes (bowl may still be slightly warm to touch). Stop mixer and scrape down bowl with spatula. Add vinegar, cornstarch, and vanilla and whip on high speed until combined, about 10 seconds.

(continued)

individual pavlovas with mango, kiwi, and mint topping

Omit berry topping. Toss 1 mango, peeled, pitted, and cut into ½-inch pieces; 1 large kiwi, peeled, quartered lengthwise, and sliced crosswise ¼ inch thick ; and 1 teaspoon sugar together in bowl. Set fruit aside for 30 minutes. Just before serving, toss 1 tablespoon chopped fresh mint into fruit mixture and garnish each pavlova with 2 small mint leaves.

3   Spoon about ¼ teaspoon meringue onto each corner of small rimmed baking sheet. Line sheet with parchment paper, pressing on corners to secure. Divide meringue into 2 evenly spaced piles on sheet. Spread each meringue pile with back of spoon to form 5½-inch disk with slight depression in center.

4   Bake meringues until exteriors are dry and crisp and meringues release cleanly from parchment when gently lifted at edges with thin metal spatula, about 1 hour. Meringues should be quite pale (a hint of creamy color is OK). Turn off oven, prop door open with wooden spoon, and let meringues cool in oven for 1½ hours. Remove from oven and let cool completely, about 15 minutes. (Cooled meringues can be wrapped tightly in plastic wrap and stored at room temperature for up to 1 week.)

5   **For the topping:** Hull strawberries, if using, and halve lengthwise if small or quarter if large. Halve blackberries larger than ¾ inch, if using. Toss berries with sugar, lime zest and juice, and salt in bowl; set aside for 30 minutes.

6   Carefully peel meringue away from parchment and place on serving plates. Spoon whipped cream into center of meringue. Just before serving, stir chopped basil into mixed berries. Using slotted spoon, spoon berries in even layer over pavlovas. Garnish with basil leaves. Let stand for at least 5 minutes or up to 1 hour. Before serving, drizzle pavlovas with any juice from bowl.

making pavlovas

Divide meringue into 2 evenly spaced piles on sheet. Spread each meringue pile with back of spoon to form 5½-inch disk with slight depression in center.

strawberry shortcakes

serves 2 • **total time** 45 minutes, plus 20 minutes cooling and resting

shortcakes

½ cup (2½ ounces) all-purpose flour

1¼ teaspoons granulated sugar, divided

½ teaspoon baking powder

Pinch baking soda

⅛ teaspoon table salt

⅓ cup heavy cream, warm (100 degrees)

strawberries and cream

8 ounces strawberries, hulled and sliced ¼ inch thick

1 tablespoon granulated sugar

½ teaspoon lemon juice

Pinch table salt

1 recipe Whipped Cream (page 85)

Confectioners' sugar, for dusting (optional)

---

bake in your air fryer

Line air-fryer basket with aluminum foil, crimping edges. Space biscuits at least ½ inch apart in prepared basket. Place basket in air fryer, set temperature to 350 degrees, and bake for 8 to 10 minutes.

why this recipe works Shortcakes are a classic expression of an early-summer strawberry dessert. This version for two is fresh, yielding just two perfect tender biscuit shortcakes, without bushels of berries to work through and no leftovers to stale. We wanted a sophisticated look without rolling out dough for just two biscuits; we found that packing the dough into a ⅓-cup measure and unmolding it onto the baking sheet gives the biscuits a structured look. Slicing the berries helps the sugar do its work to make them juicy and shortcake-ready in the time it takes to bake and cool the biscuits.

1 **For the shortcakes:** Adjust oven rack to upper-middle position and heat oven to 450 degrees. Line rimmed baking sheet with parchment paper. Whisk flour, ¾ teaspoon granulated sugar, baking powder, baking soda, and salt together in medium bowl. Using wooden spoon or rubber spatula, stir warm cream into flour mixture until soft, uniform dough forms.

2 Using spoon, transfer half of dough to greased ⅓-cup dry measuring cup, pressing to fill bottom of cup (cup will not be completely filled). Run butter knife around edge of cup and deposit dough onto prepared sheet. Repeat with remaining dough. If portions are misshapen, use your fingers to gently reshape dough into level cylinders. Sprinkle remaining ½ teaspoon granulated sugar over shortcakes. Bake until tops are light golden brown, 8 to 10 minutes, rotating sheet halfway through baking. Transfer to wire rack and let cool completely, about 20 minutes.

3 **For the strawberries and cream:** Combine strawberries, granulated sugar, lemon juice, and salt in medium bowl. Using potato masher, mash one-third of strawberries. Let rest, stirring occasionally, until sugar is dissolved and strawberries are juicy, about 20 minutes.

4 Split shortcakes crosswise and place bottoms on plates. Place half of strawberry mixture on bottom of each shortcake. Top each portion with half of whipped cream. Cap with shortcake tops and dust with confectioners' sugar, if desired. Serve.

whipped cream

makes *about 1½ cups*
total time *5 minutes*

Whipping cream in this time frame will produce soft to stiff peaks; you should hand-whisk to your desired consistency as the whipped cream volume is too small for a stand mixer. But you can use a hand mixer if you prefer: Beat at medium-low speed until foamy, about 1 minute, then increase speed to high and beat to desired consistency.

- ¼ cup heavy cream, chilled
- ¼ teaspoon confectioners' sugar

Add cream and sugar to deep bowl. Tilt bowl so cream pools on one side and whisk vigorously, in a side-to-side motion, until thick and nearly doubled in volume, 30 to 60 seconds.

variations

brown sugar–berry shortcakes

Omit lemon juice. Substitute 8 ounces blackberries, blueberries, and/or raspberries for strawberries and 3 to 5 tablespoons packed light brown sugar (depending on sweetness of berries) for granulated sugar. Halve blackberries if larger than ¾ inch.

rhubarb shortcakes

If you want to air-fry the roasted rhubarb, set temperature to 250 degrees and bake rhubarb as directed.

Substitute 8 ounces rhubarb, trimmed and cut into ¾-inch pieces, for strawberries. Increase sugar to ¼ cup (1¾ ounces). Adjust oven rack to upper-middle position and heat oven to 325 degrees. Toss rhubarb with sugar, lemon juice, and salt then transfer to 8-inch baking dish. Cover with aluminum foil and bake until paring knife inserted into rhubarb meets little resistance, about 20 minutes. Remove foil, stir rhubarb mixture, and continue to bake until rhubarb is tender but still intact, not mushy or jammy, 15 to 20 minutes. Let rhubarb mixture cool completely in dish, about 1 hour. Assemble shortcakes with rhubarb mixture as directed.

berry gratins

serves 2 • **total time** 45 minutes

berry mixture

- 8 ounces blackberries, blueberries, raspberries, and/or strawberries
- 1 teaspoon granulated sugar
- Pinch table salt

zabaglione

- 1 large egg yolk
- 1 tablespoon granulated sugar, divided
- 1 tablespoon dry white wine
- 2 teaspoons packed light brown sugar
- 2 tablespoons heavy cream, chilled

---

pan swap

Recipe can be made in a single gratin dish or 2½- to 3½-cup broiler-safe casserole dish.

why this recipe works When the occasion demands something more dressed-up than berries and cream (but without requiring much time), think gratins: fresh berries blanketed with a lightly browned zabaglione (which is easy to make in small amounts) and quickly broiled. Gentle cooking over barely simmering water gives the Italian custard the smoothest consistency; folding in a little whipped cream turns the texture cloudlike. Broiling browns the top quickly and preserves the berries' fresh flavor. Do not substitute frozen berries. Make sure to cook the egg mixture in a glass bowl over water that is barely simmering. To prevent scorching, pay close attention to the gratins when broiling.

1   **For the berry mixture:** Line rimmed baking sheet with aluminum foil. Hull strawberries, if using, and halve lengthwise if small or quarter if large. Halve blackberries larger than ¾ inch, if using. Gently toss berries, granulated sugar, and salt together in bowl. Divide berry mixture evenly between 2 shallow 6-ounce gratin dishes and set on prepared sheet; set aside.

2   **For the zabaglione:** Whisk egg yolk, 2 teaspoons granulated sugar, and wine in medium glass bowl until sugar is dissolved, about 1 minute. Set bowl over small saucepan of barely simmering water (water should not touch bottom of bowl) and cook, whisking constantly, until mixture is frothy.

3   Continue to cook, whisking constantly, until mixture is slightly thickened, creamy, and glossy, 5 to 10 minutes (mixture will form loose mounds when dripped from whisk). Remove bowl from saucepan and whisk constantly for 30 seconds to cool slightly. Transfer bowl to refrigerator and chill until egg mixture is completely cool, about 10 minutes.

4   Meanwhile, adjust oven rack 6 inches from broiler element and heat broiler. Combine remaining 1 teaspoon granulated sugar and brown sugar in bowl.

5   In separate small bowl, whisk cream until soft peaks begin to form, about 60 seconds. Using rubber spatula, gently fold whipped cream into cooled egg mixture until incorporated and no streaks remain. Spoon zabaglione over berries and sprinkle sugar mixture evenly on top; let sit at room temperature until sugar dissolves, about 10 minutes.

6   Broil gratins until sugar is bubbly and caramelized, 1 to 4 minutes. Serve immediately.

lemon, blueberry, and almond parfaits

serves 2 • **total time** 40 minutes, plus 20 minutes cooling

crumble

- 2 tablespoons all-purpose flour
- 2 tablespoons old-fashioned rolled oats
- 2 tablespoons chopped whole almonds
- 1½ tablespoons packed brown sugar
- 1½ teaspoons granulated sugar
- ⅛ teaspoon table salt
- 1½ tablespoons unsalted butter
- ½ teaspoon water

mousse

- ⅓ cup lemon curd
- ½ teaspoon grated lemon zest plus 2 teaspoons juice
- Pinch table salt
- ½ cup heavy cream, chilled
- 5 ounces (1 cup) blueberries, divided

why this recipe works When you want a fruit dessert (in the summer, that could be every day), but you don't have either the time to bake or a crowd to feed, turn to parfaits. Not yogurt parfaits, but this truly indulgent and elegant dish with a silky lemony mousse, juicy fresh berries, and a crunchy baked crumble that takes 40 minutes to make and 20 minutes to wait for. We start by making a simple oat and almond crumble, pulled together with a drizzle of browned butter (and a tiny bit of water to replace the moisture lost when browning the butter). While the nutty-tasting crumble cools, we fold pillowy whipped cream into store-bought lemon curd (fortified with a bit of lemon juice and zest) for the easiest-ever lemon mousse. To finish, we layer our creamy and crunchy layers with sweet-tart blueberries. Our favorite jarred lemon curd is Wilkin & Sons Tiptree Lemon Curd. Other varieties of jarred lemon curd can taste cloying, so purchase carefully. You will need two 10-ounce glasses or Mason jars for this recipe.

1 For the crumble: Adjust oven rack to middle position and heat oven to 350 degrees. Line rimmed baking sheet with parchment paper. Combine flour, oats, almonds, brown sugar, granulated sugar, and salt in medium bowl. Melt butter in 8-inch skillet over medium-high heat and cook, scraping up browned bits with rubber spatula, until butter is browned and has nutty aroma, 3 to 5 minutes. Stir butter and water into flour mixture until completely moistened. Spread into even layer on prepared sheet and bake until golden brown, 10 to 15 minutes. Transfer sheet to wire rack and let cool completely, about 20 minutes. Break crumble into bite-size pieces.

2 For the mousse: Whisk lemon curd, lemon zest and juice, and salt together in medium bowl. Whisk cream in separate bowl until soft peaks form, about 90 seconds. Gently whisk one-third of whipped cream into lemon curd mixture until combined. Using rubber spatula, gently fold in remaining whipped cream until homogeneous. (Mousse can be refrigerated for up to 24 hours.)

3 Spoon half of chilled mousse evenly into bottoms of two 10-ounce glasses. Top evenly with ½ cup blueberries, followed by half of crumble. Repeat layering process with remaining mousse, blueberries, and crumble. Serve.

guava, strawberry, and tahini parfaits

serves 2 • **total time** 40 minutes, plus 20 minutes cooling

crumble

2 tablespoons all-purpose flour

2 tablespoons old-fashioned rolled oats

1½ tablespoons packed brown sugar

1½ teaspoons granulated sugar

1½ teaspoons black sesame seeds

⅛ teaspoon table salt

1 tablespoon unsalted butter, melted

2 teaspoons tahini

½ teaspoon water

mousse

4 ounces guava paste, chopped into ½-inch pieces

¼ teaspoon grated lime zest plus 1 tablespoon juice

Pinch table salt

¾ cup heavy cream, chilled, divided

5 ounces strawberries, hulled and chopped (1 cup), divided

why this recipe works Aromatic, floral, and sticky-sweet guava paste—a solidified conserve made from guava pulp and sugar—delivers this highly seasonal tropical fruit direct to your pantry all year long. For uniquely delicious parfaits for two, we melt a small amount of guava paste in the microwave and incorporate the liquefied syrup into whipped cream for a quick, easy, and irresistible mousse. We add tahini and a sprinkle of visually stunning, intensely nutty black sesame seeds to an oat-based crumble, adding complex flavor and a touch of earthy bitterness (and beauty to boot) to contrast the sweetness of the guava mousse. To finish, we layer the mousse and crumble with chopped up strawberries, which complement guava's strawberry-like notes, for a balanced bite. Look for guava paste with guava pulp as the first ingredient. While we prefer the look and flavor of black sesame seeds, you can substitute white sesame seeds. You will need two 10-ounce glasses or Mason jars for this recipe.

1 **For the crumble:** Adjust oven rack to middle position and heat oven to 350 degrees. Line rimmed baking sheet with parchment paper. Combine flour, oats, brown sugar, granulated sugar, sesame seeds, and salt in medium bowl. Stir in melted butter, tahini, and water until completely moistened. Spread into even layer on prepared sheet and bake until golden brown, 10 to 15 minutes. Transfer sheet to wire rack and let cool completely, about 20 minutes. Break crumble into bite-size pieces.

2 **For the mousse:** Microwave guava paste, lime juice, and salt in medium bowl until guava paste liquefies, 1 to 1 ½ minutes, whisking every 30 seconds. Whisk mixture until completely smooth, then gradually whisk in ¼ cup heavy cream. Refrigerate until cool, about 15 minutes.

3 Whisk remaining ½ cup cream in bowl until soft peaks form, about 90 seconds. Gently whisk one-third of whipped cream into chilled guava mixture until combined. Using rubber spatula, gently fold in remaining whipped cream until homogeneous. (Mousse can be refrigerated for up to 24 hours.)

4 Toss strawberries with lime zest. Spoon half of chilled mousse evenly into bottoms of two 10-ounce glasses. Top evenly with ½ cup strawberries, followed by half of crumble. Repeat layering process with remaining mousse, strawberries, and crumble. Serve.

crème brûlée

serves 2 • **total time** 1½ hours, plus 6 hours cooling and chilling

½ vanilla bean

⅔ cup heavy cream

¼ cup (1¾ ounces) plus 1 teaspoon sugar, divided

Pinch table salt

2 large egg yolks

---

pan swap
Recipe can be made in two 4-ounce ramekins; increase baking time to 50 minutes to 1 hour.

why this recipe works Crème brûlée is a restaurant standard, but we wanted to make the sophisticated dessert without making restaurant quantities. To streamline the dessert for two people, we eliminate the water bath and instead cook the custard partway on the stovetop before filling the dishes to bake. Transferring the dishes to a low-temperature oven to finish cooking the custard yields an evenly cooked, silky-smooth custard. For a shatteringly crisp crust, we fortify the topping by torching two layers of sugar. Vanilla bean gives the custard the purest vanilla flavor, but ½ teaspoon vanilla extract, whisked into the yolks in step 3, can be used instead. It is important to bring the custard to 180 degrees twice—first on the stovetop and again in the oven—to thicken it and achieve a creamy texture without a water bath. You will need a kitchen torch for this recipe.

1   Adjust oven rack to middle position and heat oven to 225 degrees. Arrange 2 shallow 4-ounce fluted dishes on rimmed baking sheet.

2   Using paring knife, split vanilla bean in half lengthwise and scrape seeds from pods. Combine cream, 2 tablespoons sugar, salt, and vanilla bean seeds and pod in small saucepan. Bring to simmer over medium heat, stirring occasionally. Cook until sugar is dissolved, about 1 minute. Remove saucepan from heat and let sit for 15 minutes.

3   Whisk yolks and 2 tablespoons sugar in medium bowl until pale yellow in color, about 1 minute. Whisking gently, slowly add cream mixture to yolk mixture until thoroughly combined.

4   Set fine-mesh strainer in 4-cup liquid measuring cup, pitcher, or clean medium bowl. Return cream-yolk mixture to now-empty saucepan and cook over medium-low heat, stirring constantly with rubber spatula, until mixture thickens slightly and registers 180 degrees, about 2 minutes. Immediately pour custard through prepared strainer; discard solids. Using spoon, skim any bubbles or foam from top of custard. Pour or ladle custard evenly between fluted dishes, filling nearly to top of each dish.

roasted sesame crème brûlée

Substitute 1 tablespoon tahini for vanilla bean. An equal amount of smooth, natural peanut butter can be used in place of tahini.

tea-infused crème brûlée

Substitute 2 Irish Breakfast tea bags, tied together, for vanilla bean; after steeping tea in cream, squeeze bags with tongs or press into fine-mesh strainer to extract all liquid. Whisk ¼ teaspoon vanilla extract into egg yolks in step 3.

5 Carefully transfer sheet with dishes to oven. Bake until centers of custards register 180 degrees (custards will have set up slightly but will remain jiggly throughout), 40 to 45 minutes. (If custards do not reach 180 degrees after 40 minutes, check every 5 minutes until they reach 180 degrees.)

6 Transfer dishes to wire rack and let cool completely, about 2 hours. Set dishes on rimmed baking sheet, cover sheet tightly with plastic wrap, and refrigerate until cold, at least 4 hours. (Custards can be refrigerated for up to 7 days.)

7 Remove plastic. (If any condensation has collected on custards, gently dab paper towel on surface to absorb moisture.) Sprinkle each custard with ¼ teaspoon sugar, tilting and tapping dishes to evenly distribute sugar and dumping out any excess sugar.

8 Ignite torch. Holding flame 4 to 5 inches from surface of custard, sweep flame over surface to melt sugar (sugar should look transparent but not caramelized). Sprinkle each custard with another ¼ teaspoon sugar. Reignite torch. Holding flame close to surface, move flame over custard, starting from edges and moving into center, to evenly caramelize sugar. (Caramelized crème brûlée can be refrigerated for up to 45 minutes.) Serve.

caramelizing crème brûlée

1 Sprinkle each custard with ¼ teaspoon sugar, tilting and tapping dish for even coverage and dumping out any excess sugar. Holding flame 4 to 5 inches away, melt sugar.

2 Repeat tilting and tapping with additional ¼ teaspoon sugar and, holding flame close to ramekin, evenly caramelize sugar.

Crème Brûlée

Flan

flan

serves 2 • **total time** 1¼ hours, plus 4 hours cooling and chilling

3 tablespoons water

3 tablespoons sugar

1 large egg plus 1 large yolk, room temperature

½ cup milk

½ cup sweetened condensed milk

⅛ teaspoon grated lemon zest

why this recipe works Flan is a surprisingly simple, classic Spanish custard. It boasts a light, ultracreamy texture and a thin layer of caramel that pools over the custard when it is unmolded. To adapt this recipe for two, we swap out the large cake pan that's often used for two individual ramekins. A bonus: It's easier to evenly cook these smaller-scale flans than a large round flan. A quick caramel lines the bottoms of the ramekins. One whole egg plus one yolk gives the custard the perfect rich flavor and tender texture. Sweetened condensed milk makes the flan rich and creamy but not overly heavy, and a touch of lemon zest adds a balancing brightness. Any type of milk can be used in this recipe, resulting in varying degrees of richness. It's important to use a metal pan for the water bath—a glass baking pan may crack when you add the boiling water. Note that the custard will look barely set when it is ready to be removed from the oven.

1 Adjust oven rack to middle position and heat oven to 350 degrees. Place dish towel in bottom of 8-inch square baking pan. Grease two 6-ounce ramekins and place them on towel (they should not touch).

2 Pour 3 tablespoons water into small saucepan, then pour sugar into center of saucepan (don't let it hit saucepan sides). Gently stir sugar with clean spatula to wet it thoroughly. Bring to boil over medium-high heat and cook, without stirring, until sugar has dissolved completely and liquid has faint golden color (about 300 degrees), about 4 minutes.

3 Reduce heat to medium-low and continue to cook, stirring occasionally, until caramel has a dark amber color (about 350 degrees), 1 to 2 minutes. Carefully pour caramel evenly into ramekins and let cool until hardened, about 5 minutes. Bring kettle of water to boil.

4   Whisk egg and yolk together in medium bowl. Whisk in milk, sweetened condensed milk, and lemon zest until thoroughly combined. Pour custard evenly into ramekins. Set pan on oven rack. Taking care not to splash water into ramekins, pour enough boiling water into pan to reach halfway up sides of ramekins. Bake until centers of custards are just barely set and register 170 to 175 degrees, 25 to 30 minutes, checking temperature 5 minutes before recommended minimum time.

5   Carefully transfer ramekins to wire rack and let custards cool to room temperature, about 2 hours. Cover ramekins tightly with plastic wrap, and refrigerate until cold, at least 2 hours or up to 1 day.

6   Run thin knife around 1 ramekin to loosen custard. Place inverted serving plate over top and quickly flip custard and plate together. Gently remove ramekin, drizzling any extra caramel sauce over top (some caramel will remain stuck in ramekin). Repeat with remaining custard and serve.

unmolding flan

1   Run thin knife around custard to loosen it, gently pressing custard away from side of dish.

2   Place inverted serving plate over top and quickly flip custard and plate together.

3   Gently remove ramekin, drizzling any extra caramel sauce on top. (Some caramel will remain stuck in ramekin.)

chapter three
cakes

molten chocolate microwave mug cakes

serves 2 • **total time** 20 minutes

- 4 tablespoons unsalted butter
- 1 ounce bittersweet chocolate, chopped, plus 1 ounce broken into 4 equal pieces
- ¼ cup (1¾ ounces) sugar
- 2 large eggs
- 2 tablespoons unsweetened cocoa powder
- 1 teaspoon vanilla extract
- ¼ teaspoon table salt
- ¼ cup (1¼ ounces) all-purpose flour
- ½ teaspoon baking powder

why this recipe works You don't need a lot of time, a cake pan, or even an oven for these personal-size molten chocolate cakes. A microwave oven and a couple of mugs put you on the fast track to a crave-able dessert for two. A combination of cocoa powder and bittersweet chocolate gives these easy cakes deep flavor. Simply pressing two squares of chocolate into each cake halfway through microwaving produces that trademark molten chocolate center. We developed this recipe in a full-size, 1200-watt microwave. If you're using a compact microwave with 800 watts or fewer, increase the cooking time to 90 seconds for each interval. For either size microwave, reset to 50 percent power at each stage of cooking. Use mugs that hold at least 12 ounces, or the batter will overflow. Sprinkle with flake sea salt if desired.

1 Microwave butter and chopped chocolate in large bowl at 50 percent power, stirring often, until melted, about 1 minute. Whisk sugar, eggs, cocoa, vanilla, and salt into chocolate mixture until smooth. In separate bowl, combine flour and baking powder. Whisk flour mixture into chocolate mixture until combined. Divide batter evenly between two 12-ounce coffee mugs.

2 Place mugs on opposite sides of microwave turntable. Microwave at 50 percent power for 45 seconds. Stir batter and microwave at 50 percent power for 45 seconds (batter will rise to just below rim of mug).

3 Press 2 chocolate pieces into center of each cake until chocolate is flush with top of cake. Microwave at 50 percent power for 30 seconds to 1 minute (chocolate pieces should be melted and cake should be slightly wet around edges of mug and somewhat drier toward center). Let cakes sit for 2 minutes before serving.

variations

molten mocha microwave mug cakes

Add 1 tablespoon instant espresso powder along with sugar to chocolate mixture in step 1.

s'mores molten microwave mug cakes

Omit 1 ounce bittersweet chocolate, broken into 4 pieces. In step 3, press 1 marshmallow into center of each cake until marshmallow is flush with top of cake. Sprinkle top of each cake with 2 tablespoons graham cracker crumbs and top each with 2 marshmallows, pressing to adhere to top of cake. Microwave at 50 percent power for 30 seconds to 1 minute (marshmallows should be softened and puffed). Let cakes sit for 2 minutes. Sprinkle each with 2 tablespoons graham cracker crumbs and garnish each with ½ graham cracker, broken in half.

vanilla cupcakes

makes 4 cupcakes • **total time** 45 minutes, plus 1 hour 10 minutes cooling

¾ cup (3 ounces) cake flour

¼ teaspoon baking powder

⅛ teaspoon baking soda

⅛ teaspoon table salt

¼ cup (1¾ ounces) sugar

1 large egg, room temperature

3 tablespoons unsalted butter, melted and cooled

¼ cup buttermilk, room temperature

½ teaspoon vanilla extract

1 cup frosting (see pages 125–127)

---

pan swap
Recipe can be made in a 4-cup, 6-cup, or 12-cup muffin tin, or in four 4-ounce ramekins placed on a rimmed baking sheet.

why this recipe works Cupcakes are a natural choice when you want a small-scale dessert, but most recipes produce at least a dozen. We wanted a recipe for just four fluffy, tender, snowy-white cupcakes. Using cake flour and both baking powder and soda ensures that our cupcakes have golden, rounded tops and a tender crumb. Buttermilk provides the tangy richness we love in vanilla cupcakes and contributes to the fluffy texture. We add melted butter to the cupcake batter and simply stir everything together by hand. Make sure not to overmix the batter or the cupcakes will be tough. We recommend using a small offset spatula to easily and neatly frost the cupcakes.

1 Adjust oven rack to middle position and heat oven to 325 degrees. Line 4 cups of muffin tin with paper or foil liners.

2 Whisk flour, baking powder, baking soda, and salt together in bowl. Whisk sugar, egg, and melted butter in medium bowl until smooth. Whisk in buttermilk and vanilla until thoroughly combined. Sift flour mixture over egg mixture in 2 additions, whisking gently after each addition until few streaks of flour remain. Continue to whisk batter until most of lumps are gone (do not overmix).

3 Using dry measuring cup or ice cream scoop, divide batter evenly among prepared muffin cups. Bake cupcakes until golden brown and toothpick inserted in center comes out clean, 18 to 22 minutes, rotating muffin tin halfway through baking.

4 Let cupcakes cool in muffin tin on wire rack for 10 minutes. Remove cupcakes from muffin tin and let cool completely on rack, about 1 hour. Spread 3 to 4 tablespoons frosting over each cooled cupcake and serve.

olive oil cake

serves 4 • **total time** 1 hour, plus 1 hour cooling

⅔ cup (3⅓ ounces) all-purpose flour

½ teaspoon baking powder

¼ teaspoon table salt

½ cup (3½ ounces) plus 2 teaspoons sugar, divided

1 large egg

⅛ teaspoon grated lemon zest

¼ cup extra-virgin olive oil

¼ cup milk

---

pan swap

Recipe can be made in a 6-inch cake pan or an 8½ by 4½-inch loaf pan. Make sling for pans following instructions on page 125.

---

bake in your air fryer

Place springform pan or cake pan in air-fryer basket. Place basket in air fryer, set temperature to 275 degrees, and bake for 40 to 45 minutes.

why this recipe works Odds are, you've got the ingredients for this sophisticated yet homey little cake in your kitchen right now. And that's a good thing because this is a cake you'll want to make often. It has a light, plush, fine-textured crumb and a delicate, crackly sugared topping. A tiny bit of lemon zest supplements the subtle fruitiness of the olive oil. It's scaled to make four portions, and leftovers are no problem because the cake stays nice and moist for a few days thanks to the oil. You'll need a hand mixer for this recipe because the batter volume is too small for a stand mixer. For the best flavor, use a fresh, high-quality extra-virgin olive oil.

1 Adjust oven rack to middle position and heat oven to 350 degrees. Grease 6-inch springform pan. Whisk flour, baking powder, and salt together in bowl.

2 Using hand mixer, mix ½ cup sugar, egg, and lemon zest in bowl on low speed until combined. Increase speed to high and whip until mixture is fluffy and pale yellow, about 2 minutes. Reduce speed to medium and, with mixer running, slowly pour in oil. Mix until oil is fully incorporated, about 30 seconds. Add half of flour mixture and mix on low speed until incorporated, about 30 seconds. Add milk and mix until combined, about 30 seconds. Add remaining flour mixture and mix until just incorporated, about 30 seconds, scraping down bowl as needed.

3 Transfer batter to prepared pan. Sprinkle remaining 2 teaspoons sugar over entire surface. Bake until cake is deep golden brown and toothpick inserted in center comes out with few crumbs attached, about 30 minutes, rotating pan halfway through baking.

4 Transfer pan to wire rack and let cool for 15 minutes. Remove side of pan and let cake cool completely, about 1 hour. Cut into wedges and serve.

coconut snack cake

serves 4 • **total time** 1¼ hours, plus 1 hour cooling

¾ cup (3¾ ounces) all-purpose flour

¾ teaspoon baking powder

¼ teaspoon table salt

½ cup cream of coconut

¼ cup milk

1 large egg

2 tablespoons unsalted butter, melted and cooled

¾ teaspoon vanilla extract

¼ teaspoon coconut extract

¼ cup sweetened shredded coconut, toasted, divided

1 cup Cream Cheese Frosting (page 127)

---

pan swap

Recipe can be made in an 8½ by 4½-inch loaf pan; bake for about 30 minutes.

why this recipe works This cake has all the flavor and appeal of a traditional multilayered coconut layer cake, a Southern favorite—but with a much more manageable stature. It earns its coconut name three ways: Mild sweetened shredded coconut adds toasted coconut flavors and subtle texture to the cake. Coconut extract boosts the aroma without being overwhelming. And cream of coconut—a sweetened, emulsified product used in desserts and cocktail mixes—provides enough sweetness that we don't need any sugar. We whip up the traditional cream cheese frosting for a salty, tangy, sweet topping to our coconutty confection and then sprinkle more toasted coconut on top for nutty, sweet crunch. We tested this recipe using Coco López brand cream of coconut, which is often found in the soda and drink-mix aisle of the grocery store. Make sure to shake or stir it well before measuring because it separates as it stands. To toast the coconut, spread it on a rimmed baking sheet and bake in a 325-degree oven, stirring often, until golden brown, about 10 minutes.

1 Adjust oven rack to middle position and heat oven to 325 degrees. Grease 6-inch cake pan. Whisk flour, baking powder, and salt together in medium bowl. Whisk cream of coconut, milk, egg, melted butter, vanilla, and coconut extract together in second bowl. Whisk coconut mixture into flour mixture until fully combined then stir in 2 tablespoons toasted coconut until evenly distributed.

2 Transfer batter to prepared pan. Bake until toothpick inserted in center of cake comes out clean, 40 to 45 minutes, rotating pan halfway through baking.

3 Let cake cool in pan on wire rack for 15 minutes. Remove cake from pan and let cool completely on rack, about 1 hour. Spread frosting evenly over top of cake, then sprinkle with remaining 2 tablespoons toasted coconut. Serve.

whole-wheat carrot snack cake

serves 4 • **total time** 1 hour, plus 1 hour cooling

6   ounces carrots, peeled

⅓   cup (2⅓ ounces) sugar

1   large egg

2   tablespoons vegetable oil

2   tablespoons milk

1   teaspoon vanilla extract

¾   teaspoon ground cinnamon

½   teaspoon baking powder

¼   teaspoon baking soda

¼   teaspoon ground nutmeg

¼   teaspoon table salt

⅔   cup (3⅔ ounces) whole-wheat flour

1   cup Cream Cheese Frosting (page 127)

pan swap

Recipe can be made in an 8½ by 4½-inch loaf pan.

why this recipe works Smart ingredient choices make for a simple, satisfying carrot cake that lives up to its wholesome image and is a joy to eat. We keep the carrots front and center by packing in a generous amount, and we complement their flavor with nutty whole-wheat flour. A modest amount of sugar supports the natural sweetness and moisture of the carrots, and oil (rather than butter) further contributes to a luscious, moist crumb. Using a food processor both to shred the carrots and mix the batter stream-lines recipe prep. With a blanket of cream cheese frosting, this cake works equally well as a dessert or snack for two (and you'll each have a slice to look forward to the next day). Since you use the food processor to make the batter, it makes sense to shred the carrots using the shredding disk, but you could shred the carrots by hand using a box grater if you prefer.

1   Adjust oven rack to middle position and heat oven to 350 degrees. Grease 6-inch cake pan. Use food processor fitted with shredding disk to shred carrots; transfer to bowl (you should have about 1¾ cups).

2   Fit now-empty processor with chopping blade. Process sugar, egg, oil, milk, vanilla, cinnamon, baking powder, baking soda, nutmeg, and salt until sugar is mostly dissolved and mixture is emulsified, 10 to 12 seconds, scraping down sides of bowl as needed. Add shredded carrots and pulse until combined, about 3 pulses. Add flour and pulse until just incorporated, about 5 pulses; do not overmix.

3   Transfer batter to prepared pan and smooth top. Bake until cake is light golden and toothpick inserted in center comes out clean, 30 to 40 minutes, rotating pan halfway through baking.

4   Let cake cool in pan on wire rack for 15 minutes. Remove cake from pan and let cool completely on rack, about 1 hour. Spread frosting evenly over top of cake and serve.

blueberry buckle

serves 4 • **total time** 1¼ hours, plus 50 minutes cooling

¼   cup (1¼ ounces) all-purpose flour

¼   cup packed (1¾ ounces) light brown sugar

1   tablespoon granulated sugar

⅛   teaspoon ground cinnamon

    Pinch table salt

2   tablespoons unsalted butter, melted and cooled slightly

cake

¾   cup (3¾ ounces) all-purpose flour

¾   teaspoon baking powder

4   tablespoons unsalted butter, melted and cooled slightly

⅓   cup (2⅓ ounces) granulated sugar

1   large egg

¾   teaspoon vanilla extract

¼   teaspoon table salt

¼   teaspoon grated lemon zest

10   ounces (2 cups) blueberries

why this recipe works This rustic confection starts with blueberries held together in a buttery cake batter that is then topped with a crisp brown-sugar streusel. The cake, burdened as it is with fruit and topping, is said to buckle on the surface as it bakes—thus the name. Accordingly, we pack 2 full cups of fresh blueberries into our scaled-down version of this American classic. With such a small amount of cake in play, we skip creaming the batter with a mixer and instead use melted butter so we can simply stir the ingredients together. The batter will be extremely thick and heavy, and some effort will be required to spread it in the prepared pan. This buckle is best made with fresh blueberries, not frozen ones, which are too moist.

1   **For the streusel:** Combine flour, brown sugar, granulated sugar, cinnamon, and salt in medium bowl, stirring with fork until no lumps remain. Stir in melted butter until mixture resembles wet sand.

2   **For the cake:** Adjust oven rack to lower-middle position and heat oven to 350 degrees. Grease 8½ by 4½-inch loaf pan, line with parchment sling (see page 125 for more information), and grease parchment.

3   Whisk flour and baking powder together in small bowl. Whisk melted butter, granulated sugar, egg, vanilla, salt, and lemon zest together in medium bowl. Add flour mixture and stir until smooth. Gently fold in blueberries until evenly distributed.

4   Transfer batter to prepared pan; spread batter evenly to pan edges and smooth top. Squeeze handful of streusel in your hand to form large cohesive clump; break up clump with your fingers and sprinkle evenly over batter. Repeat with remaining streusel. Bake until deep golden brown and toothpick inserted in center comes out clean, about 50 minutes, rotating pan halfway through baking.

5   Let cake cool in pan on wire rack for 20 minutes (cake will fall slightly as it cools). Using parchment overhang, remove cake from pan. Discard parchment and let cake cool for about 30 minutes. Serve warm or at room temperature.

cinnamon streusel coffee cake

serves 4 • **total time** 1 hour, plus 30 minutes cooling

streusel

- 6 tablespoons packed (2⅔ ounces) dark brown sugar
- ¼ cup (1¼ ounces) all-purpose flour
- 1½ teaspoons ground cinnamon
- ¼ teaspoon table salt
- 2 tablespoons unsalted butter, melted

cake

- 1 cup plus 2 tablespoons (5⅔ ounces) all-purpose flour
- ⅔ cup (3⅓ ounces) granulated sugar
- ¾ teaspoon baking powder
- ¼ teaspoon baking soda
- ½ teaspoon table salt
- ½ cup milk
- 6 tablespoons unsalted butter, melted
- 1 large egg
- 1 teaspoon vanilla extract

---

pan swap

Recipe can be made in an 8½ by 4½-inch loaf pan. Make sling for pan following instructions on page 125.

why this recipe works The classic companion for any coffee (or tea) break, this cinnamon-scented cake always hits the spot. Rich with the flavors of butter and sweet vanilla, the delectable cake marries perfectly with the slightly salty and crunchy brown-sugar streusel and is just the right size to yield four satisfying servings. We recommend using dark brown sugar here for a bigger flavor but light brown sugar will also work.

1 **For the streusel:** Combine brown sugar, flour, cinnamon, and salt in medium bowl, stirring with fork until no lumps remain. Stir in melted butter until mixture resembles wet sand.

2 **For the cake:** Adjust oven rack to middle position and heat oven to 350 degrees. Grease 6-inch cake pan, line with foil sling (see page 125 for more information), and grease parchment.

3 Whisk flour, granulated sugar, baking powder, baking soda, and salt together in medium bowl. Whisk milk, melted butter, egg, and vanilla together in second bowl. Add to flour mixture and stir until just combined. Transfer batter to prepared pan and smooth top.

4 Squeeze handful of streusel in your hand to form large cohesive clump; break up clump with your fingers and sprinkle evenly over batter. Repeat with remaining streusel then press in streusel lightly.

5 Bake until center of cake is set and toothpick inserted in center comes out with few moist crumbs attached, about 40 minutes, rotating pan halfway through baking.

6 Let cake cool in pan on wire rack for 10 minutes. Using foil overhang, remove cake from pan. Discard parchment and let cake cool for about 30 minutes. Serve warm or at room temperature.

pound cakes

serves 4 • **total time** 40 minutes, plus 1 hour cooling

¾ cup (3 ounces) cake flour

½ teaspoon baking powder

¼ teaspoon table salt

⅔ cup (4⅔ ounces) sugar

2 large eggs, room temperature

¾ teaspoon vanilla extract

8 tablespoons unsalted butter, melted and hot

pan swap

Recipe can be made in a 6-inch round cake pan; bake for 20 to 30 minutes.

why this recipe works A slab of pound cake makes a fine snack or casual dessert. But you can elevate this minimalist classic—literally—by baking the batter in mini Bundt pans so that each diner has their own cake. The simple, scaled-down recipe uses hot melted butter and a food processor for a beautifully emulsified batter that bakes up into moist, fine-grained mini cakes. While these pound cakes are delicious on their own, they're even better served with Blueberry Compote (recipe follows) and Whipped Cream (page 85).

1 Adjust oven rack to middle position and heat oven to 350 degrees. Spray four ¾- to 1-cup Bundt pans with baking spray with flour. Whisk flour, baking powder, and salt together in bowl.

2 Process sugar, eggs, and vanilla in food processor until combined, about 5 seconds. With processor running, add hot melted butter in steady stream until incorporated. Transfer to large bowl. Sift flour mixture over egg mixture in 3 additions, whisking to combine after each addition until no streaks of flour remain. Continue to whisk batter until no lumps remain.

3 Divide batter evenly among prepared pans, smooth tops, and gently tap pans on counter to release air bubbles. Bake until toothpick inserted in center of cakes comes out with few crumbs attached, 15 to 20 minutes.

4 Let cakes cool in pans on wire rack for 10 minutes. Remove cakes from pans and let cool completely on rack, about 1 hour. Serve.

variations

lemon pound cakes

Add 1 tablespoon grated lemon zest and 1 teaspoon juice to food processor with sugar, eggs, and vanilla in step 2.

ginger pound cakes

Add 1½ tablespoons minced crystallized ginger, ¾ teaspoon ground ginger, and ¼ teaspoon ground mace or nutmeg to food processor with sugar, eggs, and vanilla in step 2.

blueberry compote

makes *about ½ cup*
total time *15 minutes*

You can substitute fresh blueberries for frozen: Crush one-third of them against the side of the saucepan with a wooden spoon before bringing to a boil. If you can get them, wild blueberries are particularly nice in this.

5	ounces (1 cup) frozen blueberries
1	tablespoon sugar plus extra for seasoning
1	tablespoon water
	Pinch salt
½	teaspoon lemon juice

Bring blueberries, sugar, water, and salt to boil in small saucepan over medium heat. Reduce heat to medium-low and simmer, stirring occasionally, until reduced to ½ cup, 3 to 6 minutes. Off heat, stir in lemon juice and season with extra sugar to taste.

cider-glazed apple-spelt mini bundt cakes

serves 4 • **total time** 1¼ hours, plus 1 hour cooling

1⅓ cups apple cider

1¼ cups (6¼ ounces) spelt flour

½ teaspoon table salt

½ teaspoon baking powder

⅛ teaspoon baking soda

¼ teaspoon ground cinnamon

⅛ teaspoon ground allspice

¼ cup (1 ounce) confectioners' sugar

½ cup packed (3½ ounces) dark brown sugar

5 tablespoons unsalted butter, melted

1 large egg

1 teaspoon vanilla extract

1 large Fuji apple, peeled, cored, and shredded (1 cup)

why this recipe works With their moist, tender crumb, beautiful fall flavors, sweet glaze, and adorable profile, you'll love having one of these Bundt cakes all for yourself. They're made with spelt flour for a unique nutty and slightly toasty flavor. After experimenting with the ratio of all-purpose flour to spelt flour, we realized we could forgo the all-purpose flour altogether without sacrificing the cake's structure. Achieving unmistakable apple flavor doesn't mean packing the tiny cakes with extra apples, as too many make the crumb soggy and dense. We opt to include a potent reduction of apple cider that we mix into the batter, brush onto the warm exteriors of the baked cakes, and stir into the icing. We like a Fuji apple here but you can use any other sweet apple, like Gala, if you prefer. If storing these cakes, hold off on icing them until just before serving.

1 Adjust oven rack to middle position and heat oven to 350 degrees. Spray four ¾- to 1-cup Bundt pans with baking spray with flour. Bring cider to boil in 10-inch skillet over high heat; cook until reduced to ⅓ cup, about 6 minutes. Meanwhile, whisk flour, salt, baking powder, baking soda, cinnamon, and allspice together in medium bowl.

2 Whisk 2 teaspoons cider reduction and confectioners' sugar together to form smooth icing; cover with plastic wrap and set aside.

3 Whisk 2 tablespoons cider reduction, brown sugar, melted butter, egg, and vanilla until smooth. Set aside remaining cider reduction. Stir sugar mixture into flour mixture until almost fully combined. Stir in apples until evenly distributed. Divide batter evenly among prepared pans and smooth tops. Bake until toothpick inserted in center of cakes comes out clean, 15 to 20 minutes.

4 Transfer pans to wire rack set in rimmed baking sheet and brush exposed surface of cakes lightly with 1 teaspoon reserved cider reduction. Let cakes cool for 10 minutes, then remove cakes from pan and transfer to wire rack, flat sides down. Brush exterior of cakes with remaining reserved cider reduction, then let cakes cool for 10 minutes. Stir reserved icing to loosen, then drizzle decoratively over cakes. Let cakes cool completely, about 1 hour, before serving.

vanilla cake

serves 2 • **total time** 1¼ hours, plus 30 minutes cooling

1 large egg white, room temperature

⅓ cup (2⅓ ounces) sugar, divided

½ cup (2 ounces) cake flour

¼ teaspoon baking powder

Pinch baking soda

⅛ teaspoon table salt

¼ cup buttermilk, room temperature

3 tablespoons unsalted butter, melted and cooled

½ teaspoon vanilla extract

1 cup frosting (see pages 125–127)

---

pan swap

Recipe can be made in a 16-ounce ramekin or a 9 by 6-inch rimmed baking sheet. If using rimmed baking sheet, decrease baking time to 10 to 15 minutes.

why this recipe works   When there are just two of you, an appropriately sized cake can feel more special than a large one, because it's tailor-made for the occasion. This bespoke vanilla cake is a prime example. Using cake flour and doubling up on leaveners creates a golden crust and tender crumb. Buttermilk contributes tangy richness. Be sure to bring all of the ingredients to room temperature before beginning the recipe. Measure out the full amount of sugar, then use 2 tablespoons from that quantity for whipping the egg whites in step 1. The remaining sugar will be used with the flour mixture in step 2. Using a wide, shallow bowl to fold in the egg whites in step 2 is the easiest way to minimize deflation. If you'd like to slice and layer the cake, see pages 122–124 for guidance.

1   Adjust oven rack to middle position and heat oven to 350 degrees. Grease 6-inch cake pan. Using stand mixer fitted with whisk attachment or using hand mixer, beat egg white on medium-low speed until foamy, about 1 minute. Increase speed to medium-high and beat white to soft, billowy mounds, 1 to 2 minutes. With mixer running, slowly add 2 tablespoons sugar and beat until glossy, stiff peaks form, 2 to 4 minutes, scraping down sides of bowl occasionally; set aside.

2   Whisk flour, baking powder, baking soda, salt, and remaining sugar together in wide, shallow, medium bowl. Whisk buttermilk, melted butter, and vanilla together in second bowl then add to bowl with flour mixture and whisk until well combined. Whisk one-third of whipped white into batter, then add remaining white and gently fold into batter until no white streaks or lumps remain. Transfer batter to prepared pan and smooth top.

3   Bake until cake is golden brown, center of cake is firm to touch, and toothpick inserted in center comes out clean, 25 to 30 minutes, rotating pan halfway through baking.

4   Let cake cool in pan on wire rack for 10 minutes. Remove cake from pan and let cool completely, about 30 minutes. Frost and serve.

chocolate cake

serves 2 • **total time** 35 minutes, plus 20 minutes cooling

6 tablespoons (1¾ ounces)
all-purpose flour

6 tablespoons (2⅔ ounces) sugar

3 tablespoons unsweetened
cocoa powder

¼ teaspoon baking soda

⅛ teaspoon baking powder

¼ teaspoon table salt

¼ cup buttermilk

1 large egg

1 tablespoon vegetable oil

½ teaspoon vanilla extract

1 cup frosting (see pages 125–127)

---

pan swap

Recipe can be made in a 16-ounce ramekin
or a 6-inch round cake pan; increase baking time to 25 to 30 minutes and cooling
time to 30 minutes.

why this recipe works You don't need to forgo the "wow" factor of multiple layers when you're baking for two. Using an eighth sheet pan is an easy way to make an impressively tall cake with four layers. The cake, trimmed to a neat rectangle, is divided into four smaller rectangles that are slathered with frosting and stacked. See pages 122–124 for guidance in slicing and layering cakes. The simple stir-together batter uses cocoa for a straightforward, deeply chocolaty flavor. It's a classic no matter how you choose to frost it. If a more traditional round cake is what you're after, the same batter can be baked in a round pan or large ramekin.

1   Adjust oven rack to middle position and heat oven to 325 degrees. Grease 9 by 6-inch rimmed baking sheet. Whisk flour, sugar, cocoa, baking soda, baking powder, and salt together in medium bowl. Whisk buttermilk, egg, oil, and vanilla together in second bowl. Stir buttermilk mixture into flour mixture until smooth batter forms. Transfer batter to prepared sheet and smooth top.

2   Bake until center of cake is firm to touch and toothpick inserted in center comes out with moist crumbs attached, 10 to 15 minutes, rotating sheet halfway through baking.

3   Let cake cool in baking sheet on wire rack for 10 minutes. Turn cake onto wire rack and let cool completely, about 20 minutes. Frost and serve.

crafting a cake for two

You can bake our vanilla and chocolate layer cake batters in a 6-inch round cake pan, a rectangular eighth sheet pan (9 by 6 inches), or a tall 16-ounce ramekin. Each pan creates a striking (and darling) result. Leave a 6-inch cake whole or slice it into two layers. Cut the sheet pan cake into four pieces and stack into layers for a super-sleek rectangular layer cake. Or make the classic three-layer birthday cake affair in miniature from the ramekin. Whatever pan you have will yield a beautiful cake for two.

for cake made in a 6-inch cake pan

1 To create level top layer, use serrated knife to trim mounded top from cake. Discard trimmings.

2 Cover edges of plate or cake stand with 4 strips of parchment paper (remove them before serving). Center cake on plate, adjusting parchment strips as needed.

3 Using long serrated knife, score 1 horizontal line around side of cake.

4 Following scored line, cut into 2 even layers.

5 Using mini offset spatula or large spoon, transfer 2 to 3 tablespoons filling of choice to center of 1 cake layer and spread evenly over surface, leaving ¼-inch border around edge.

6 Place remaining cake layer on top and frost top and sides of cake with remaining frosting as desired.

for cake made in an eighth sheet pan

1 Place cake on cutting board. Trim ¼ inch from edges for a supremely neat look, then cut cake into four 4 by 2½-inch rectangles.

2 To keep serving plate clean, cover edges of plate or cake stand with 4 strips of parchment paper (remove them before serving). Center first cake rectangle on plate, adjusting parchment strips as needed.

3 Using mini offset spatula or large spoon, transfer 1 to 2 tablespoons filling of choice to center of cake rectangle and spread evenly over surface, leaving ¼-inch border around edge.

4 Place second cake rectangle on top of filling, pressing gently to adhere. Repeat, spreading filling evenly over second cake layer.

5 Spread filling evenly over third cake layer.

6 Place final cake rectangle on top, pressing gently to adhere. Chill cake for 10 minutes if filling has softened, then frost top and sides of cake as desired.

crafting a cake for two

for cake made in a 16-ounce ramekin

1 For a totally flat top layer, use serrated knife to trim mounded top off of cake. Discard trimmings.

5 Following remaining scored line, cut cake into remaining layers. Carefully remove top layer and set aside.

2 Cover edges of plate or cake stand with 4 strips of parchment paper (remove them before serving).

6 Using mini offset spatula or large spoon, transfer 1 to 2 tablespoons filling of choice to center of cake layer on plate and spread evenly over surface, leaving ¼-inch border around edge.

3 Center cake on plate, adjusting parchment strips as needed. Using long serrated knife, score 2 evenly spaced horizontal lines around sides of cake layer.

7 Place second cake layer on top and press gently to adhere. Repeat, spreading filling evenly over second cake layer.

4 Following top scored line, use serrated knife to cut first layer of cake. Carefully remove layer and set aside.

8 Top with final cake layer, pressing gently to adhere. Chill cake for 10 minutes if filling has softened, then frost top and sides of cake as desired.

small pan special prep

When a cake can't be inverted after baking, such as those with a delicate crumb or a topping, we use a springform pan. But you can often just as easily use a regular round pan or loaf pan with the aid of a foil or parchment sling following these instructions.

6-inch cake foil sling

1 Cut two 1-inch-wide by 12-inch-long strips of aluminum foil. Lay sheets of foil in 6 by 2-inch cake pan perpendicular to each other, with extra foil hanging over edge of pan. Push into corners and up sides of pan, smoothing foil flush to pan. Press overhang against outside of pan. Spray lightly with vegetable oil spray.

2 Fit 6-inch circle of parchment paper over foil sling and spray with vegetable oil spray.

loaf pan parchment sling

Spray 8½ by 4½-inch loaf pan with vegetable oil spray. Line pan with 10½ by 8½-inch sheet of parchment, smoothing it up long sides of pan. Spray parchment.

frostings and fillings

You can choose any perfectly scaled frosting you like from the following to pair with your petite cake; or you can spread each layer with jam or curd (we love our Passion Fruit Curd [page 127] but store-bought works too) and save the frosting for the top and sides of your cake. Depending on the filling you choose, you may use less of it than we recommend, which is OK! For example, we typically use less jam in between layers than we do frosting since it has such concentrated flavor and sweetness. Or maybe you want to frost the top of your cake and leave the sides bare. Ultimately, when it comes to these cakes, there's no wrong answer: Just follow what your eyes and palate tell you is best, and have fun making your dream cake. (We do not recommend using a 6-quart stand mixer for these recipes.)

vanilla frosting

makes *about 1 cup*
total time *15 minutes*

Consider stirring in a few drops of food coloring.

10	tablespoons unsalted butter, softened
1¼	cups (5 ounces) confectioners' sugar
	Pinch table salt
1	tablespoon heavy cream
¾	teaspoon vanilla extract

Using stand mixer fitted with paddle or using hand mixer, beat butter at medium-high speed until smooth, 30 to 60 seconds. Add sugar and salt and beat at medium-low speed until most of sugar is moistened, about 45 seconds. Scrape down sides of bowl and beat at medium speed until mixture is fully combined, about 15 seconds longer; scrape down bowl. Add heavy cream and vanilla and beat at medium speed until incorporated, 10 to 30 seconds. Increase speed to medium-high and beat until light and fluffy, 4 to 5 minutes, scraping down bowl once or twice during mixing.

frostings and fillings

coffee frosting

Add 2 teaspoons instant espresso powder or instant coffee powder to cream.

coconut frosting

Add 1 teaspoon coconut extract to cream.

orange frosting

Add ¾ teaspoon grated orange zest and 2 teaspoons orange juice to bowl with butter.

raspberry buttercream

makes *about 1 cup*
total time *15 minutes*

Freeze-dried berries can be found with the dried fruit in most markets. Use whatever freeze-dried fruit you prefer; we particularly like cherry and strawberry in addition to raspberry. Leftover fruit powder is great added to yogurt or smoothies.

- 10 tablespoons unsalted butter, softened
- 1¼ cups (5 ounces) confectioners' sugar
- Pinch table salt
- 1 tablespoon heavy cream
- ½ teaspoon vanilla extract
- ⅓ cup freeze-dried raspberries

1 Using stand mixer fitted with paddle or using hand mixer, beat butter at medium-high speed until smooth, 30 to 60 seconds. Add sugar and salt and beat at medium-low speed until most of sugar is moistened, about 45 seconds. Scrape down sides of bowl and beat at medium speed until mixture is fully

combined, about 15 seconds longer; scrape down bowl. Add heavy cream and vanilla and beat at medium speed until incorporated, 10 to 30 seconds. Increase speed to medium-high and beat until light and fluffy, 4 to 5 minutes, scraping down bowl once or twice during mixing.

2 Meanwhile, grind raspberries in spice grinder until reduced to fine powder. Sift powder through fine-mesh strainer set over small bowl. Add 1 tablespoon powder to buttercream and beat on medium speed until fully incorporated, about 30 seconds. Add more raspberry powder to taste, as desired.

chocolate ermine frosting

makes *about 1 cup*
total time *20 minutes, plus 30 minutes cooling*

This frosting produces the silkiest, fluffiest chocolate frosting you've ever tasted. That's thanks to the offbeat, old-fashioned cooked milk method. Using a flat or mini whisk makes it easier to incorporate the ingredients and get into the corners of the saucepan in step 1.

- ¼ cup (1¾ ounces) sugar
- 1 tablespoon cornstarch
- 2 teaspoons Dutch-processed cocoa powder
- ⅛ teaspoon table salt
- ⅛ teaspoon instant espresso powder (optional)
- ¼ cup milk
- ¼ cup (1½ ounces) bittersweet or semisweet chocolate chips
- 4 tablespoons unsalted butter, softened

1 Whisk sugar, cornstarch, cocoa, salt, and espresso powder, if using, together in small saucepan. Slowly whisk in milk until smooth, being sure to get into corners of pan. Cook over medium heat, whisking constantly, until mixture is very thick and glossy and looks like pudding, 3 to 6 minutes. Off heat, add chocolate chips and whisk until smooth. Transfer to medium bowl, cover tightly with plastic wrap, and let cool completely, at least 30 minutes (do not refrigerate).

2 Using stand mixer fitted with paddle or using hand mixer, beat butter on medium speed until soft and light, about 1 minute. Scrape down bowl and paddle and add chocolate mixture. Beat on medium speed until well combined, about 1 minute. Scrape down bowl and paddle thoroughly. Continue to mix on medium speed until mixture is slightly fluffy and looks like dark chocolate mousse, 30 to 60 seconds.

cream cheese frosting

makes *about 1 cup*
total time *10 minutes*

Using softened butter and cream cheese keeps this frosting smooth and lump-free.

- 4 ounces cream cheese, cut into 8 pieces and softened
- 2 tablespoons unsalted butter, softened
- ½ teaspoon vanilla extract
- Pinch table salt
- ½ cup (2 ounces) confectioners' sugar

Using stand mixer fitted with whisk attachment or using hand mixer, beat cream cheese, butter, vanilla, and salt on medium-high speed until smooth, 1 to 2 minutes, scraping down sides of bowl as needed. Reduce speed to medium-low, gradually add sugar, and beat until smooth, 2 to 3 minutes. Scrape down sides of bowl, increase speed to medium-high, and beat until frosting is pale and fluffy, 2 to 3 minutes.

passion fruit curd

makes *about ½ cup*
total time *10 minutes, plus 30 minutes chilling*

Passion fruit puree is sometimes sold as passion fruit pulp; if using pulp, be sure yours doesn't include the seeds. If it does contain seeds, strain the pulp before using. This recipe makes enough to fill two 4-inch tarts or to use as layers in a layer cake (with a little leftover for a treat another day).

- ¼ cup passion fruit puree
- 3 tablespoons sugar
- 1 tablespoon cornstarch
- 1½ ounces white chocolate, chopped
- 3 tablespoons unsalted butter, cut into ½-inch pieces

Whisk passion fruit puree, sugar, and cornstarch together in small saucepan. Cook over medium-low heat, stirring constantly, until thick paste forms, 2 to 4 minutes. Off heat, add chocolate and whisk until melted, then whisk in butter in 2 additions until mixture is smooth and glossy. Transfer to bowl, press lightly greased parchment against surface of curd, and refrigerate until firm, about 30 minutes. (Curd can be refrigerated for up to 3 days.)

financiers

serves 4 to 6 • **total time** 35 minutes, plus 20 minutes cooling

2½ tablespoons unsalted butter

⅓ cup (1½ ounces) almond flour

¼ cup (1¾ ounces) sugar

1 tablespoon all-purpose flour

Pinch table salt

1½ ounces egg whites (about 2 large eggs)

¼ cup sliced almonds, lightly toasted (optional)

variations

chocolate chunk financiers

Substitute twelve ½-inch dark chocolate chunks for sliced almonds, placing 1 chocolate chunk on top of each cake (do not press into batter) before baking.

plum financiers

Substitute ½ small pitted plum, cut into 3 wedges, for sliced almonds. Slice plum wedges crosswise ¼ inch thick, then shingle 2 slices on top of each cake (do not press into batter) before baking.

raspberry financiers

Substitute 12 small raspberries for sliced almonds, placing 1 raspberry on its side of top of each cake (do not press into batter) before baking.

why this recipe works Financiers are tiny cakes that leave a big impression: One bite, and the cake's lightly crunchy shell gives way to a moist, cakey center rich with the nuttiness of browned butter and almonds. Although their flavor is complex, the recipe is simple. Just whisk together almond flour, all-purpose flour, sugar, and salt; stir in egg whites and browned butter; and bake in a mini-muffin tin. Prepping the tin with baking spray with flour helps the sides of the cakes rise along with the centers, preventing doming. You'll need a 12-cup mini-muffin tin for this recipe, or use only half of a 24-cup tin. Because egg whites can vary in size, measuring the whites by weight is essential. You can store financiers at room temperature for up to 3 days.

1 Adjust oven rack to middle position and heat oven to 375 degrees. Generously spray mini-muffin tin with baking spray with flour. Melt butter in 8-inch skillet over medium-high heat. Cook, stirring and scraping skillet constantly with rubber spatula, until milk solids are dark golden brown and butter has nutty aroma, 1 to 3 minutes. Immediately transfer butter to heatproof bowl.

2 Whisk almond flour, sugar, all-purpose flour, and salt together in separate medium bowl. Add egg whites. Using rubber spatula, stir until combined, mashing any lumps against side of bowl until mixture is smooth. Stir in butter until incorporated. Distribute batter evenly among 12 muffin cups (cups will be about half full). Sprinkle sliced almonds, if using, on top of cakes.

3 Bake until edges are well browned and tops are golden, about 14 minutes, rotating muffin tin halfway through baking. Immediately invert wire rack on top of muffin tin. Using towels or oven mitts, invert rack and tin; carefully remove tin. Turn cakes right side up and let cool for 20 minutes. Serve warm or at room temperature.

chocolate-raspberry torte

serves 4 • **total time** 1 hour, plus 1½ hours cooling and chilling

cake and filling

- 4 ounces bittersweet chocolate, chopped fine
- 6 tablespoons unsalted butter, cut into ½-inch pieces
- 1 teaspoon vanilla extract
- ⅛ teaspoon instant espresso powder
- ¾ cup sliced almonds, lightly toasted, divided
- 2 tablespoons all-purpose flour
- ¼ teaspoon table salt
- 2 large eggs plus 1 large white
- ⅓ cup (2⅓ ounces) sugar
- ¼ cup fresh raspberries, plus 8 to 12 individual berries for garnishing cake
- 2 tablespoons seedless raspberry jam
- 2 (6-inch) cardboard rounds

glaze

- 2½ ounces bittersweet chocolate, chopped fine
- 4½ tablespoons heavy cream

why this recipe works Many small-scale desserts are cute, but this mini chocolate-raspberry torte delivers elegance and drama—perfect for a special occasion for two. We use a nearly flourless chocolate cake as the base, adding ground toasted almonds for flavor and structure. Our tangy-sweet filling combines raspberry jam with mashed fresh raspberries. After giving the torte a glossy bittersweet chocolate coat, we dot fresh raspberries around the circumference and press toasted sliced almonds onto its sides. This is a real beauty—inside and out. You will need two 6-inch round cake pans for this recipe.

1 For the cake and filling: Adjust oven rack to middle position and heat oven to 325 degrees. Line bottoms of two 6-inch round cake pans with parchment paper; set aside. Microwave chocolate and butter in large bowl at 50 percent power, stirring often, until melted, 2 to 4 minutes. Let cool completely, about 20 minutes, then stir in vanilla and espresso powder.

2 Pulse ¼ cup almonds in food processor until coarsely chopped, about 6 pulses; set aside. Process remaining ½ cup almonds until very finely ground, about 30 seconds. Add flour and salt and continue to process until combined, about 15 seconds. Transfer almond-flour mixture to medium bowl.

3 Process eggs and white in now-empty processor until lightened in color and almost doubled in volume, about 3 minutes. With processor running, slowly add sugar until thoroughly combined, about 15 seconds. Gently fold egg mixture into chocolate mixture until few streaks of egg remain. Sprinkle half of almond-flour mixture over chocolate-egg mixture and gently whisk until just combined. Sprinkle in remaining almond-flour mixture and gently whisk until just combined.

4 Divide batter evenly between prepared pans and smooth tops. Bake until center is firm and toothpick inserted in center comes out with few moist crumbs attached, 14 to 16 minutes, rotating pans halfway through baking.

5 Let cakes cool completely in pans on wire rack, about 30 minutes. Run paring knife around sides of cakes to loosen. Invert cakes onto cardboard rounds and remove parchment paper. Using wire rack, reinvert 1 cake so top faces up; slide back onto cardboard round.

6 Coarsely mash ¼ cup raspberries in medium bowl using fork. Stir in jam until just combined. Spread raspberry mixture onto cake layer with top facing up. Top with second cake layer, bottom side up. Transfer assembled torte, still on cardboard round, to wire rack set in rimmed baking sheet.

7 **For the glaze:** Microwave chocolate and cream in bowl at 50 percent power, stirring often, until chocolate is melted, 2 to 4 minutes. Remove from heat and whisk until smooth. Pour glaze onto center of torte and spread evenly over top, then spread glaze along sides of torte to coat evenly.

8 Using fine-mesh strainer, sift reserved almonds to remove any fine bits. Holding bottom of torte on cardboard round with your hand, gently press sifted almonds onto torte sides with your other hand. Arrange remaining raspberries around circumference of cake. Refrigerate torte on rack until glaze is set, at least 1 hour or up to 24 hours. Transfer torte to serving platter and serve.

rustic peach cake

serves 4 • **total time** 50 minutes, plus 1¼ hours cooling

¼ cup (1¾ ounces) granulated sugar, divided

⅛ teaspoon ground cinnamon

1 peach, peeled, halved, pitted, and cut into 8 wedges

½ cup (2½ ounces) all-purpose flour

½ teaspoon baking powder

¼ teaspoon table salt

¼ cup vegetable oil

2 tablespoons packed light brown sugar

1 large egg, room temperature

2 tablespoons milk

½ teaspoon vanilla extract

why this recipe works This cake is unmistakably summer, with a pretty peach pinwheel pattern on top, and it's so simple to make—the perfect dessert on a lazy late-season day. We envisioned a moist cake, so we opted for vegetable oil instead of butter; unlike butter, oil doesn't solidify at room temperature after the cake is baked and cooled. Using vegetable oil also eliminates the need for equipment to mix the batter. We scrape the batter into a 6-inch cake pan and arrange the peach slices that have been rolled in cinnamon sugar on top. Since overly ripe peaches will make the cake soggy, we recommend looking for a barely ripe peach, one that gives only slightly to the touch.

1 Adjust oven rack to middle position and heat oven to 350 degrees. Grease 6-inch cake pan. Combine 2 tablespoons granulated sugar and cinnamon in medium bowl. Measure out and reserve 1 tablespoon cinnamon sugar. Add peach wedges to bowl with remaining cinnamon sugar and toss to coat; set aside.

2 Whisk flour, baking powder, and salt together in medium bowl. Whisk oil, brown sugar, egg, milk, vanilla, and remaining 2 tablespoons granulated sugar in separate bowl until combined, then stir milk mixture into flour mixture until just combined.

3 Transfer batter to prepared pan, smooth top, and gently tap pan on counter to release air bubbles. Arrange reserved sugared peach wedges in pinwheel pattern in cake batter, then sprinkle reserved 1 tablespoon cinnamon sugar mixture evenly over peaches.

4 Bake until top of cake is golden brown and toothpick inserted in center comes out with few moist crumbs attached, 30 to 40 minutes, rotating pan halfway through baking.

5 Let cake cool in pan on wire rack for 20 minutes. Remove cake from pan and let cool completely on rack, about 1 hour. Serve.

french apple cake

serves 4 • **total time** 1¾ hours, plus 2 hours cooling

12 ounces Granny Smith apples, peeled, cored, cut into 8 wedges, and sliced ⅛ inch thick crosswise

1½ teaspoons Calvados

½ teaspoon lemon juice

½ cup (2½ ounces) plus 1 tablespoon all-purpose flour, divided

½ cup (3½ ounces) plus 1½ teaspoons granulated sugar, divided

1 teaspoon baking powder

¼ teaspoon table salt

½ cup vegetable oil

½ cup whole milk

1 large egg, separated

½ teaspoon vanilla extract

Confectioners' sugar

why this recipe works This small-scale take on a simple yet seemingly luxurious classic French dessert still offers the best of both worlds: a custardy, apple-rich base sitting beneath a light, cake-like topping. To ensure that the apple slices soften fully, we microwave them briefly to break down the enzyme responsible for firming up pectin. The addition of Calvados (French apple brandy) to the apples brings out their flavors. To create two different textured layers out of the same batter, we divide the batter and add an egg yolk to one part (to make the custardy base) and flour the other part (to form the cake layer above it). The resulting cake has a timeless subtle glamour befitting afternoon tea for two, or a few. Don't be alarmed if you experience leaking from the springform pan as the cake bakes. The microwaved apples should be pliable but not completely soft when cooked. To test for doneness, take one apple slice and try to bend it. If it snaps in half, it's too firm; microwave it for an additional 30 seconds and test again. If Calvados is unavailable, 1½ teaspoons of apple brandy or white rum can be substituted.

1 Adjust oven rack to lower-middle position and heat oven to 325 degrees. Grease 6-inch springform pan. Place prepared pan on aluminum foil–lined rimmed baking sheet. Place apples in bowl, cover, and microwave until apples are pliable and slightly translucent, about 3 minutes. Toss apples with Calvados and lemon juice and let cool for 15 minutes.

2 Whisk ½ cup flour, ½ cup granulated sugar, baking powder, and salt together in bowl. Whisk oil, milk, egg white, and vanilla in medium bowl until smooth. Add flour mixture to milk mixture and whisk until just combined.

3 Transfer ½ cup batter to third bowl; set aside. Add egg yolk to remaining batter in medium bowl and whisk to combine. Using spatula, gently fold in cooled apples. Transfer batter to prepared pan; spread batter evenly to pan edges and gently press on apples to create even, compact layer with smooth surface.

4 Whisk remaining 1 tablespoon flour into reserved ½ cup batter. Pour over batter in pan, spreading evenly to pan edges and smoothing surface. Sprinkle remaining 1½ teaspoons granulated sugar evenly over top. Bake until center of cake is set, toothpick inserted in center comes out clean, and top is golden brown, about 50 minutes, rotating pan halfway through baking.

5 Let cake cool in pan on wire rack for 5 minutes. Run thin knife around edge of pan to loosen cake, then let cool completely, 2 to 3 hours. Remove side of pan and slide thin metal spatula between cake bottom and pan bottom to loosen, then slide cake onto platter. Dust cake lightly with confectioners' sugar before serving.

semolina and ricotta cake

serves 4 • **total time** 1½ hours, plus 9 hours cooling, chilling, and sitting

2 tablespoons unsalted butter, plus softened butter for pan

⅓ cup (2⅔ ounces) granulated sugar, plus extra for pan

2 large eggs

6 ounces (¾ cup) whole-milk ricotta cheese

1 tablespoon orange liqueur

1 teaspoon vanilla extract

3 tablespoons semolina flour

1½ cups whole milk

1 tablespoon grated lemon zest

2¼ teaspoons grated orange zest

½ teaspoon ground cardamom

¼ teaspoon table salt

Confectioners' sugar

why this recipe works This convenient make-ahead semolina and ricotta cake will fill your kitchen with bright, sweet, and warm notes while you wait to serve it. Inspired by the style prepared in Naples, this intoxicatingly aromatic, slightly sweet, and velvety dessert has a texture somewhere between that of a cheesecake and a cake. We start by cooking a porridge of semolina flour, milk, butter, sugar, lemon and orange zests, and ground cardamom. Next, we combine this warm porridge with a mixture of ricotta, eggs, vanilla, and orange liqueur. After baking, we refrigerate the cake to ensure that it is firm enough to slice, so you can prepare the cake the day before your dessert date.

1 Adjust oven rack to middle position and heat oven to 425 degrees. Grease 6-inch springform pan with softened butter, then dust with granulated sugar and knock out excess.

2 Using stand mixer fitted with paddle or using hand mixer, beat eggs on medium-low speed until just combined, 1 to 2 minutes. Add ricotta, liqueur, and vanilla and mix on medium speed until smooth, 2 to 4 minutes, scraping down bowl as needed.

3 Whisk semolina and granulated sugar together in small bowl. Heat butter, milk, lemon zest, orange zest, cardamom, and salt in small saucepan over medium-low heat, stirring occasionally, until mixture registers 180 degrees, about 7 minutes. Off heat, pour semolina mixture into milk mixture in very slow stream, whisking constantly, until smooth. Return saucepan to heat and stir constantly with wooden spoon until mixture pulls away from side of saucepan, 2 to 4 minutes.

4 Add one-third of semolina mixture to ricotta mixture and mix on medium speed until incorporated. Add remaining semolina mixture in 2 additions, mixing after each addition until incorporated. Continue to mix, scraping down bowl as needed, until mostly smooth (it's OK if some small lumps remain), 3 to 5 minutes longer.

5 Set prepared pan in rimmed baking sheet and transfer batter to pan. Bake until edges are puffed (some slight cracking is OK) and center registers 200 degrees and is slightly jiggly, about 35 minutes, rotating pan halfway through baking.

6 Let cake cool in pan, still on sheet, on wire rack for 10 minutes. Run knife around edge of cake to loosen. Unlock pan ring, but leave ring in place. Let cool completely, about 2 hours. Refasten ring. Refrigerate cake until firm and thoroughly chilled, at least 6 hours or up to 24 hours.

7 To unmold cake, remove pan ring. Slide thin metal spatula between cake and pan bottom to loosen, then slide cake onto serving platter. Let cake stand at room temperature for 1 to 2 hours, gently dab surface with paper towels to remove any moisture, then sprinkle with confectioners' sugar. To slice, dip sharp knife in very hot water and wipe dry after each cut. Serve.

cranberry upside-down cake

serves 4 • **total time** 1¼ hours, plus 30 minutes chilling

topping

2	tablespoons unsalted butter
5	ounces (1¼ cups) fresh or frozen cranberries, thawed
⅓	cup (2⅓ ounces) sugar
1	tablespoon seedless raspberry jam
⅛	teaspoon vanilla extract

cake

½	cup (2½ ounces) all-purpose flour
½	teaspoon baking powder
⅛	teaspoon table salt
¼	cup whole milk
½	teaspoon vanilla extract
3	tablespoons unsalted butter, softened
⅓	cup (2⅓ ounces) sugar
1	large egg, separated, plus 1 large yolk
	Pinch cream of tartar

why this recipe works It's worth keeping a bag of cranberries in the freezer for this little jewel of a cake. Cooking the cranberries with raspberry jam and sugar brings out their juices and tames their tart edge. The topping of glossy, ruby-red fruit is supported and complemented by a tender, buttery vanilla cake.

1 **For the topping:** Adjust oven rack to middle position and heat oven to 350 degrees. Spray 6-inch cake pan with baking spray with flour, line bottom with parchment paper, and grease parchment. Melt butter in 8-inch nonstick skillet over medium-low heat. Add cranberries, sugar, and jam and cook, stirring gently, until cranberries are just softened, about 3 minutes. Off heat, stir in vanilla. Pour berries with juice into prepared pan, gently spread into even layer, and refrigerate for 30 minutes.

2 **For the cake:** Whisk flour, baking powder, and salt together in medium bowl. Whisk milk and vanilla together in separate bowl.

3 Using stand mixer fitted with paddle or using hand mixer, beat butter and sugar together on medium-high speed until pale and fluffy, 3 to 4 minutes, scraping down bowl as needed. Add egg yolks, one at a time, and beat until combined, scraping down bowl after each addition. Reduce speed to low and add flour mixture in 3 additions, alternating with milk mixture in 2 additions, scraping down bowl as needed. Give batter final stir by hand, then transfer batter to large bowl.

4 Using clean, dry mixer bowl and whisk attachment or using hand mixer, whip egg white and cream of tartar on medium-low speed until foamy, about 1 minute. Increase speed to medium-high and whip until soft peaks form, 2 to 4 minutes, scraping down sides of bowl occasionally. Whisk one-third of whipped white into batter, then add remaining white and gently fold into batter until no white streaks or lumps remain.

5 Pour batter over chilled cranberry mixture and smooth top. Bake until toothpick inserted in center of cake comes out clean, 35 to 40 minutes, rotating pan halfway through baking. Let cake cool in pan on wire rack for 10 minutes. Run paring knife around edge of cake and invert onto serving platter. Remove parchment, and serve warm or at room temperature.

pear-walnut upside-down cake

serves 4 • **total time** 1½ hours, plus 1½ hours cooling

topping

2 tablespoons unsalted butter, melted

¼ cup packed (1¾ ounces) dark brown sugar

1 teaspoon cornstarch

Pinch table salt

1 large ripe but firm Bosc pear (8 ounces)

cake

½ cup walnuts, toasted

¼ cup (1¼ ounces) all-purpose flour

¼ teaspoon table salt

⅛ teaspoon baking powder

Pinch baking soda

½ cup (3½ ounces) granulated sugar

1 large egg

2 tablespoons unsalted butter, melted

2 tablespoons vegetable oil

why this recipe works With sweet, dense flesh that holds its shape during baking, Bosc pears are an inspired choice for a fruit upside-down cake. Instead of a typical yellow cake, we incorporate ground toasted walnuts into the batter, which makes a cake that is light but sturdy, mildly sweet, and visually attractive. To fit plenty of pear in a 6-inch pan we arrange the wedges in staggered horizontal stripes. Removing the cake from the pan after 15 minutes allows the top to set while preventing the bottom from steaming and turning soggy. We strongly recommend baking this cake in a light-colored cake pan with sides that are at least 2 inches tall. Serve with crème fraîche or Whipped Cream (page 85).

1 **For the topping:** Adjust oven rack to middle position and heat oven to 300 degrees. Grease 6-inch round cake pan and line bottom with parchment paper. Pour melted butter over bottom of pan and swirl to evenly coat. Combine brown sugar, cornstarch, and salt in small bowl and sprinkle evenly over melted butter.

2 Peel, halve, and core pear. Cut pear halves into 3 wedges each. Arrange pear wedges, tapered ends pointing inward, in staggered horizontal lines across cake pan.

3 **For the cake:** Process walnuts, flour, salt, baking powder, and baking soda in food processor until walnuts are finely ground, about 20 seconds. Transfer walnut mixture to bowl.

4 Process granulated sugar and egg in now-empty processor until very pale yellow, about 2 minutes. With processor running, add melted butter and oil in steady stream until incorporated. Add walnut mixture and pulse to combine, 4 or 5 pulses. Pour batter evenly over pears (some pear may show through; cake will bake up over fruit).

5 Bake until center of cake is set and bounces back when gently pressed and toothpick inserted in center comes out clean, 50 minutes to 1 hour, rotating pan halfway through baking.

6 Let cake cool in pan on wire rack for 15 minutes. Run paring knife around edge of cake and invert onto serving platter. Remove parchment and let cake cool completely, about 1½ hours. Serve.

individual new york cheesecakes

serves 2 • **total time** 1 hour, plus 3½ hours cooling, chilling, and sitting

crust

- 3 whole graham crackers, broken into 1-inch pieces
- 3 tablespoons unsalted butter, melted and cooled, divided
- 1 tablespoon sugar

filling

- 10 ounces cream cheese, softened
- ⅓ cup (2⅓ ounces) sugar, divided
- Pinch table salt
- 4 teaspoons sour cream
- ½ teaspoon lemon juice
- ½ teaspoon vanilla extract
- 1 large egg plus 1 large yolk

---

bake in your air fryer

Place pans in air-fryer basket. Place basket in air fryer, set temperature to 200 degrees, and bake for 45 minutes.

why this recipe works New York cheesecake is unapologetically rich—that's why we love it. But it's also why a full-size one can be too much of a good thing for a small household—so we adapted our recipe to produce two individual cheesecakes. A full 10 ounces of cream cheese gives the little cakes an impressive stature, allowing for a range in texture, from firm to creamy. To produce the bronzed surface that's a hallmark of this style of cheesecake, we start them in the oven at 500 degrees and then turn the heat down to 200. Baked this way, they're done in about 15 minutes. Once chilled, the mini cheesecakes are everything an authentic New York cheesecake should be. To make the cheesecakes in a toaster oven, start by setting the temperature to 500 degrees (or the highest temperature your toaster oven reaches) and bake for 2 minutes; reduce the temperature to 200 degrees and increase the bake time to 45 to 50 minutes to account for the toaster oven's rapid heat loss.

1 **For the crust:** Adjust oven rack to middle position and heat oven to 325 degrees. Process graham cracker pieces in food processor to fine, even crumbs, about 30 seconds. Sprinkle 2 tablespoons melted butter and sugar over crumbs and pulse to incorporate, about 5 pulses. Divide mixture evenly between two 4½-inch springform pans. Using bottom of spoon, press crumbs firmly into even layer on bottom of pans, keeping sides as clean as possible. Bake crusts until fragrant and beginning to brown, about 10 minutes. Let crusts cool in pans on wire rack while making filling.

2 **For the filling:** Increase oven temperature to 500 degrees. Using stand mixer fitted with paddle or using hand mixer, beat cream cheese at medium-low speed until smooth, 1 to 2 minutes. Scrape down sides of bowl. Add ¼ cup sugar and salt and beat until combined, 30 to 60 seconds. Scrape down bowl, add remaining sugar, and beat until combined, 30 to 60 seconds. Scrape down bowl, add sour cream, lemon juice, and vanilla, and beat until combined, 15 to 30 seconds. Scrape down bowl, add egg and egg yolk, and beat until combined, 30 to 60 seconds.

3 Being careful not to disturb baked crusts, brush inside of pans with remaining 1 tablespoon melted butter and place pans on rimmed baking sheet. Pour filling evenly into cooled crusts, smooth tops, and bake cheesecakes for 2 minutes. Without opening oven door, reduce oven temperature to 200 degrees and continue to bake until cakes register 150 degrees, 12 to 17 minutes, rotating sheet halfway through baking.

4 Let cheesecakes cool in pans on wire rack for 5 minutes, then run thin knife around edge of each cake. Let cakes cool completely, about 1 hour. Wrap pans tightly in plastic wrap and refrigerate until cold, about 2 hours.

5 To unmold cheesecakes, wrap hot dish towel around pans and let sit for 1 minute. Remove sides of pans. Slide thin metal spatula between crusts and pan bottoms to loosen, then slide cakes onto individual serving plates. Let cakes sit at room temperature for 30 minutes before serving.

basque cheesecake

serves 4 to 6 • **total time** 1 hour, plus 2 hours cooling

4 large eggs, room temperature

1 cup (7 ounces) sugar

1 pound cream cheese, room temperature

½ cup heavy cream, room temperature

2 tablespoons all-purpose flour

---

bake in your air fryer
Place pan in air-fryer basket. Place basket in air fryer, set temperature to 300 degrees, and bake for 1¼ hours.

why this recipe works It takes only a few ingredients to make this decadent and iconic cheesecake. The recipe is a mini version of the original, which was adapted from the celebrated recipe developed more than 30 years ago by Santiago Rivera at the La Viña bar and restaurant in Donostia–San Sebastián, Basque Country, Spain. This cheesecake is baked in a hot oven without a water bath, yielding a cake with a caramelized exterior and ultracreamy interior. The milky, sweet, and slightly tangy interior is beautifully complemented by the added complex notes from the caramelized top. We recommend keeping a close eye on the internal temperature by sticking the thermometer exactly in the center of the cake to prevent an interior that's too loose or overbaked. Moistening crumpled parchment for lining the pan makes the paper supple and easy to work with. Do not use cream cheese spread, whipped or low-fat cream cheese, or Neufchâtel in this recipe. If baking the cheesecake in a toaster oven, decrease the baking time by about 5 minutes.

1 Adjust oven rack to middle position and heat oven to 425 degrees. Spray or lightly sprinkle 1 approximately 16 by 12-inch piece of parchment paper evenly with cold water. Crumple parchment into ball, then gently uncrumple. Press parchment onto bottom and sides of 6-inch springform pan. Fold overhanging parchment outward, over edge of pan. Using kitchen shears, trim overhanging parchment to about 1 inch past edge of pan.

2 Process eggs and sugar in food processor until mixture is frothy and pale yellow, about 1 minute. Add cream cheese, heavy cream, and flour and pulse until cream cheese is broken into large, even pieces, about 6 pulses. Process until mixture is completely smooth, about 1 minute.

3 Transfer batter to prepared pan and place pan on rimmed baking sheet. Bake until top of cheesecake is deeply browned, edges are set, and center of cheesecake registers 155 degrees, about 50 minutes (center will be jiggly). Remove cheesecake from oven and transfer to wire rack. Let cheesecake cool in pan for 2 hours.

4 Remove side of pan. Gently peel parchment away from sides of cheesecake until parchment is flush with counter. To slice, dip sharp knife in very hot water and wipe dry after each cut. Serve slightly warm or at room temperature.

chapter four
pies and tarts

fried peach hand pies

makes 8 hand pies • **total time** 1 hour, plus 20 minutes chilling

4 ripe peaches, peeled, halved, pitted, and cut into ½-inch-wide wedges

½ cup (3½ ounces) sugar

1 teaspoon table salt, divided

2 teaspoons lemon juice

2 cups (10 ounces) all-purpose flour

2 teaspoons baking powder

6 tablespoons unsalted butter, melted and cooled

½ cup whole milk

1½ quarts vegetable or peanut oil for frying

freeze and bake

At end of step 5, place pies on parchment paper–lined baking sheet and freeze until firm; transfer pies to zipper-lock bag and store in freezer for up to 1 month. Thaw completely in refrigerator before frying.

why this recipe works What could be better than your own personal peach pie? These hand pies are fried, so the crust on each is golden brown and tender with a dainty crumble. Hand pies are one of the best pastries for small households: You can fry them all, or store them in the freezer to fry whenever you want. (Be sure to thaw them first so the filling heats through during frying.) Using a saucepan rather than a Dutch oven for frying cuts down on the oil required. A soft dough made with flour, melted butter, milk, and baking powder is a breeze to roll and form. You can substitute 20 ounces of frozen peaches for the fresh; increase the cooking time in step 1 to 15 to 20 minutes.

1 Combine peaches, sugar, and ¼ teaspoon salt in medium saucepan. Cover and cook over medium heat until tender, about 5 minutes, stirring occasionally.

2 Uncover and continue to cook, stirring and mashing frequently with potato masher to coarse puree, until mixture is thickened and measures about 1⅔ cups, 7 to 13 minutes. Off heat, stir in lemon juice and let cool completely.

3 While filling cools, line rimmed baking sheet with parchment paper. Pulse flour, baking powder, and remaining ¾ teaspoon salt in food processor until combined, about 3 pulses. Add melted butter and pulse until mixture resembles wet sand, about 8 pulses, scraping down sides of bowl as needed. Add milk and process until no floury bits remain and dough looks pebbly, about 8 seconds.

4 Turn dough onto lightly floured counter, gather into 4-inch disk, and divide into 8 equal pieces. Roll each piece between your hands into ball, then press to flatten into disk. Place disks on prepared sheet, cover with plastic wrap, and refrigerate for 20 minutes.

5 Working with 1 dough disk at a time on floured counter, roll into 6- to 7-inch circle about ⅛ inch thick. Place 3 tablespoons filling in center of circle. Brush edges of dough with water and fold dough over filling to create half-moon shape, lightly pressing out air at seam. Trim any ragged edges and crimp edges with floured fork to seal. Return pies to prepared sheet, cover with plastic, and refrigerate until ready to fry. (Pies can be covered and refrigerated for up to 24 hours.)

6 Line platter with triple layer of paper towels. Add oil to large saucepan until it measures about 1½ inches deep and heat over medium-high heat to 375 degrees. Carefully place 3 pies in hot oil and fry until golden brown, about 3 minutes, using slotted spatula or spider skimmer to flip halfway through frying. Adjust burner, if necessary, to maintain oil temperature between 350 and 375 degrees. Transfer pies to prepared platter. Return oil to 375 degrees and repeat with remaining 5 pies in 2 batches. Let cool for 10 minutes before serving. (Cooled hand pies can be stored at room temperature for up to 3 days; rewarm in a 300-degree oven for about 10 minutes.)

sweet cherry pie

serves 4 • **total time** 1¼ hours, plus 2 hours chilling, freezing, and cooling

2 disks Foolproof All-Butter Pie Dough (page 166)

14 ounces fresh sweet cherries, pitted and halved

1 red plum, quartered and pitted

¼ cup (1¾ ounces) sugar

2 teaspoons instant tapioca, ground

1½ teaspoons lemon juice

Pinch table salt

Pinch ground cinnamon (optional)

1 tablespoon unsalted butter, cut into ¼-inch pieces

1 large egg white, lightly beaten

why this recipe works As with all fruit pie, cherry pie's allure—the contrast of textures between flaky crust and vibrant, juicy filling—is not built to last, and you definitely want to eat this pie fresh. A pint-size cherry pie, scaled to fit a 6-inch pie plate, lets you enjoy the fruits of your labors at their peak, and looks darn cute too. Sour cherries are the archetypal pie cherry; to make this pie with easy-to-source sweet cherries, we cut them in half and puree a portion of them along with a tart plum. This helps bring out their juices and flavor for a filling with an intense jamminess to rival the best sour cherry pie. We skip the traditional (and fussy) lattice-top crust in favor of a simple vented crust. We like the buttery flavor and flaky texture of homemade pie dough here; however, you can substitute two 9-inch store-bought pie dough rounds, if desired. You can substitute 12 ounces frozen sweet cherries for the fresh cherries; thaw them only partway before using. Grind the tapioca to a fine powder in a spice grinder or a mini food processor.

1 Adjust oven rack to lowest position and heat oven to 425 degrees. Roll 1 dough disk into 9-inch circle on floured counter. Loosely roll dough circle around rolling pin and gently unroll it onto 6-inch pie plate, letting excess dough hang over edge. Ease dough into plate by gently lifting edge of dough with your hand while pressing into plate bottom with your other hand. Leave any dough that overhangs plate in place. Wrap dough-lined pie plate loosely in plastic wrap and refrigerate until dough is firm, about 30 minutes. Roll other dough disk into 9-inch circle on floured counter, then transfer to parchment paper–lined baking sheet; cover with plastic and refrigerate for 30 minutes.

2 While dough chills, process ½ cup cherries and plum in food processor until smooth, about 1 minute, scraping down sides of bowl as necessary. Strain puree through fine-mesh strainer into large bowl, pressing on solids to extract liquid; discard solids. Stir remaining cherries, sugar, ground tapioca, lemon juice, salt, and cinnamon, if using, into puree and let sit for 15 minutes.

3 Transfer cherry mixture with its juices to dough-lined pie plate, mounding it slightly in middle (pie plate will be very full). Scatter butter pieces over top. Loosely roll remaining dough circle around rolling pin and gently unroll it onto filling. Trim overhang to ½ inch beyond lip of pie plate. Pinch edges of top and bottom crusts firmly together. Tuck overhang under itself; folded edge should be flush with edge of pie plate. Crimp dough evenly around edge of pie plate using your fingers. Cut five 1-inch vents in center of top crust. Brush surface with beaten egg white and freeze for 20 minutes.

4 Place pie on foil-lined rimmed baking sheet and bake until crust is light golden brown, 20 to 25 minutes. Reduce oven temperature to 350 degrees, rotate sheet, and continue to bake until juices are bubbling and crust is deep golden brown, 25 to 35 minutes. Let pie cool on wire rack until filling has set, about 1½ hours; serve slightly warm or at room temperature.

lemon ricotta pie

serves 4 • **total time** 1¾ hours, plus 2 hours chilling and cooling

8 ounces (1 cup) whole-milk ricotta cheese

1 disk Foolproof All-Butter Pie Dough (page 166)

¼ cup heavy cream

¼ cup (1¾ ounces) granulated sugar

1 large egg

1 teaspoon grated lemon zest

½ teaspoon vanilla extract

Pinch table salt

1⅔ ounces (⅓ cup) blackberries, blueberries, and/or raspberries

Confectioners' sugar

why this recipe works A traditional Italian ricotta pie is typically baked like a cheesecake; we re-envisioned the concept, encasing the sweetened, rich ricotta filling (reminiscent of a fine Italian cannoli) in a buttery, flaky pie crust. We give the pie shell a head start in the oven before adding the filling so the crust is perfectly crispy. Pressing out excess water from the ricotta before combining it with the rich cream and egg also helps to keep our pie crust from getting soggy under the filling. We perfume the filling with lemon zest and vanilla, and top the pie with berries dusted with confectioners' sugar just before serving for an elegant petite treat. We like the buttery flavor and flaky texture of homemade pie dough here; however, you can substitute one 9-inch store-bought pie dough round, if desired. It is important to add the ricotta filling to the crust while it is still warm; if the crust has cooled, rewarm it in the oven for 5 minutes before adding the filling.

1 Line large plate with triple layer of paper towels. Spread ricotta on paper towels into even layer, then cover with second triple layer of paper towels. Place second large plate on top and weight with several heavy cans. Let ricotta sit for at least 30 minutes or up to 2 hours. Discard top layer of paper towels, then transfer ricotta to food processor bowl.

2 Roll dough disk into 9-inch circle on floured counter. Loosely roll dough around rolling pin and gently unroll it onto 6-inch pie plate, letting excess dough hang over edge. Ease dough into plate by gently lifting edge of dough with your hand while pressing into plate bottom with your other hand.

3 Trim overhang to ½ inch beyond lip of plate. Tuck overhang under itself; folded edge should be flush with edge of plate. Crimp dough evenly around edge of plate. Wrap dough-lined plate loosely in plastic wrap and refrigerate until firm, about 30 minutes. Adjust oven rack to middle position and heat oven to 350 degrees.

4 Line chilled pie shell with double layer of aluminum foil, covering edges to prevent burning, and fill with pie weights. Bake on foil-lined rimmed baking sheet until edges are set and just beginning to turn lightly golden, 25 to 30 minutes, rotating sheet halfway through baking. Remove foil and weights, rotate sheet, and continue to bake crust until starting to turn golden brown on inside bottom, 15 to 20 minutes longer. Transfer sheet to wire rack. (Crust must still be warm when filling is added.) Increase oven temperature to 400 degrees.

5 While crust bakes, process cream, granulated sugar, egg, lemon zest, vanilla, and salt with ricotta in food processor until well combined and smooth, about 30 seconds. With pie plate still on sheet, pour mixture into warm crust, smoothing top with clean spatula into even layer. Bake until center of pie registers 160 degrees, about 30 minutes, shielding edges with aluminum foil during last 10 minutes of baking if crust is getting too dark. Transfer pie to wire rack and let cool completely, about 1½ hours.

6 Top cooled pie with berries, then sprinkle with confectioners' sugar. Serve.

icebox strawberry pie

serves 4 • **total time** 1¼ hours, plus 6 hours cooling and chilling

1 disk Foolproof All-Butter Pie Dough (page 166)

filling

8 ounces (1¾ cups) frozen strawberries

¾ teaspoon unflavored gelatin

1½ teaspoons lemon juice

1 teaspoon water

⅓ cup (2⅓ ounces) sugar

Pinch table salt

5 ounces fresh strawberries, hulled and sliced thin (¾ cup)

topping

½ cup heavy cream, chilled

1 ounce cream cheese, softened

1 tablespoon sugar

¼ teaspoon vanilla extract

why this recipe works Frozen strawberries, cooked until juicy and flavorful, form the base of this refreshing strawberry pie, a diner favorite that looks extra special in miniature form. A bit of unflavored gelatin produces a clean-slicing, not-too-bouncy pie. Fresh strawberries, stirred into the mixture off the heat, bring big berry flavor to the scaled-down dessert. The crowning touch of whipped cream topping gets some rich body from cream cheese, along with a mild tanginess that offsets the sweet berry filling nicely. We like the buttery flavor and flaky texture of homemade pie dough here; however, you can substitute one 9-inch store-bought pie dough round, if desired. In step 4, be sure to cook the strawberry mixture until it measures ½ cup in a liquid measuring cup.

1 Roll dough disk into 9-inch circle on floured counter. Loosely roll dough circle around rolling pin and gently unroll it onto 6-inch pie plate, letting excess dough hang over edge. Ease dough into plate by gently lifting edge of dough with your hand while pressing into plate bottom with your other hand.

2 Trim overhang to ½ inch beyond lip of plate. Tuck overhang under itself; folded edge should be flush with edge of plate. Crimp dough evenly around edge of plate. Wrap dough-lined plate loosely in plastic wrap and refrigerate until firm, about 30 minutes. Adjust oven rack to lower-middle position and heat oven to 375 degrees.

3 Line chilled pie shell with double layer of aluminum foil, covering edges to prevent burning, and fill with pie weights. Bake until edges are set and just beginning to turn lightly golden, 25 to 30 minutes, rotating plate halfway through baking. Remove foil and weights, rotate plate, and continue to bake crust until deep golden brown, 10 to 12 minutes. Transfer plate to wire rack and let crust cool completely, about 1 hour.

4 **For the filling:** While crust cools, cook frozen strawberries in small saucepan over low heat until berries begin to release their juice, about 3 minutes. Increase heat to medium-low and continue to cook, stirring frequently, until mixture measures ½ cup and is thick and jam-like, 10 to 15 minutes.

5   Sprinkle gelatin over lemon juice and water in bowl and let sit until gelatin softens, about 5 minutes. Stir gelatin mixture, sugar, and salt into cooked berry mixture in saucepan, return to simmer, and cook for 1 minute. Transfer to medium bowl and let cool to room temperature, about 30 minutes.

6   Fold fresh strawberries into cooled berry mixture. Spread filling evenly over bottom of baked and cooled pie crust and refrigerate until set, at least 4 hours or up to 24 hours.

7   **For the topping:** Using stand mixer fitted with whisk attachment or hand mixer set at medium-low speed, beat cream, cream cheese, sugar, and vanilla until combined, about 1 minute. Increase speed to high and beat until stiff peaks form, 1 to 3 minutes. Spread topping evenly over pie and serve.

banana cream pie

serves 4 • **total time** 1¼ hours, plus 8 hours cooling and chilling

1 disk Foolproof All-Butter Pie Dough (page 166)

2 ripe bananas, divided

2 tablespoons unsalted butter, divided

1¼ cups half-and-half

5 tablespoons (2¼ ounces) sugar

3 large egg yolks

⅛ teaspoon table salt

1 tablespoon cornstarch

½ teaspoon vanilla extract

1 recipe Whipped Cream (page 85)

why this recipe works A creamy, cool, and luscious concoction, banana cream pie is a treat you should be able to enjoy anytime, without waiting for a crowd to share it with. To make sure the pie is banana in more than just name, we layer it with banana slices, and we infuse the pastry cream with the flavor of a ripe sautéed banana. A fluffy cloud of whipped cream is the finishing touch. We like the buttery flavor and flaky texture of homemade pie dough here; however, you can substitute one 9-inch store-bought pie dough round, if desired. Peel and slice the bananas just before using. It's important to take the temperature of the custard in multiple spots to get an accurate reading; the thickness of the custard is a good indicator of doneness. When straining the half-and-half mixture in step 5, do not press on the bananas or the custard will turn gray as it sits.

1 Roll dough disk into 9-inch circle on floured counter. Loosely roll dough circle around rolling pin and gently unroll it onto 6-inch pie plate, letting excess dough hang over edge. Ease dough into plate by gently lifting edge of dough with your hand while pressing into plate bottom with your other hand.

2 Trim overhang to ½ inch beyond lip of plate. Tuck overhang under itself; folded edge should be flush with edge of plate. Crimp dough evenly around edge of plate. Wrap dough-lined plate loosely in plastic wrap and refrigerate until firm, about 30 minutes. Adjust oven rack to lower-middle position and heat oven to 375 degrees.

3 Line chilled pie shell with double layer of aluminum foil, covering edges to prevent burning, and fill with pie weights. Bake until edges are set and just beginning to turn lightly golden, 25 to 30 minutes, rotating plate halfway through baking. Remove foil and weights, rotate plate, and continue to bake crust until deep golden brown, 10 to 12 minutes. Transfer plate to wire rack and let crust cool completely, about 1 hour.

4 While crust cools, peel and slice 1 banana ½ inch thick. Melt 1 tablespoon butter in small saucepan over medium-high heat. Add banana slices and cook until beginning to soften, about 2 minutes. Add half-and-half, bring to boil, and cook for 30 seconds. Remove pot from heat, cover, and let sit for 40 minutes.

5 Whisk sugar, egg yolks, and salt in medium bowl until smooth. Whisk in cornstarch. Strain cooled half-and-half mixture through fine-mesh strainer into yolk mixture—do not press on banana—and whisk until incorporated; discard cooked banana.

6 Transfer mixture to clean saucepan. Cook over medium heat, whisking constantly, until mixture registers 180 degrees and is thickened to consistency of warm pudding, 4 to 6 minutes. Off heat, whisk in remaining 1 tablespoon butter and vanilla. Transfer pastry cream to bowl, press greased parchment directly against surface, and let cool for about 1 hour.

7 Peel and slice remaining banana ¼ inch thick and place over bottom of baked and cooled pie crust. Whisk pastry cream briefly, then transfer to pie crust and smooth top. Spread whipped cream attractively over center of pie. Refrigerate until set, at least 5 hours or up to 24 hours. Serve.

key lime pie

serves 4 • **total time** 45 minutes, plus 4½ hours resting, cooling, and chilling

filling

- 2 large egg yolks
- 2 teaspoons grated lime zest plus ¼ cup juice (2 limes)
- ⅔ cup sweetened condensed milk

crust

- 4 whole graham crackers, broken into 1-inch pieces
- 2 tablespoons unsalted butter, melted and cooled
- 4 teaspoons sugar

- 1 recipe Whipped Cream (page 85)

why this recipe works Key lime pie is a classic dessert whose sum is exponentially greater than its parts—which, by the way, are all kitchen staples that you can easily keep on hand. The filling uses just three ingredients—egg yolks, sweetened condensed milk, and ordinary fresh limes. The process is streamlined: Whisk these ingredients together, let the mixture sit while you make and parbake the easy graham cracker crust, and then bake the filling in the crust for a mere 15 minutes. Enjoy the chilled pie with a dollop of whipped cream. We developed our recipe using regular supermarket Persian limes. Feel free to use key limes if desired; note that you'll need about 10 key limes to yield ¼ cup juice. It is important to add the filling to the crust while it is still warm; if the crust has cooled, rewarm it in the oven for 5 minutes before adding the filling.

1 **For the filling:** Whisk egg yolks and lime zest in medium bowl until mixture has light green tint, about 1 minute. Whisk in condensed milk until smooth, then whisk in lime juice. Cover mixture and set aside at room temperature until thickened, about 30 minutes.

2 **For the crust:** Meanwhile, adjust oven rack to middle position and heat oven to 325 degrees. Process graham cracker pieces in food processor to fine, even crumbs, about 30 seconds. Sprinkle melted butter and sugar over crumbs and pulse to incorporate, about 5 pulses.

3 Sprinkle mixture into 6-inch pie plate. Using bottom of measuring cup, press crumbs into even layer on bottom and up sides of plate. Bake until crust is fragrant and beginning to brown, 13 to 18 minutes. Transfer plate to wire rack; do not turn oven off. (Crust must still be warm when filling is added.)

4 Pour thickened filling into warm pie crust. Bake pie until center is firm but jiggles slightly, 15 to 20 minutes. Let pie cool slightly on wire rack, about 1 hour; cover loosely with plastic wrap and refrigerate until filling is chilled and set, about 3 hours.

5 Serve chilled pie with whipped cream.

classic cheese quiche

serves 4 • **total time** 1¼ hours, plus 1 hour chilling and cooling

1 disk Foolproof All-Butter Pie Dough (page 166)

⅔ cup half-and-half

2 large eggs, lightly beaten

2 teaspoons minced fresh chives or parsley

⅛ teaspoon table salt

⅛ teaspoon pepper

2 ounces cheddar cheese, shredded (½ cup)

variations

ham and swiss quiche

Substitute 2 ounces Swiss cheese for cheddar cheese. Stir 2 ounces thinly sliced deli ham, cut into ¼-inch pieces, into egg mixture with cheese in step 4.

quiche lorraine

While crust bakes in step 3, cook 2 slices bacon, cut into ¼-inch pieces, in 8-inch skillet over medium-low heat until crisp, about 10 minutes. Using slotted spoon, transfer bacon to paper towel–lined plate. Pour off all but 1 tablespoon fat from skillet, add ¼ cup finely chopped onion, and cook over medium heat until softened and lightly browned, 5 to 7 minutes. Substitute 2 ounces Gruyère cheese for cheddar cheese and whisk bacon and onion into egg mixture in step 4.

why this recipe works Simple yet satisfying, cheese quiche needs nothing more than a green salad to make an ideal light meal for two today and a pleasing leftover lunch tomorrow. Success depends on a fully baked crust married with a softly set filling. We add the filling to the warm crust and bake just until slightly soft; as it cools, it sets up to become a velvety, cheesy custard. We like the buttery flavor and flaky texture of home-made pie dough here; however, you can substitute one 9-inch store-bought pie dough round, if desired. It is important to add the custard to the crust while it is still warm; if the crust has cooled, rewarm it in the oven for 5 minutes before adding the custard.

1 Roll dough disk into 9-inch circle on floured counter. Loosely roll dough circle around rolling pin and gently unroll it onto 6-inch pie plate, letting excess dough hang over edge. Ease dough into plate by gently lifting edge of dough with your hand while pressing into plate bottom with your other hand.

2 Trim overhang to ½ inch beyond lip of pie plate. Tuck overhang under itself; folded edge should be flush with edge of plate. Crimp dough evenly around edge of plate. Wrap dough-lined plate loosely in plastic wrap and refrigerate until firm, about 30 minutes. Adjust oven rack to lower-middle position and heat oven to 375 degrees.

3 Line chilled pie shell with double layer of aluminum foil, covering edges to prevent burning, and fill with pie weights. Bake on foil-lined rimmed baking sheet until edges are set and just beginning to turn lightly golden, 25 to 30 minutes, rotating sheet halfway through baking. Remove foil and weights. Transfer sheet to wire rack. (Crust must still be warm when custard filling is added.)

4 Reduce oven temperature to 350 degrees. Whisk half-and-half, eggs, chives, salt, and pepper together in 4-cup liquid measuring cup. Stir in cheddar until well combined.

5 With pie plate still on sheet, carefully pour egg mixture into warm crust until it reaches about ½ inch from top edge of crust (you may have extra egg mixture). Bake quiche until top is lightly browned, very center still jiggles and looks slightly underdone, and knife inserted about 1 inch from edge comes out clean, 30 to 40 minutes. Let quiche cool on wire rack for 30 minutes to 1 hour. Serve slightly warm or at room temperature.

chocolate-pecan slab pie

serves 4 to 6 • **total time** 2 hours, plus 2 hours chilling and cooling

1 recipe Slab Pie Dough (page 166)

filling

4 tablespoons unsalted butter

1½ ounces unsweetened chocolate, chopped fine

½ cup light corn syrup

½ cup packed (3½ ounces) brown sugar

2 large eggs

2 teaspoons vanilla extract

¼ teaspoon table salt

1⅓ cups pecans, toasted and chopped coarse

bourbon whipped cream

½ cup heavy cream, chilled

1½ tablespoons packed brown sugar

1 tablespoon bourbon

¼ teaspoon vanilla extract

why this recipe works Slab pies, rectangular pies that fit in a baking sheet, serve a crowd—unless you make them in an eighth sheet pan. So what are the benefits of these shrunken slabs? A pie that can be portioned into sturdy portable slices you can eat out of hand, a pleasing ratio of buttery crust to filling, lots of great textures, a flexible serving size, and good looks. This chocolate-pecan slab pie holds just enough of an ultrarich filling and is studded with lots of crunchy nuts. The deep, buttery flavors go well with dollops of bourbon whipped cream. You will need one 9 by 6-inch rimmed baking sheet (an eighth sheet) for this recipe. We like the buttery flavor and flaky texture of homemade pie dough; however, you can substitute two 9-inch store-bought pie dough rounds if desired; brush half of one dough round with water and then overlap with the second dough round before rolling to a 12½ by 10½-inch rectangle.

1 Line large rimmed baking sheet with parchment paper. Roll pie dough into 12½ by 10½-inch rectangle on floured counter and place on prepared sheet. Cover loosely with plastic wrap and refrigerate until dough is firm but still pliable, about 10 minutes.

2 Spray 9 by 6-inch rimmed baking sheet with vegetable oil spray. Using parchment as sling, transfer chilled dough rectangle to counter; discard parchment. Starting at short side of dough rectangle, loosely roll around rolling pin, then gently unroll over prepared sheet, leaving about 2 inches of dough overhanging edges.

3 Ease dough into sheet by gently lifting edges of dough with your hand while pressing into sheet bottom with your other hand. Trim overhang to ½ inch beyond edge of sheet. Tuck overhang under itself; folded edge should rest on edge of sheet. Crimp dough evenly around edge of sheet. Cover loosely with plastic and refrigerate until firm, about 30 minutes. Adjust oven racks to lower middle and middle positions and heat oven to 350 degrees.

4 Line chilled pie shell with double layer of aluminum foil, covering edges to prevent burning, and fill with pie weights. Bake crust on upper rack until edges are set and just beginning to turn lightly golden, about 30 minutes, rotating sheet halfway through baking. Remove foil and weights, rotate sheet, and continue to bake crust until center is golden brown, 20 to 25 minutes longer. Transfer sheet to wire rack (crust does not need to be completely cool before filling). Decrease oven temperature to 325 degrees.

5 **For the filling:** Microwave butter and chocolate in medium bowl at 50 percent power, stirring occasionally, until melted, 1½ to 2 minutes. Add corn syrup, sugar, eggs, vanilla, and salt to chocolate mixture and whisk until well combined and smooth. Stir in pecans.

6 Pour filling into shell and spread into even layer. Place large sheet of aluminum foil directly on lower rack (to catch any bubbling filling). Place pie on upper rack and bake until firm pecan layer forms on top and puffs slightly, and filling in center of pie registers 185 to 190 degrees, 35 to 40 minutes, rotating sheet halfway through baking. Let pie cool on wire rack until set, about 1½ hours.

7 **For the bourbon whipped cream:** Using stand mixer fitted with whisk attachment or hand mixer set at medium-low speed, whip cream, sugar, bourbon, and vanilla until foamy, about 1 minute. Increase speed to high and whip until soft peaks form, 1 to 3 minutes. Serve pie with whipped cream.

triple-berry slab pie with ginger-lemon streusel

serves 4 to 6 • **total time** 2½ hours, plus 2 hours chilling and cooling

1   recipe Slab Pie Dough (page 166)

streusel

6   tablespoons (1¾ ounces) all-purpose flour

2   tablespoons packed brown sugar

2   tablespoons crystallized ginger, chopped fine

1   tablespoon granulated sugar

¾   teaspoon ground ginger

¼   teaspoon grated lemon zest

Pinch table salt

3   tablespoons unsalted butter, melted

filling

¼   cup (1¾ ounces) granulated sugar

1½   tablespoons instant tapioca, ground

¼   teaspoon grated lemon zest

Pinch table salt

6   ounces (1¼ cups) blackberries

6   ounces (1¼ cups) blueberries

6   ounces (1¼ cups) raspberries

why this recipe works This berry slab pie is striking—and a cinch to prepare. We start by tossing no-prep berries—blueberries, raspberries, and blackberries—with sugar and lemon zest. Instead of applying a top crust, which would hide the beautiful berry hues and trap moisture, we sprinkle on a streusel that we flavor liberally with more lemon zest as well as some crystallized ginger. You will need one 9 by 6-inch rimmed baking sheet (an eighth sheet) for this recipe. We like the buttery flavor and flaky texture of homemade pie dough; however, you can substitute two 9-inch store-bought pie dough rounds if desired; brush half of one dough round with water and then overlap with the second dough round before rolling to a 12½ by 10½-inch rectangle. Grind the tapioca to a powder in a spice grinder or a mini food processor.

1   Line large rimmed baking sheet with parchment paper. Roll pie dough into 12½ by 10½-inch rectangle on floured counter and place on prepared sheet. Cover loosely with plastic wrap and refrigerate until dough is firm but still pliable, about 10 minutes.

2   Spray 9 by 6-inch rimmed baking sheet with vegetable oil spray. Using parchment as sling, transfer chilled dough rectangle to counter; discard parchment. Starting at short side of dough rectangle, loosely roll around rolling pin, then gently unroll over prepared sheet, leaving about 2 inches of dough overhanging edges.

3   Ease dough into sheet by gently lifting edges of dough with your hand while pressing into sheet bottom with your other hand. Trim overhang to ½ inch beyond edge of sheet. Tuck overhang under itself; folded edge should rest on edge of sheet. Crimp dough evenly around edge of sheet. Cover loosely with plastic and refrigerate until firm, about 30 minutes. Adjust oven racks to lower middle and middle positions and heat oven to 350 degrees.

4   Line chilled pie shell with double layer of aluminum foil, covering edges to prevent burning, and fill with pie weights. Bake crust on upper rack until edges are set and just beginning to turn lightly golden, about 30 minutes, rotating sheet halfway through baking. Remove foil and weights, rotate sheet, and continue to bake crust until bottom is starting to turn golden brown, about 15 minutes longer. Transfer sheet to wire rack (crust does not need to be completely cool before filling). Increase oven temperature to 375 degrees.

5 **For the streusel:** Meanwhile, combine flour, brown sugar, crystallized ginger, granulated sugar, ground ginger, lemon zest, and salt in bowl. Stir in melted butter until mixture is completely moistened; set aside.

6 **For the filling:** Whisk granulated sugar, tapioca, lemon zest, and salt together in medium bowl. Add blackberries, blueberries, and raspberries and gently toss to combine. Spread berry mixture evenly over parbaked pie shell. Sprinkle reserved streusel evenly over fruit, breaking up any large chunks. Place large sheet of aluminum foil directly on lower rack (to catch any bubbling juices). Place pie on upper rack and bake until crust and streusel are deep golden brown and juices are bubbling, 1 hour to 1 hour 15 minutes, rotating sheet halfway through baking, and tenting entire pie with aluminum foil for the last 20 to 30 minutes of baking if crust or streusel begin to get dark. Let pie cool on wire rack until filling has set, about 1½ hours. Serve.

pie doughs

No matter the size of the pie, pie dough is an item that can bog down bakers. And why even bother for two? While pie dough has a reputation for being finicky, our recipes are easy to handle and ensure flaky crusts every time. The most appealing part of pie dough for a small-batch baker is its storage capabilities. Have time one weekend? Make your dough, fashion it into disks, and then freeze them so the hard part is done when it comes to pie time. Making a single-crust pie? You'll have a dough disk left for your next project.

foolproof all-butter pie dough

makes 2 dough disks
total time 25 minutes, plus 2 hours chilling

This recipe's two-step process protects much of the flour from coming in contact with the water, which limits the gluten formation that makes crust tough. This dough starts out very moist, but as it chills it becomes supple. This recipe makes enough dough for two 6-inch single-crust pies or one 6-inch double-crust pie.

    9   tablespoons unsalted butter, chilled, divided
 1¼   cups (6¼ ounces) all-purpose flour, divided
    1   tablespoon sugar
  ½   teaspoon table salt
  ¼   cup ice water, divided

1   Grate 2 tablespoons butter on large holes of box grater and place in freezer. Cut remaining 7 tablespoons butter into ½-inch cubes.

2   Pulse ¾ cup flour, sugar, and salt in food processor until combined, 2 pulses. Add cubed butter and process until homogeneous paste forms, about 30 seconds. Using your hands, carefully break paste into 2-inch chunks and redistribute evenly around processor blade.

3   Add remaining ½ cup flour and pulse until mixture is broken into pieces no larger than 1 inch (most pieces will be much smaller), 4 or 5 pulses. Transfer mixture to medium bowl. Add grated butter and toss until butter pieces are separated and coated with flour.

4   Sprinkle 2 tablespoons ice water over mixture. Toss with rubber spatula until mixture is evenly moistened. Sprinkle remaining 2 tablespoons ice water over mixture and toss to combine. Press dough with spatula until dough sticks together. Using spatula, divide dough into 2 equal pieces. Transfer each portion to sheet of plastic wrap. Working with 1 portion at a time, draw edges of plastic over dough and press firmly on sides and top to form compact, fissure-free mass. Wrap in plastic and flatten to form 4-inch disk. Refrigerate dough for at least 2 hours or up to 2 days. Let chilled dough sit on counter to soften slightly, about 10 minutes, before rolling. (Wrapped dough can be frozen for up to 1 month. If frozen, let dough thaw completely on counter before rolling.)

variations

whole-grain all-butter pie dough

Substitute ¾ cup (4⅛ ounces) whole-wheat flour or rye flour for the first addition of all-purpose flour in step 2. Add ½ cup (2½ ounces) all-purpose flour to dough mixture in step 3 as directed.

slab pie dough

This recipe makes enough dough for one slab pie. You can make this following the directions for Foolproof All-Butter Pie Dough or Whole-Grain All-Butter Pie Dough.

In step 4, instead of dividing dough into 2 pieces, shape into 6 by 4-inch rectangle before refrigerating or freezing.

making pie dough

1 Pulse ¾ cup flour, sugar, and salt in food processor until combined, 2 pulses. Add cubed butter and process until homogeneous paste forms, about 30 seconds.

2 Using your hands, carefully break paste into 2-inch chunks and redistribute evenly around processor blade.

3 Add remaining ½ cup flour and pulse until mixture is broken into pieces no larger than 1 inch (most pieces will be much smaller), 4 or 5 pulses. Transfer mixture to bowl.

4 Add grated butter and toss until butter pieces are coated with flour. Sprinkle 2 tablespoons ice water over mixture. Toss with rubber spatula until mixture is evenly moistened. Sprinkle remaining 2 tablespoons water over mixture, toss to combine, and press until dough sticks together.

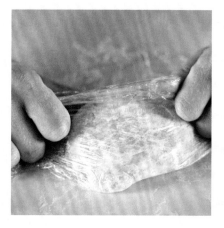

5 Divide dough in half and transfer each half to sheet of plastic wrap. Working with 1 portion at a time, draw edges of plastic over dough and press firmly on sides and top to form compact, fissure-free mass.

6 Wrap in plastic and flatten to form 4-inch disk.

pie doughs

shaping pie dough

1 Loosely roll dough around rolling pin, then gently unroll it onto pie plate, letting excess hang over plate.

2 Lift dough around edges and gently press it into corners of pie plate.

3 To finish, trim overhanging edge of crust to about ½ inch beyond lip of pie plate, then tuck overhang under itself to make it flush with edge of pie plate.

4 Use index finger of your hand and thumb and index finger of your other hand to create fluted ridges perpendicular to edge of pie plate.

shaping slab pie dough

1 Roll pie dough into 12½ by 10½-inch rectangle on floured counter. Cover loosely with plastic wrap and refrigerate until dough is firm but still pliable, about 10 minutes.

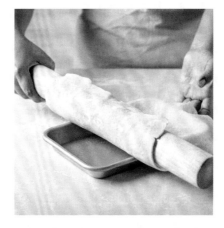

2 Starting at short side of dough rectangle, loosely roll around rolling pin, then gently unroll over prepared sheet, leaving about 2 inches of dough overhanging edges.

3 Ease dough into sheet by gently lifting edges of dough with your hand while pressing into sheet bottom with your other hand.

4 Trim overhang to ½ inch beyond edge of sheet. Tuck overhang under itself; folded edge should rest on edge of sheet.

apple galette

serves 2 • **total time** 55 minutes

½ (9½ by 9-inch) sheet puff pastry, thawed

1 large Granny Smith apple (8 ounces), peeled, cored, halved, and sliced ⅛ inch thick

½ tablespoon unsalted butter, cut into ¼-inch pieces

2 teaspoons sugar

1 tablespoon apple jelly

1 teaspoon water

why this recipe works If there's such a thing as "easier than pie," this elegant apple galette, which comes together simply and quickly with kitchen staples, deserves the title. Half a sheet of store-bought puff pastry provides the perfect amount of real estate for a for-two dessert. We thinly slice a single large Granny Smith apple and shingle the slices across the pastry. A sprinkling of sugar and dots of butter work magic in the oven, drawing out the apple's moisture and caramelizing the slices. Brushing the hot-out-of-the-oven tart with apple jelly creates an attractive sheen and adds a fruity tartness that really enhances the flavors. To thaw frozen puff pastry, let it sit either on the counter for 30 minutes to 1 hour or in the refrigerator for 24 hours. Slice the pastry in half lengthwise; the remaining half sheet can be wrapped tightly in plastic wrap and refrozen. We do not recommend baking this in a toaster oven.

1 Adjust oven rack to middle position and heat oven to 400 degrees. Line rimmed baking sheet with parchment paper. Transfer puff pastry to prepared sheet and fold edges over by ¼ inch; crimp to create ¼-inch-thick border.

2 Starting in 1 corner of pastry, shingle apple slices into crust in tidy diagonal rows, overlapping them by about half, until surface is completely covered. Dot apple with butter and sprinkle evenly with sugar. Bake until bottom of galette is deep golden brown and apple has caramelized, 40 to 45 minutes, rotating sheet halfway through baking.

3 Combine apple jelly and water in bowl and microwave until mixture begins to bubble, about 30 seconds. Brush glaze over apples and let galette cool slightly on sheet. Serve warm or at room temperature.

rustic berry tart

serves 2 • **total time** 1¼ hours, plus 20 minutes cooling

1 recipe Rustic Tart Dough
(page 188), shaped into
one 4-inch disk

8 ounces peaches, nectarines,
apricots, or plums, halved, pitted,
and cut into ½-inch wedges

2½ ounces (¼ cup) blackberries,
blueberries, or raspberries

3–5 tablespoons sugar, divided

why this recipe works Turning summer fruit pie into a free-form tart makes it both more casual and more special. And when you're making a tart for two, you don't need a bumper crop of fruit; a couple handfuls of berries and stone fruits will suffice. Our rustic tart dough is made with the fraisage method for a flaky yet sturdy texture. We mound the lightly sweetened fruit in the center of the round and loosely pleat the dough around it. A little extra sugar on top gives the tart sparkle. Taste the fruit before adding sugar; use the lesser amount if the fruit is very sweet, more if it is tart. However much sugar you use, do not add it to the fruit until you are ready to fill and form the tart. We like the buttery flavor and flaky texture of homemade tart dough here; however, you can substitute one 9-inch store-bought pie dough round, if desired. You could also shape this recipe into two smaller tarts; follow the shaping instructions on page 173.

1   Roll dough disk into 9-inch circle between 2 sheets of floured parchment paper. (If dough sticks to parchment, gently loosen and lift sticky area with bench scraper and dust parchment with additional flour.) Slide dough circle, still between parchment sheets, onto rimmed baking sheet and refrigerate until firm, 15 to 30 minutes. Adjust oven rack to middle position and heat oven to 400 degrees.

2   Gently toss peaches, blackberries, and 2 tablespoons sugar together in bowl. (If fruit tastes tart, add up to 2 tablespoons more sugar.) Remove top sheet of parchment from dough circle. (If refrigerated longer than 15 to 30 minutes and dough is hard and brittle, let sit at room temperature until pliant, about 10 minutes.) Mound fruit in center of circle, leaving 1½-inch border around edge of fruit. Being careful to leave ½-inch border of dough around edge of fruit, fold outermost 1 inch of dough over fruit, pleating it every 1 to 2 inches as needed; gently pinch pleated dough to secure, but do not press dough into fruit.

3   Return tart to parchment-lined sheet. Brush dough with water and sprinkle tart evenly with remaining 1 tablespoon sugar. Bake until crust is deep golden brown and fruit is bubbling, 35 to 45 minutes, rotating sheet halfway through baking.

4   Transfer tart with sheet to wire rack and let cool for 10 minutes, then use parchment to gently transfer tart to wire rack. Use metal spatula to loosen tart from parchment and remove parchment. Let tart cool on rack until juices have thickened, about 20 minutes; serve slightly warm or at room temperature.

one or two tarts

The Rustic Berry Tart and the Pineapple, Ginger, and Lime Tarts (page 174) can both be made as either one 6-inch tart or two 4-inch tartlets using the same dough. Start by shaping your dough into 1 or 2 disks (see the steps on page 189), and then follow the instructions below to shape as desired.

one tart

1 Roll 4-inch dough disk into 9-inch circle between 2 sheets of floured parchment.

2 Slide dough circle, still between parchment sheets, onto rimmed baking sheet and refrigerate until firm, 15 to 30 minutes.

3 Remove top sheet of parchment from dough circle. Mound fruit mixture in center of circle, leaving 1½-inch border around edge of fruit.

4 Being careful to leave ½-inch border of dough around edge of fruit, fold outermost 1 inch of dough over fruit, pleating it every 1 to 2 inches as needed; gently pinch pleated dough to secure, but do not press dough into fruit.

two tarts

1 Roll each 3-inch dough disk into 7-inch circle between 2 small sheets of floured parchment.

2 Slide dough circles, still between parchment sheets, onto rimmed baking sheet and refrigerate until firm, 15 to 30 minutes.

3 Remove top sheet of parchment from 1 dough circle; transfer to one side of second parchment-lined sheet. Mound half of fruit in center of circle, leaving 1½-inch border around edge of fruit.

4 Being careful to leave ½-inch border of dough around edge of fruit, fold outermost 1 inch of dough over fruit, pleating it every 1 to 2 inches as needed; gently pinch pleated dough to secure, but do not press dough into fruit.

pineapple, ginger, and lime tarts

serves 2 • **total time** 1¼ hours, plus 20 minutes cooling

1 recipe Rustic Tart Dough (page 188), shaped into two 3-inch disks

2½ tablespoons sugar, divided

1 teaspoon cornstarch

Pinch table salt

1 (20-ounce) can pineapple slices, drained

1½ teaspoons grated fresh ginger

½ teaspoon grated lime zest, plus extra for garnish

2 teaspoons torn fresh mint

why this recipe works Pineapple makes a terrific tart filling, and here we turn to pantry-friendly canned pineapple. It's the right amount for small-scale tarts and saves us from peeling, coring, and cutting a fresh pineapple. We chop up a portion of the pineapple and drain its excess juice so we can pack it in the filling without it running over the edges of the tart. Including fresh ginger and lime zest gives the tart pleasing warmth and aroma. Reserving a few pineapple slices to place on top gives the tarts a photo-ready finish, which is enhanced with a sprinkle of fresh lime zest and refreshing mint just before serving. You could also shape this recipe into one larger tart; follow the shaping instructions on page 173, reserving 3 pineapple slices for the top.

1 Roll each dough disk into 7-inch circles between 2 sheets of floured parchment paper. (If dough sticks to parchment, gently loosen and lift sticky area with bench scraper and dust parchment with additional flour.) Slide dough circles, still between parchment sheets, onto rimmed baking sheet and refrigerate until firm, 15 to 30 minutes. Adjust oven rack to middle position and heat oven to 400 degrees.

2 Whisk 2 tablespoons sugar, cornstarch, and salt together in medium bowl; set aside. Reserve 2 pineapple slices; finely chop remaining pineapple rings and transfer to fine mesh strainer set over second bowl. Press chopped pineapple with rubber spatula to remove excess juice (you should have about ¼ cup juice). Add drained chopped pineapple, ginger, and lime zest to bowl with sugar mixture; toss to combine.

3 Remove top sheet of parchment from 1 dough circle and transfer to 1 side of second parchment-lined sheet. (If refrigerated longer than 15 to 30 minutes and dough is hard and brittle, let sit at room temperature until pliant, about 10 minutes.) Mound half of pineapple mixture in center of circle, leaving 1½-inch border around edge of fruit. Arrange reserved pineapple slices on top. Being careful to leave ½-inch border of dough around edge of fruit, fold outermost 1 inch of dough over fruit, pleating it every 1 to 2 inches as needed; gently pinch pleated dough to secure, but do not press dough into fruit. Repeat with remaining fruit and dough circle.

4 Brush dough with water and sprinkle tart crusts evenly with remaining 1½ teaspoons sugar. Bake until crust is deep golden brown, 35 to 45 minutes, rotating sheet halfway through baking.

5 Transfer sheet to wire rack and let cool for 10 minutes, then use parchment to gently transfer tarts to wire rack. Use metal spatula to loosen tarts from parchment and remove parchment. Let tarts cool on rack until juices have thickened, about 20 minutes. Sprinkle with mint and lime zest and serve slightly warm or at room temperature.

pear and chestnut tarts

serves 2 • **total time** 1 hour

4 ounces (½ cup) mascarpone cheese, room temperature

1 teaspoon confectioners' sugar, plus extra for dusting

½ teaspoon grated lemon zest plus ½ teaspoon juice

1 (9½ by 9-inch) sheet puff pastry, thawed

1 large egg, lightly beaten

1 tablespoon unsalted butter

1 slightly underripe pear, peeled, cored, and cut into ½-inch pieces

¼ cup chestnut spread

1 tablespoon water

Pinch table salt

1 teaspoon minced fresh rosemary, divided

why this recipe works The French have a secret: It's called crème de marrons, which translates as chestnut spread, and it is little known outside of France. Inexpensive, yet made from the offcuts of pricey candied chestnuts, it is packed with vanilla-flecked chestnut flavor. It's commonly spread on toast or dolloped on yogurt, but here we put it front and center, using this convenient product to elevate what are dead-simple tarts for two. We cook a slightly underripe pear in butter (so it doesn't turn overly soft during cooking) and then make a pan sauce to coat the pear using the chestnut spread, lemon juice, and rosemary. We use store-bought puff pastry as our crust, layer it with lightly sweetened mascarpone cheese that's flavored with lemon zest to cut the richness, and then fill it with our pear mixture. We developed this recipe using Clément Faugier Chestnut Spread, which can be found in specialty stores or online in small tubes or larger tins. One 2¾-ounce tube will yield the ¼ cup needed here. Do not use unsweetened chestnut puree. To thaw frozen puff pastry, let it sit either in the refrigerator for 24 hours or on the counter for 30 minutes to 1 hour. The remaining half sheet of puff pastry can be wrapped tightly in plastic wrap and refrozen.

1 Adjust oven rack to middle position and heat oven to 400 degrees. Gently stir mascarpone, confectioners' sugar, and lemon zest in bowl until combined, then cover and refrigerate until ready to serve.

2 Cut puff pastry into 9 by 4½-inch rectangle, then roll into 10 by 5-inch rectangle on lightly floured counter (reserve remaining pastry for another use). Cut in half widthwise (you should have two 5 by 5-inch squares) and transfer to parchment paper–lined rimmed baking sheet. Poke dough all over with fork and brush surface with egg wash. Bake until puffed and golden brown, 17 to 20 minutes, rotating sheet halfway through baking.

3 Using tip of paring knife, cut ½-inch-wide border around top edge of pastries (being careful not to cut through to bottom). Transfer tart shells to wire rack and let cool while cooking pears.

pear and almond tarts

The almond paste is much thicker than the chestnut spread and will require more mashing and stirring in step 5 to become smooth.

Substitute 1½ ounces almond paste for chestnut spread. Increase water to ¼ cup.

4 Melt butter in 8-inch skillet over medium heat. Add pears and cook until well browned on most sides, 7 to 10 minutes. Transfer to bowl.

5 Off heat, add chestnut spread, water, and salt to now-empty skillet. Set over low heat and, using spatula, mash and stir until smooth. Off heat, stir in lemon juice, ½ teaspoon rosemary, and cooked pears. Return pear mixture to bowl and let cool for 10 minutes.

6 Press center of cooled tart shells down with your fingertips. Spread all but 2 tablespoons mascarpone mixture evenly over tart shells, avoiding raised border. Spoon pear topping over top then dollop with reserved mascarpone mixture. Sprinkle with remaining ½ teaspoon rosemary and dust with confectioners' sugar. Serve.

making the crust

1 Poke dough all over with fork and brush with egg wash. Bake until puffed and golden brown, 17 to 20 minutes, rotating sheet halfway through baking.

2 Using tip of paring knife, cut ½-inch-wide border around top edge of pastry (being careful not to cut through to bottom). Press center of cooled tart shells down with your fingertips.

Pear and Chestnut Tarts

Tarte Tatin

tarte tatin

serves 2 • **total time** 1¼ hours, plus 2¼ hours chilling and cooling

dough

- ½ cup (2½ ounces) all-purpose flour
- 1 teaspoon sugar
- ¼ teaspoon table salt
- 4 tablespoons unsalted butter, cut into ½-inch pieces and chilled
- 4–6 teaspoons ice water

filling

- 1 Golden Delicious or Gala apple, peeled, cored, and cut into 1½-inch wide wedges
- Pinch table salt
- ¼ cup (1¾ ounces) sugar
- 1 tablespoon light corn syrup
- 1 tablespoon water
- 1 tablespoon unsalted butter

why this recipe works If you're looking for an elegant dessert, our modified tarte tatin is an ideal choice—it's as beautiful and delicious as its instructions are simple. Traditionally, peeled apple wedges are cooked in a skillet, then a chilled dough round is set on the apples and it's baked in a hot oven until the dough is bronzed and crisp while the apple topping caramelizes. Once cooked, the pan is flipped onto a serving plate and the sauce and apple coat the crust and just start to soften its crispness. For our tarte-for-two, we found that an 8-inch skillet made too much dessert, while a 6-inch skillet couldn't even accommodate a single apple. So we changed the method, making the tarte in a 6-inch pie plate. But the apples still need precooking to set the pectin or they'll turn to mush in the oven. We give them a brief blast in the microwave and combine them in the pie plate with a caramel sauce that we make in a saucepan. We then pop a mini dough round on top before baking it all in the pie plate. It's important to match the size of your burner to the size of your saucepan when making the caramel to avoid hot spots. We bake the tarte on a 13 by 9-inch rimmed baking sheet (a quarter sheet); if you use a larger sheet you may need to increase your cook time in step 6 by up to 10 minutes.

1 **For the dough:** Process flour, sugar, and salt in food processor until combined, about 5 seconds. Scatter butter over top and pulse until mixture resembles coarse crumbs and butter pieces are about size of small peas, 7 to 10 pulses. Continue to pulse, adding 1 teaspoon ice water at a time, until dough begins to form small curds and holds together when pinched with your fingers (dough will be crumbly), 4 to 6 pulses.

2 Turn dough crumbs onto lightly floured counter and gather into rectangular pile about 6 inches long and 3 inches wide, with short side facing you. Starting at farthest end, use heel of your hand to smear small amount of dough against counter. Continue to smear dough until all crumbs have been worked. Gather smeared crumbs together into another rectangular pile and repeat process.

3   Line large flat plate with parchment paper. Shape dough into 5-inch disk, pressing any cracked edges back together. Roll dough into 7-inch circle, flouring counter and dough as needed. Transfer to prepared plate. Invert 6-inch pie plate onto dough and press gently to form indentation. Remove pie plate and, using paring knife, cut dough circle, following inner ridge of indentation; discard scraps. Cut three 2-inch slits in center of dough. (If, at any point during rolling, the dough gets too soft to work with, refrigerate for 10 minutes before continuing.) Cover dough with plastic wrap and refrigerate until dough is very firm, at least 2 hours or up to 2 days.

4   **For the filling:** Adjust oven rack to upper-middle position and heat oven to 375 degrees. Spray 6-inch pie plate with vegetable oil spray. Toss apples and pinch salt together in bowl. Cover and microwave until apples are warm to touch, 45 to 60 seconds, stirring once halfway through microwaving. Let apples sit, covered, for 5 minutes. Arrange apple slices in prepared pie plate, cut side down. (You may have 1 extra apple slice, depending on the size of your apple.)

5   Bring sugar, corn syrup, and water to boil in small saucepan over medium-high heat. Cook, without stirring, until mixture begins to turn straw-colored around edge of saucepan, 3 to 5 minutes. Reduce heat to medium-low and continue to cook, swirling saucepan occasionally, until mixture is amber-colored and registers 360 to 370 degrees, 1 to 3 minutes longer. (To take temperature, tilt saucepan to 1 side and stir with thermometer to equalize hotter and cooler spots, avoiding bottom of saucepan.)

6   Off heat, carefully stir in butter (mixture will bubble and steam). Working quickly, pour caramel over apples in pie plate. Place chilled dough over apples. Set pie plate on 13 by 9-inch rimmed baking sheet and bake until thick, syrupy bubbles form around edge and crust is golden brown, 35 to 45 minutes. Transfer to wire rack and let sit for 20 minutes.

7   Run paring knife around edge of pie plate to loosen tart. Invert serving plate over pie plate. Swiftly and carefully invert tart onto serving plate (if apples shift or stick to pie plate, rearrange with spoon), scraping any sauce clinging to pie plate over top of tart. Serve warm or at room temperature.

lemon tartlets

serves 2 • **total time** 30 minutes, plus 1½ hours cooling

1 large egg plus 3 large yolks

⅓ cup (2⅓ ounces) granulated sugar

1 tablespoon grated lemon zest plus ¼ cup juice (2 lemons)

Pinch table salt

2 tablespoons unsalted butter, cut into 2 pieces

1 tablespoon heavy cream, chilled

1 recipe Browned-Butter Tart Shells (page 188), still warm

Confectioners' sugar

why this recipe works Individual lemon tartlets, with their colorful centers and sleek fluted shapes, are pastry case darlings. There's no denying the appeal of re-creating these impressive pastries to enjoy at home, and we found a way to make this happen for two. Rather than rolling out dough rounds and then painstakingly fitting them into the small tart pans, we start with an easy press-in dough that uses melted butter, which we first brown for a nutty flavor boost. We parbake the crusts so they don't shrink and remain crisp after baking. The lemon curd comes together quickly on the stovetop, and is baked briefly in the warm tart shells. A dusting of confectioners' sugar adds understated elegance. Once the lemon curd ingredients are combined, cook the curd immediately; otherwise, it will have a grainy consistency. It is important to add the filling to the tart shells while they are still warm; if the shells have cooled, rewarm them in the oven for 5 minutes before adding the filling.

1 Adjust oven rack to middle position and heat oven to 375 degrees. Whisk egg and yolks together in small saucepan. Whisk in granulated sugar until combined, then whisk in lemon zest and juice and salt. Add butter and cook over medium-low heat, stirring constantly, until mixture registers 170 degrees and has thickened slightly, 5 to 7 minutes. Immediately pour mixture through fine-mesh strainer into bowl and stir in cream.

2 Divide warm lemon filling evenly between warm prebaked tart shells and smooth tops. Place tarts on rimmed baking sheet and bake until filling is opaque and centers jiggle slightly when gently shaken, about 10 minutes, rotating sheet halfway through baking.

3 Transfer tarts with sheet to wire rack and let cool completely, about 1½ hours. To serve, remove outer metal ring of tart pans, slide thin metal spatula between tarts and tart pan bottoms, and carefully slide tarts onto individual plates. Dust with confectioners' sugar. Serve.

walnut tartlets

serves 2 • **total time** 1¼ hours, plus 2 hours chilling and cooling

tart shells

- ½ cup (2½ ounces) all-purpose flour
- 2 tablespoons packed light brown sugar
- 2 tablespoons coarsely chopped walnuts, toasted
- ⅛ teaspoon baking powder
- ⅛ teaspoon table salt
- 4 tablespoons unsalted butter, cut into ½-inch pieces and chilled

filling

- ⅓ cup packed (2⅓ ounces) light brown sugar
- 3 tablespoons light corn syrup
- 2 tablespoons unsalted butter, melted and cooled
- 2 teaspoons bourbon or dark rum
- ½ teaspoon vanilla extract
  - Pinch table salt
- 1 large egg
- ⅓ cup walnuts, chopped coarse

why this recipe works These walnut tarts make a sophisticated finish to a special meal for two, yet they're surprisingly easy to prepare thanks to a very simple filling, which is similar to pecan pie filling but with less sugar, a hefty amount of vanilla, and a splash of bourbon (or rum). The slender proportions of the tarts ensure that the flavor is more about the nuts than the custard. To reinforce the rich, earthy, nuttiness, we use walnuts in the crust as well as the filling. Pecans can be substituted for the walnuts if desired. We like the flavor of the walnut tart shells in this recipe, but you can use our recipe for Browned-Butter Tart Shells (page 188) if you prefer.

1 For the tart shells: Grease two 4-inch tart pans with removable bottoms. Process flour, sugar, walnuts, baking powder, and salt in food processor until combined, about 5 seconds. Scatter butter over top and pulse until mixture resembles coarse cornmeal, about 8 pulses.

2 Sprinkle mixture evenly into prepared pans. Using bottom of measuring cup, press crumbs firmly into even layer on bottom and up sides of pans. Use your thumb to level off top edges and remove excess crumbs. Use excess crumbs to patch any holes. Place crumb-lined tart pans on large plate, cover with plastic wrap, and freeze until fully chilled and firm, at least 30 minutes or up to 1 day. Adjust oven rack to middle position and heat oven to 350 degrees.

3 Set chilled crumb-lined tart pans on rimmed baking sheet. Press double layer of aluminum foil into frozen tart shells, covering edges to prevent burning, and fill with pie weights. Bake tart shells until golden brown and set, 20 to 25 minutes, rotating sheet halfway through baking. Remove foil and weights; transfer tarts with sheet to wire rack and let cool slightly while making filling.

4 For the filling: Whisk sugar, corn syrup, melted butter, bourbon, vanilla, and salt in medium bowl until sugar dissolves. Whisk in egg until combined. Pour filling evenly into tart shells and sprinkle with walnuts. Bake tarts until filling is set and walnuts begin to brown, 25 to 30 minutes, rotating sheet halfway through baking.

5 Transfer tarts with sheet to wire rack and let cool completely, about 1½ hours. To serve, remove outer metal ring of tart pans, slide thin metal spatula between tarts and tart pan bottoms, and carefully slide tarts onto individual plates.

chocolate-passion fruit tartlets

serves 2 • **total time** 20 minutes, plus 1 hour chilling

curd

¼ cup passion fruit puree

3 tablespoons sugar

1 tablespoon cornstarch

1½ ounces white chocolate, chopped

3 tablespoons unsalted butter, cut into ½-inch pieces

1 recipe Browned-Butter Tart Shells (page 188), cooled

ganache

1½ ounces milk chocolate, chopped

2 tablespoons heavy cream

Pinch table salt

Flake sea salt

why this recipe works These individual-size desserts are visually stunning, incredibly delicious, and shockingly easy. Floral and mouth-puckeringly tart, fresh passion fruits are hard to find in much of the United States, but a puree made from their pulp can commonly be found in your freezer aisle. Heating just a few tablespoons of puree with cornstarch and sugar before blending with white chocolate and butter makes a lusciously textured and vibrantly flavored curd that we layer into two baked tart shells. To pair with the assertively flavored curd, we make a three-ingredient milk chocolate ganache in the microwave in less than a minute and then pour it over the chilled layer of curd. It sets to a beautifully glossy sheen, hiding the sunny yellow passion fruit layer within. Look for passion fruit puree with the other frozen fruit in your grocery store; it may also be sold as "passion fruit pulp," but make sure it is seedless. Do not remove the tart shells from the tins until they are filled. If you've got one, use a flat or mini whisk to get into the corners of the saucepan when making the curd in step 1.

1 For the curd: Whisk passion fruit puree, sugar, and cornstarch together in small saucepan. Cook over medium-low heat, stirring constantly, until thick paste forms, 2 to 4 minutes. Off heat, add white chocolate and whisk until melted, then whisk in butter in 2 additions until mixture is smooth and glossy. Divide curd evenly between cooled tart shells and smooth tops with small offset spatula. Refrigerate, uncovered, until firm, about 30 minutes.

2 For the ganache: Microwave milk chocolate, cream, and salt in bowl at 50 percent power, whisking frequently, until chocolate is melted, 30 seconds to 1 minute. Divide ganache evenly between tart shells, spreading into smooth, even layer with clean offset spatula. Refrigerate, uncovered, until set, about 30 minutes.

3 To serve, remove outer metal ring of tart pans, slide thin metal spatula between tarts and tart pan bottoms, and carefully slide tarts onto individual plates. Sprinkle with flake sea salt.

tart doughs

Tarts for two are so darn cute that they deserve great-tasting and great-textured doughs.

rustic tart dough

makes *enough for two 4-inch tartlets or one 6-inch tart*
total time *15 minutes, plus 1 hour chilling*

Without the support of a pie plate or tart pan, the crust for a free-form tart is prone to leaking juice, resulting in a soggy tart bottom. The answer to satisfying structure is a French pastry method called fraisage; pieces of butter are smeared into the flour in long, thin sheets, creating lots of long, flaky layers when the dough is baked. These long layers are tender for eating yet sturdy and impermeable, making the crust ideal for supporting a generous filling of juicy fruit.

- ¾ cup (3¾ ounces) all-purpose flour
- ¼ teaspoon table salt
- 5 tablespoons unsalted butter, cut into ½-inch pieces and chilled
- 2–3 tablespoons ice water

1 Process flour and salt in food processor until combined, about 5 seconds. Scatter butter over top and pulse until mixture resembles coarse crumbs and butter pieces are about size of small peas, 6 to 8 pulses. Continue to pulse, adding 1 tablespoon ice water at a time, until dough begins to form small curds and holds together when pinched with fingers (dough will be crumbly), 7 to 10 pulses.

2 Turn dough crumbs onto lightly floured counter and gather into rectangular pile about 8 inches long and 3 inches wide, with short side facing you. Starting at farthest end, use heel of your hand to smear small amount of dough against counter. Continue to smear dough until all crumbs have been worked. Gather smeared crumbs together into another rectangular pile and repeat process.

3 For one 6-inch tart, shape dough into 4-inch disk. For two 4-inch tarts, divide dough in half and form each half into 3-inch disk. Wrap disk(s) tightly in plastic wrap and refrigerate for 1 hour. Let chilled dough sit on counter to soften slightly, about 10 minutes, before rolling. (Wrapped dough can be refrigerated for up to 2 days or frozen for up to 2 months. If frozen, let dough thaw completely on counter before rolling.)

browned-butter tart shells

makes *two 4-inch tart shells*
total time *45 minutes, plus 30 minutes cooling*

For a tart dough that doesn't need to be rolled and can be parbaked without pie weights, we start by stirring melted butter into flour, sugar, and salt to create a malleable dough that can be simply pressed into the pan. For extra flavor, we first brown the butter and add back the water that had cooked off so that there is enough moisture for the flour to form gluten (the protein network that gives the dough structure).

- ½ cup (2½ ounces) all-purpose flour
- 1 tablespoon plus 2 teaspoons sugar
- Pinch table salt
- 4 tablespoons unsalted butter
- 1 tablespoon water

1 Adjust oven rack to middle position and heat oven to 350 degrees. Spray two 4-inch tart pans with removable bottoms with vegetable oil spray; set aside. Whisk flour, sugar, and salt together in medium bowl. Melt butter in small saucepan over medium-high heat, swirling saucepan occasionally, until foaming subsides. Cook, stirring and scraping bottom of saucepan with spatula, until milk solids are dark golden brown and butter has nutty aroma, 1 to 3 minutes. Remove saucepan from heat and carefully add water (mixture will sputter and steam). When bubbling subsides, add butter to bowl with flour mixture and stir until well combined. Let dough rest until just warm to the touch, about 5 minutes.

2 Divide dough in half, then transfer each half to prepared tart pans. Use your hands to evenly press and smooth dough over bottom and up side of pan (using two-thirds of dough for each bottom crust and remaining third for sides). Place pans on wire rack set in rimmed baking sheet and bake until crusts are golden brown, 23 to 28 minutes, rotating sheet halfway through baking. Use tart shells while warm or let cool completely, about 30 minutes, according to individual recipe.

variation

browned-butter whole-wheat tart shells

Substitute ½ cup (2¾ ounces) whole-wheat flour for all-purpose flour and increase water to 4 teaspoons.

making rustic tart dough

1 Process flour and salt in food processor until combined, about 5 seconds. Scatter butter over top and pulse until mixture resembles coarse crumbs and butter pieces are about size of small peas, 6 to 8 pulses.

2 Continue to pulse, adding 1 tablespoon ice water at a time, until dough begins to form small curds and holds together when pinched with fingers (dough will be crumbly), 7 to 10 pulses.

3 Turn dough crumbs onto lightly floured counter and gather into rectangular-shaped pile about 8 inches long and 3 inches wide, with short side facing you. Starting at farthest end, use heel of your hand to smear small amount of dough against counter.

4 Gather smeared crumbs together into another rectangular pile and repeat process.

5 For one 6-inch tart, shape dough into 4-inch disk. Wrap tightly in plastic wrap and refrigerate for 1 hour.

6 For two 4-inch tarts, divide dough in half and form each half into 3-inch disk. Wrap tightly in plastic wrap and refrigerate for 1 hour.

chapter five
pastries and pockets

easy apple turnovers

makes 4 turnovers • **total time** 1½ hours

2 Fuji, Gala, or Golden Delicious apples, cored and cut into ½-inch pieces

2 tablespoons packed light brown sugar, divided

1 (9½ by 9-inch) sheet puff pastry, thawed

1 large egg, lightly beaten with 1 tablespoon water

½ teaspoon ground cinnamon

why this recipe works Apple turnovers—with their umpteen crispy, flaky layers wrapped around a glossy fruit-packed filling—look like they'd be hard to make, but we found a way to make the easy handheld treats with just a few ingredients. Sautéing the apples with light brown sugar does most of the work of cooking them so they hold their shape in the pastry through baking. It also does wonders for flavor: After just a few minutes, the apples release their juices, which reduce to a syrup that coats the fruit evenly, fortifying that crisp apple taste. Baking the filling in store-bought puff pastry sprinkled with a dash of cinnamon sugar gives the turnovers the warmth of a homemade apple pie with little effort. Once baked, the four turnovers hold up for four days, so you can have little treats throughout the week. To thaw frozen puff pastry, let it sit either in the refrigerator for 24 hours or on the counter for 30 minutes to 1 hour.

1 Combine apples and 1½ tablespoons sugar in 12-inch nonstick skillet. Cover and cook over medium heat, stirring frequently, until apples are tender but still hold their shape, 5 to 7 minutes. (Apples and juices should gently simmer during cooking.) Transfer apples and any accumulated juices to medium plate and let cool completely, about 10 minutes.

2 Line rimmed baking sheet with parchment paper. Dust counter lightly with flour. Unfold pastry and roll into 10-inch square. Cut pastry into four 5-inch squares. Space pastry squares evenly on prepared sheet. Divide apple filling evenly among pastry squares, mounding filling in center of each. Brush edges of pastry with some of egg wash. Fold pastry over filling to form triangle. Using fork, crimp edges of pastry to seal. Cut three 1-inch-long slits on top of each turnover (do not cut through filling). Freeze turnovers until filling and pastry are firm, about 15 minutes.

3 Adjust oven rack to middle position and heat oven to 400 degrees. Combine remaining 1½ teaspoons sugar and cinnamon in bowl. Brush tops of pies with remaining egg wash and sprinkle with cinnamon sugar. Bake pies until puffed and deep golden brown, 15 to 20 minutes, rotating sheet halfway through baking. Let turnovers cool on wire rack for 15 minutes. Serve warm or at room temperature. (Cooled turnovers can be stored at room temperature for up to 4 days; if desired, rewarm in 300-degree oven for about 6 minutes.)

guava and cheese pastelitos

makes 4 pastelitos • **total time** 1 hour

2 ounces cream cheese, cut into 2 pieces and softened

1½ teaspoons milk

¼ teaspoon lemon juice

1 (9½ by 9-inch) sheet puff pastry, thawed

3 ounces guava paste, cut into four 3-inch-long by ¼-inch-thick slices

1 large egg, lightly beaten with 1 tablespoon water

Confectioners' sugar (optional)

freeze and bake

At end of step 2, place all or a portion of pastelitos on parchment-lined baking sheet and freeze until firm; wrap individually in plastic wrap, transfer to zipper-lock bag, and store in freezer for up to 1 month. Do not thaw before baking.

why this recipe works Pastelitos ("little pastries" in Spanish) are a common bakery treat in Cuba and Puerto Rico, typically referring to pastries filled with sweet and floral guava paste and tangy, rich cream cheese. The contrast between the flavors of the filling, plus the contrasting textures of the filling and ultracrisp pastry, make pastelitos an irresistible treat for anytime, especially when paired with a cup of coffee (even better if it's café con leche). Our small batch starts with a sheet of store-bought puff pastry cut into squares to make four folded pockets. We fill them with a dollop of cream cheese mixed with a bit of lemon juice (to offset the guava paste's sweetness) and a small rectangle of guava paste. In the oven, the guava paste melts a bit, so sweet and salty flavors meld inside the flaky pocket. Bake all four to share with a friend, or save a couple in the freezer for another day's indulgence. Look for guava paste with guava puree as the first ingredient. To thaw frozen puff pastry, let it sit either in the refrigerator for 24 hours or on the counter for 30 minutes to 1 hour.

1 Adjust oven rack to middle position and heat oven to 400 degrees. Line rimmed baking sheet with parchment paper. Whisk cream cheese, milk, and lemon juice in small bowl until smooth.

2 Dust counter lightly with flour. Unfold pastry and roll into 10-inch square. Cut pastry into four 5-inch squares. Space pastry squares evenly on prepared sheet. Divide cream cheese mixture evenly among pastry squares, mounding filling on 1 half of each square. Spread cream cheese mixture into 3 by 1½-inch rectangle, then top with 1 slice guava paste. Brush edges of pastry with some of egg wash. Fold pastry over filling to form rectangle. Press edges of pastry to seal. Cut four 1-inch-long slits on top of each pastelito (do not cut through filling). Brush tops of pastelitos with remaining egg wash.

3 Bake pastelitos until puffed and deep golden brown, 20 to 25 minutes, rotating sheet halfway through baking. Let pastelitos cool on wire rack for 15 minutes. Dust with confectioners' sugar, if using, and serve warm or at room temperature. (Cooled pastelitos can be stored at room temperature for up to 4 days; if desired, rewarm in 300-degree oven for about 10 minutes.)

everything bagel danish

makes 4 danish • **total time** 50 minutes

1 (5.2-ounce) package Boursin Garlic & Fine Herbs cheese, softened

1 (9½ by 9-inch) sheet puff pastry, thawed

1 large egg, lightly beaten with 1 tablespoon water

1 tablespoon everything bagel seasoning

2 teaspoons minced fresh chives

freeze and bake

At end of step 2, place all or a portion of Danish on parchment-lined baking sheet and freeze until firm; wrap Danish individually in plastic wrap, transfer to zipper-lock bag, and store in freezer for up to 1 month. Do not thaw before baking.

why this recipe works This savory mash-up combines the best features of two breakfast favorites in one: the allium-forward, nutty crunch of an everything bagel schmeared with cream cheese, plus the flaky richness of a cheese Danish. We start with store-bought puff pastry, which stands in for the laminated dough traditionally used in Danish pastry but that is prepped in a fraction of the time and with minimal effort. A quick dollop of soft and spreadable Boursin cheese, already flavored with garlic and herbs, makes for a creamy center. The pastry then gets the "everything" treatment with a sprinkling of bagel seasoning before baking. Our recipe makes enough for four, but if you're serving breakfast for just one or two, freeze a couple Danish to bake and enjoy another day. You can substitute a combination of 1 teaspoon each toasted sesame seeds, kosher salt, and dried minced onion or garlic for the bagel seasoning. To thaw frozen puff pastry, let it sit either in the refrigerator for 24 hours or on the counter for 30 minutes to 1 hour.

1 Adjust oven rack to middle position and heat oven to 400 degrees. Line rimmed baking sheet with parchment paper. Whisk Boursin cheese in small bowl until smooth.

2 Dust counter lightly with flour. Unfold pastry and roll into 10-inch square. Cut pastry into four 5-inch squares. Space pastry squares evenly on prepared sheet. Divide Boursin evenly among pastry squares, mounding filling in center of each square, and spread into 3-inch circle. Brush edges of pastry with egg wash, then sprinkle with bagel seasoning.

3 Bake Danish until puffed and deep golden brown, 15 to 20 minutes, rotating sheet halfway through baking. Let Danish cool on wire rack for 15 minutes. Sprinkle with chives and serve warm or at room temperature. (Cooled Danish can be stored at room temperature for up to 4 days; if desired, rewarm in 300-degree oven for about 10 minutes.)

goat cheese, sun-dried tomato, and basil danish

makes 4 danish • **total time** 55 minutes

4 ounces goat cheese, softened

1 ounce cream cheese, softened

1 large egg yolk; plus 1 large egg, lightly beaten with 1 tablespoon water

⅛ teaspoon table salt

Pinch pepper

⅔ cup oil-packed sun-dried tomatoes, chopped coarse

¼ teaspoon red pepper flakes

1 garlic clove, minced

1 (9½ by 9-inch) sheet puff pastry, thawed

4 teaspoons shredded fresh basil

freeze and bake

At end of step 2, place all or a portion of Danish on parchment-lined sheet and freeze until firm; wrap Danish individually in plastic wrap, transfer to zipper-lock bag, and store in freezer for up to 1 month. Do not thaw before baking.

why this recipe works Small-batch baked goods come together quickly and without waste when you use store-bought puff pastry, and they can serve a number of purposes, not just breakfast or dessert. This savory treat is perfect for a late afternoon pick-me-up or even as a dinner or lunch when served with a salad. Umami-rich sun-dried tomatoes, zesty pepper flakes, and fresh basil complement a base of tangy goat cheese that we blend with a bit of always-on-hand cream cheese for spreadability. To thaw frozen puff pastry, let it sit either in the refrigerator for 24 hours or on the counter for 30 minutes to 1 hour.

1 Adjust oven rack to middle position and heat oven to 400 degrees. Line rimmed baking sheet with parchment paper. Whisk goat cheese, cream cheese, egg yolk, salt, and pepper in small bowl until smooth. Combine tomatoes, pepper flakes, and garlic in separate small bowl.

2 Dust counter lightly with flour. Unfold pastry and roll into 10-inch square. Cut pastry into four 5-inch squares. Space pastry squares evenly on prepared sheet. Divide goat cheese mixture evenly among pastry squares, mounding filling in center of each square, and spread into 3-inch circle. Divide tomato mixture evenly over each goat cheese circle. Brush edges of pastry with egg wash.

3 Bake Danish until puffed and deep golden brown, 15 to 20 minutes, rotating sheet halfway through baking. Let Danish cool on wire rack for 15 minutes. Sprinkle with basil and serve warm or at room temperature. (Cooled Danish can be stored at room temperature for up to 4 days; if desired, rewarm in 300-degree oven for about 10 minutes.)

working with puff pastry

Puff pastry is a small household's best baking friend. You can make gorgeous, rewarding treats without the hassle of the food processor or the mess of rolling dough. Keep a box (or a few) in your freezer at all times and you can easily make something elegant when unexpected company comes by. Or make pastry, from sweet desserts like turnovers (see page 192) to dinner-worthy Danish (see page 199), a possibility on a weeknight. The following are our best practices for working with this dough.

thaw
When we have the foresight, we like to thaw frozen puff pastry in the refrigerator for 24 hours. That said, if a baking project calls out of the blue, you can let the pastry sit on the counter for 30 minutes to an hour. (Avoid this if your kitchen is very warm as it can overheat the dough and melt the layers of butter.) Don't unfold a sheet of pastry before it's fully thawed or it could crack.

cut to size
Puff pastry often comes in 9½ by 9-inch sheets. If your sheets are larger, cut them to the dimensions specified in the recipe.

Sometimes a recipe calls for just half a sheet of puff pastry (see page 171). In those cases, it's totally fine to thaw the pastry, slice it in half, and then return the half you won't be using to the freezer for future use. In testing, we've found that there is little difference between dough frozen once and dough frozen twice; pastry made with all butter (rather than butter and shortening) won't rise quite as high after a double freeze, but the effect is minimal.

To return a puff pastry sheet to the freezer, you can keep it flat and wrap it in a double layer of plastic wrap. If freezer space is a concern, you can fold the sheets back along their original folds; place strips of parchment between the folds to prevent the pastry from freezing to itself.

Slice pastry sheet in half.

get ready to roll
Lightly flour the surface you're working on before you roll out the puff pastry to the proper dimensions. If your thawed puff has some condensation on it, dab it away before rolling.

watch where you roll
When rolling out your dough to the correct size, try not to flatten the edges of the sheet, which inhibits those areas from puffing.

stay sharp
Be sure to use a sharp knife or bench scraper to score and slice puff pastry dough. If the knife drags through the dough rather than cutting it cleanly, it will pinch the edges together and prevent them from puffing.

chill out
If the dough is getting too soft to work with at any time, pop it in the refrigerator to rechill for 15 minutes or so. Firm butter ensures flaky layers.

working with phyllo dough

Phyllo dough is a convenient pastry used to make many Mediterranean and Middle Eastern baked items, both sweet and savory, but it's also just a great choice for making delicate pastries for two without making a complicated dough.

Frozen packaged phyllo is thin and fragile, so you can benefit from learning some best practices to make working with it easy. Here are some of our strategies for working with the dough.

warm up slowly

For even thawing, let the phyllo defrost overnight in the refrigerator, then let it rest on the counter for 30 minutes before opening the package and unrolling the leaves. If necessary, you can thaw it completely on the counter for 4 to 5 hours.

keep covered

To keep phyllo from drying out, most recipes recommend covering the stack with a damp towel, but the dough can easily turn sticky. We prefer to cover the stack with plastic wrap and then a damp towel to weigh it down and keep the plastic flush against the phyllo.

stagger cracks

Because phyllo is so fragile, some sheets inevitably crack or tear while still in the box. Don't worry—just adjust the orientation of the sheets as you stack them so cracks in different sheets don't line up.

trim stuck edges

When phyllo sheets emerge from the box fused at their edges, don't try to separate the sheets. Instead, trim the fused portions and discard them.

Stagger sheets so cracks don't line up.

Trim edges that are stuck together.

hortopita

serves 2 • **total time** 1¾ hours

¼ cup extra-virgin olive oil, divided

1 leek, white and light green parts only, halved lengthwise, sliced thin, and washed thoroughly

1 garlic clove, minced

¼ teaspoon table salt

⅛ teaspoon pepper

8 ounces chopped frozen kale, thawed and thoroughly squeezed dry

3 ounces feta cheese, crumbled (¾ cup)

1 large egg, lightly beaten with 1 tablespoon water

2 tablespoons minced fresh dill

1 tablespoon minced fresh mint

7 (14 by 9-inch) sheets phyllo, thawed

½ teaspoon sesame seeds and/or nigella seeds (optional)

why this recipe works Hortopita is one of many treasured Greek phyllo pies. Here we make the greens-packed pastry petite to serve two. Hortopita more traditionally relies on a variety of wild greens (horta), including dandelion, mustard, chicory, and sorrel, as well as fennel and dill fronds, all commonly foraged by Greek cooks. While we encourage you to experiment with your favorite greens, this recipe uses frozen kale for simplicity. We found that the heartier green matched perfectly with fresh dill and mint, sweet leeks, and a sprinkling of briny feta. The filling is complex and aromatic, perfectly encased in thin sheets of phyllo dough that's enriched with olive oil and sprinkled with sesame seeds at the finish. Frozen kale is sometimes sold in 10-ounce bags; if so, feel free to use it all in the recipe. Phyllo dough is also available in larger 18 by 14-inch sheets; if using, cut them in half to make 14 by 9-inch sheets. Thaw phyllo in the refrigerator overnight or on the counter for 4 to 5 hours; don't thaw it in the microwave.

1 Heat 2 tablespoons oil in 12-inch skillet over medium heat until shimmering. Add leek, garlic, salt, and pepper and cook until leek is softened, 4 to 6 minutes. Transfer to large bowl and stir in kale until combined. Let cool slightly, about 10 minutes, then stir in feta, egg mixture, dill, and mint.

2 Adjust oven rack to upper-middle position and heat oven to 400 degrees. Line rimmed baking sheet with parchment paper. Place 16½ by 12-inch sheet of parchment paper on counter with long side parallel to counter edge. Place 1 phyllo sheet on parchment with long side parallel to counter edge. Lightly brush sheet with some of remaining 2 tablespoons oil. Repeat with remaining 6 phyllo sheets and oil (you may not use all the oil), stacking sheets one on top of other as you go.

3 Arrange kale mixture in 10 by 2½-inch rectangle, 2 inches from bottom of phyllo, and about 2 inches from each side. Using parchment, fold sides of phyllo over filling, then fold bottom edge of phyllo over filling. Brush folded portions of phyllo with oil. Fold top edge over filling, making sure top and bottom edges overlap by about 1 inch. (If they do not overlap, unfold, rearrange filling into slightly narrower strip, and refold.) Press firmly to seal. Using thin metal spatula, transfer hortopita to prepared sheet. Lightly brush top and sides of hortopita with remaining oil. Using sharp knife, make 6 evenly spaced ¼-inch-deep slashes, 2 inches long, on top of hortopita. Sprinkle with sesame and/or nigella seeds, if using.

4 Bake hortopita until golden brown, 30 to 35 minutes, rotating sheet halfway through baking. Let hortopita cool on sheet for 15 minutes. Slice and serve.

eggplant and tomato phyllo pie

serves 2 • **total time** 1¼ hours

1 tomato, cored and sliced ¼ inch thick

¾ teaspoon table salt, divided

8 ounces eggplant, sliced into ¼-inch-thick rounds

¼ cup extra-virgin olive oil, divided

6 (14 by 9-inch) sheets phyllo, thawed and halved crosswise

2 teaspoons minced fresh oregano

1 small garlic clove, minced

¼ teaspoon pepper

2 ounces mozzarella cheese, shredded (½ cup)

1 tablespoon grated Parmesan cheese

1 tablespoon chopped fresh basil

why this recipe works Phyllo dough is a fast pass to a visually stunning tart for two, with golden brown, shatteringly crisp, paper-thin dough layers baked around a filling of eggplant, tomatoes, melty mozzarella, and a little nutty Parmesan. It's a delightful dinner to share. Broiling the eggplant slices before assembling the tart gives them deeper flavor and a delightful char. To capture the tomatoes' appealing juiciness while avoiding a soggy tart, we salt the slices and let them sit in a colander to draw out excess moisture. Layering 12 sheets of phyllo dough in an offset pattern creates a beautiful crust that's also sturdy enough to stand up to the abundance of vegetables. For the best results, look for a tomato that weighs 6 to 8 ounces and is roughly 3 inches in diameter. Phyllo dough is also available in larger 18 by 14-inch sheets; if using, cut them in half to make 14 by 9-inch sheets. Thaw phyllo in the refrigerator overnight or on the counter for 4 to 5 hours; don't thaw it in the microwave.

1 Sprinkle tomato with ½ teaspoon salt in colander and set aside to drain for 30 minutes.

2 Meanwhile, adjust oven rack 6 inches from broiler element and heat broiler. Arrange eggplant in single layer on aluminum foil–lined rimmed baking sheet and brush both sides with 1 tablespoon oil. Broil eggplant until softened and beginning to brown, 8 to 10 minutes, flipping eggplant halfway through broiling. Set aside to cool slightly, about 10 minutes.

3 Heat oven to 375 degrees. Line second rimmed baking sheet with parchment paper. Place 2 tablespoons oil in small bowl. Place 1 phyllo sheet on prepared sheet, then lightly brush phyllo with prepared oil. Turn baking sheet 30 degrees and place second phyllo sheet on first phyllo sheet, leaving any overhanging phyllo in place. Brush second phyllo sheet with oil. Repeat turning baking sheet and layering remaining 10 phyllo sheets in pinwheel pattern, brushing each with oil (you should have 12 total layers of phyllo).

assembling phyllo pie

1 Place 1 phyllo sheet on prepared baking sheet then lightly brush with oil.

2 Turn baking sheet 30 degrees and place second phyllo sheet on first phyllo sheet. Brush second phyllo sheet with oil. Repeat process with remaining sheets.

4 Shake colander to rid tomato of excess juice. Combine tomato, oregano, garlic, pepper, remaining ¼ teaspoon salt, and remaining 1 tablespoon oil in bowl. Sprinkle mozzarella in even 6-inch round in center of phyllo. Shingle tomato and eggplant on top of mozzarella in concentric circles, alternating tomatoes and eggplant as you go. Sprinkle Parmesan cheese over top of vegetables.

5 Gently fold edges of phyllo over vegetable mixture, pleating every 2 to 3 inches as needed. Bake until phyllo is crisp and golden brown, 20 to 25 minutes. Let pie cool for 15 minutes on sheet. Slide pie onto cutting board or serving platter and sprinkle with basil. Cut into wedges and serve. (Leftover phyllo pie can be refrigerated for up to 3 days; reheat in 300-degree oven for 8 to 10 minutes.)

3 Gently fold edges of phyllo over vegetable mixture, pleating every 2 to 3 inches as needed.

4 Bake until phyllo is crisp and golden brown, 20 to 25 minutes. Let pie cool for 15 minutes on sheet. Sprinkle with basil before serving.

apple strudel

serves 2 • **total time** 1¼ hours, plus 20 minutes cooling

14 ounces Fuji, Gala, or Golden Delicious apples, peeled, cored, and cut into ½-inch pieces

1½ tablespoons granulated sugar

¼ teaspoon grated lemon zest plus 1 teaspoon juice

⅛ teaspoon ground cinnamon

⅛ teaspoon ground ginger

⅛ teaspoon table salt, divided

¼ cup pine nuts, toasted and chopped

2 tablespoons golden raisins

1 tablespoon panko bread crumbs

4 tablespoons unsalted butter, melted

2 teaspoons confectioners' sugar, plus extra for serving

7 (14 by 9-inch) phyllo sheets, thawed

why this recipe works Bursting with warm-spiced apples and dotted with plump golden raisins, strudel tastes celebratory, yet it's easy enough to be an everyday dessert, this one in an attractive for-two package. Microwaving the apples ahead of time makes them tender and allows you to drain off the juice so the filling isn't too soggy. Panko bread crumbs soak up any liquid released during baking. For a tender crust that's flaky but not flyaway, use just seven sheets of phyllo and sprinkle confectioners' sugar between the layers; this fuses the pastry while baking. And that apple liquid that was drained off? We use it to seal the phyllo package and brush it on top for a deep golden finish. Phyllo dough is also available in larger 18 by 14-inch sheets; if using, cut them in half to make 14 by 9-inch sheets. Thaw phyllo in the refrigerator overnight or on the counter for 4 to 5 hours; don't thaw it in the microwave.

1 Toss apples, granulated sugar, lemon zest and juice, cinnamon, ginger, and pinch salt together in large bowl. Cover and microwave until apples are softened, 2 to 4 minutes, stirring once halfway through microwaving. Let apples sit, covered, for 5 minutes. Transfer apples to colander set in second large bowl and let drain, reserving liquid. Return apples to now-empty bowl and stir in pine nuts, raisins, and panko; set aside.

2 Adjust oven rack to lowest position and heat oven to 350 degrees. Spray rimmed baking sheet with vegetable oil spray. Stir remaining pinch salt into melted butter.

3 Place confectioners' sugar in fine-mesh strainer. Place 16½ by 12-inch sheet of parchment paper on counter with long side parallel to counter edge. Place 1 phyllo sheet on parchment with long side parallel to counter edge. Lightly brush sheet with melted butter mixture and dust sparingly with confectioners' sugar. Repeat with remaining 6 phyllo sheets, melted butter, and confectioners' sugar, stacking sheets one on top of other as you go.

(continued)

4 Arrange reserved apple mixture in 10 by 2½-inch rectangle, 2 inches from bottom of phyllo, and about 2 inches from each side. Using parchment, fold sides of phyllo over filling, then fold bottom edge of phyllo over filling. Brush folded portions of phyllo with reserved apple liquid. Fold top edge over filling, making sure top and bottom edges overlap by about 1 inch. (If they do not overlap, unfold, rearrange filling into slightly narrower strip, and refold.) Press firmly to seal. Using thin metal spatula, transfer strudel to prepared sheet. Lightly brush top and sides of strudel with remaining reserved apple liquid.

5 Bake until golden brown, 25 to 30 minutes, rotating sheet halfway through baking. Using thin metal spatula, immediately transfer strudel to cutting board. Let cool for 3 minutes. Slice strudel and let cool for at least 20 minutes. Serve warm or at room temperature, dusting with extra confectioners' sugar before serving.

assembling apple strudel

1 Mound filling along bottom third of 7 layered phyllo sheets on parchment paper, leaving 2-inch border at bottom edge and sides of phyllo.

2 Using parchment, fold sides of phyllo over filling, then fold over bottom edge of phyllo. Brush folded portions with apple liquid.

3 Fold top edge of phyllo over mounded filling, which should overlap the bottom edge by about 1 inch. Press to seal.

bean and cheese pupusas

makes 8 pupusas • **total time** 1¼ hours, plus 20 minutes resting

2 cups (8 ounces) masa harina

1 teaspoon table salt, divided

2 cups boiling water, plus warm tap water as needed

2 teaspoons vegetable oil, divided

1 (15-ounce) can kidney beans, rinsed

5 ounces Monterey Jack cheese, shredded (1¼ cups)

½ teaspoon ground cumin

½ teaspoon dried oregano

⅛ teaspoon cayenne pepper

---

freeze and bake

Place all or a portion of uncooked pupusas on parchment-lined baking sheet and freeze until firm. Wrap pupusas individually in plastic, transfer to zipper-lock bag, and store in freezer for up to 1 month. Do not thaw before cooking; increase cooking time by 1 minute per side.

why this recipe works Pupusas, the national dish of El Salvador, are enticing packages of masa dough stuffed with a savory cheese filling and fried in a skillet. Getting them perfectly round, level, and evenly filled can take some practice, but this recipe flattens the learning curve: Using boiling water gives you a well-hydrated dough that's easy to work with. Pressing the dough into a disk, placing the filling in the center and enclosing it in the dough, and then pressing the stuffed pupusas into 4-inch disks between sheets of plastic ensures uniform thickness with filling in every bite. Cook as many as you like now (up to four will fit in a 12-inch skillet) and freeze the rest for a quick savory bite anytime you like. For an accurate measurement of boiling water, bring a full kettle of water to a boil and then measure out the desired amount. An occasional leak while cooking the pupusas is to be expected, and the resulting browned cheese is delicious. Serve with your favorite fresh tomato salsa and Curtido (recipe follows), a punchy, quick pickled Salvadoran slaw.

1   Using permanent marker, draw 4-inch circle in center of 1 side of 1-quart or 1-gallon zipper-lock bag. Cut open seams along both sides of bag, but leave bottom seam intact so bag opens completely. Set aside until ready to assemble pupusas.

2   Using rubber spatula, combine masa harina and ½ teaspoon salt in medium bowl. Add boiling water and 1 teaspoon oil and mix with spatula until soft dough forms. Cover dough and let rest for 20 minutes.

3   Meanwhile, line rimmed baking sheet with parchment paper. Place beans in medium bowl and mash with potato masher or fork until chunky paste forms. Add Monterey Jack, cumin, oregano, cayenne, and remaining ½ teaspoon salt and stir until evenly mixed. Form mixture into 8 balls, weighing about 1½ ounces each, and place balls on 1 half of prepared sheet.

(continued)

curtido

makes *about 3 cups*
total time *20 minutes, plus 1 hour chilling*

- ½ cup cider vinegar
- ¼ cup water
- 1½ teaspoons sugar
- ¾ teaspoon table salt
- 3 cups shredded green cabbage
- ½ onion, sliced thin
- 1 small carrot, peeled and shredded
- ½ jalapeño chile, minced
- ½ teaspoon dried oregano
- ½ cup chopped fresh cilantro

Whisk vinegar, water, sugar, and salt in large bowl until sugar is dissolved. Add cabbage, onion, carrot, jalapeño, and oregano and toss to combine. Cover and refrigerate for at least 1 hour or up to 24 hours. Toss slaw, then drain. Return slaw to bowl and stir in cilantro.

4 Knead dough in bowl for 15 to 20 seconds. Test dough's hydration by flattening golf ball–size piece. If cracks larger than ¼ inch form around edges, add extra warm tap water, 2 teaspoons at a time, until dough is soft and slightly tacky. Transfer dough to counter, shape into large ball, and divide into 8 equal pieces. Using your damp hands, roll 1 dough piece into ball and place on empty half of prepared sheet. Cover with damp dish towel. Repeat with remaining dough pieces.

5 Place open cut bag marked side down on counter. Place 1 dough ball in center of circle. Fold other side of bag over ball. Using glass pie plate or 8-inch square baking dish, gently press dough to 4-inch diameter, using circle drawn on bag as guide. Turn out disk into your palm and place 1 ball of filling in center. Bring sides of dough up around filling and pinch top to seal. Remoisten your hands and roll ball until smooth, smoothing any cracks with your damp fingertip. Return ball to bag and slowly press to 4-inch diameter. Pinch closed any small cracks that form at edges. Return pupusa to sheet and cover with damp dish towel. Repeat with remaining dough and filling.

6 Heat remaining 1 teaspoon oil in 12-inch nonstick skillet over medium-high heat until shimmering. Wipe skillet clean with paper towels. Carefully lay up to 4 pupusas in skillet and cook until spotty brown on both sides, 2 to 4 minutes per side. Transfer to platter and repeat with remaining 4 pupusas. Serve warm.

chicken and potato empanadas

makes 8 empanadas • **total time** 2¼ hours

filling

- 1 Yukon Gold potato (8 ounces), peeled and cut into ½-inch pieces
- 1 teaspoon table salt, divided
- 8 ounces boneless skinless chicken thighs, trimmed
- 1 tablespoon vegetable oil, divided
- 4 scallions, sliced thin
- 2 garlic cloves, minced
- ¾ teaspoon ground cumin
- 1½ plum tomatoes, cored and chopped fine

dough

- 1¼ cups (6 ⅞ ounces) yellow masarepa
- 1 cup plus 2 tablespoons hot tap water, plus extra as needed
- ½ teaspoon table salt

ají

- ½ serrano chile, minced
- 1 small garlic clove, minced
- ½ teaspoon table salt
- ¼ cup hot tap water
- ½ plum tomato, cored and chopped fine
- 2 scallions, sliced thin
- 2 tablespoons minced fresh cilantro
- 2 teaspoons lime juice
- 1½ quarts vegetable or peanut oil, for frying

why this recipe works Empanadas are a favorite street food and anytime snack throughout Latin America. Some are fried, others are baked, and all are filled, but with a variety of different ingredients including meat, vegetables, and cheese. Colombian empanadas are fried and unique, as they are made from corn, specifically a precooked finely ground cornmeal product called masarepa (so called because of its primary use for making the savory corn cakes, called arepas, that are also common in Colombia). These empanadas are fun to serve at a small gathering. We created a chicken and potato filling—a common combination in Colombia—flavored with cumin, tomatoes, and scallions. (Or swap out the chicken for ground beef as in our beef variation.) After tucking the filling inside cornmeal pockets, we fry the empanadas in just enough oil in a large saucepan—no need for a large Dutch oven when you're making a small batch. When the crispy pockets emerge, we serve them with their traditional accompaniment: a spicy, cilantro-forward sauce called ají. Yellow masarepa is traditionally used for this recipe; however, white masarepa can be substituted. Do not substitute masa harina for the masarepa—it will not work in this recipe. We had the best success using P.A.N. masarepa in this recipe; if you use other brands you may need to adjust the amount of water added to achieve the right dough consistency.

1 Using permanent marker, draw 5-inch circle in center of 1 side of 1-quart or 1-gallon zipper-lock bag. Cut open seams along both sides of bag, but leave bottom seam intact so bag opens completely. Set aside until ready to assemble empanadas.

2 For the filling: Place potatoes and ¼ teaspoon salt in medium bowl. Add just enough water to cover potatoes. Cover bowl and microwave until potatoes are very tender, 10 to 12 minutes. Drain potatoes well and return to now-empty bowl to cool.

3 Meanwhile, pat chicken thighs dry with paper towels and sprinkle with ¼ teaspoon salt. Heat 1 teaspoon oil in 10-inch nonstick skillet over medium heat until shimmering. Add chicken and cook until lightly browned on each side and registers at least 175 degrees, 8 to 10 minutes. Transfer chicken to cutting board, let cool slightly, then finely shred using 2 forks. Add chicken to bowl with potatoes.

4   Heat remaining 2 teaspoons oil in now-empty skillet over medium heat until shimmering. Add scallions, garlic, cumin, and remaining ½ teaspoon salt and cook until scallions are softened, about 1 minute. Stir in tomatoes and cook until softened and juices evaporate, about 4 minutes. Add tomato mixture to bowl with potatoes and chicken and stir, mashing potatoes slightly, to make cohesive filling. Set aside to cool while making dough and ají.

5   **For the dough:** Using rubber spatula, combine masarepa, hot water, and salt in medium bowl, then continue to fold mixture, using hand as needed, until homogeneous. (Dough should be soft and moist, but not wet. Add up to 1 tablespoon additional hot water, 1 teaspoon at a time, if dough feels crumbly, dry, or stiff.) Cover with plastic wrap and let sit for 15 minutes.

6   **For the ají:** In mortar and pestle, or on cutting board using flat side of chef's knife, mash serrano, garlic, and salt to coarse paste. Transfer to small bowl and stir in hot water. Stir in tomato, scallions, cilantro, and lime juice. Set aside until ready to serve. (Ají can be refrigerated for up to 3 days; bring to room temperature and stir to recombine before serving.)

7   Knead dough in bowl for about 10 seconds until soft and pliable. (If dough feels stiff or crumbly, add up to 1 tablespoon additional hot water, 1 teaspoon at a time, until dough feels smooth and moist to the touch, but not wet.) Divide dough into 8 equal pieces (about 2 ounces each), then use moistened hands to roll into balls. Place balls on one half of rimmed baking sheet and cover with damp kitchen towel.

8   Place open cut bag marked side down on counter. Place 1 dough ball in center of circle. Fold other side of bag over ball. Using glass pie plate or 8-inch square baking dish, press dough to 5-inch diameter, using circle drawn on bag as guide. Gently open bag, leaving dough round on plastic and place scant ¼ cup filling in center of dough round. Flatten filling into oval, then use bag to help fold 1 side of dough round over filling, forming half-moon shape. Gently peel plastic off empanada, then use your wet fingers to pinch and seal edge, smoothing out any small cracks. Transfer empanada to empty half of sheet, and cover with second damp kitchen towel. Repeat with remaining dough and filling.

9   Line large plate with triple layer paper towels. Add oil to large saucepan until it measures about 1½ inches deep and heat over medium-high heat to 375 degrees. Carefully add 3 empanadas to hot oil using slotted spoon and fry until crisp and golden around edges, about 7 minutes, flipping halfway through frying to ensure even browning on both sides. Adjust burner, if necessary, to maintain oil temperature between 350 and 400 degrees. Transfer empanadas to prepared plate. Return oil to 375 degrees and repeat with remaining 5 empanadas in 2 batches. Serve with ají. (Cooled empanadas can be stored in refrigerator for up to 3 days. Reheat in 400-degree oven on wire rack set in rimmed baking sheet for 10 to 15 minutes until warmed through; let cool for 5 minutes before serving.)

variation

beef and potato empanadas

In step 4, omit oil and chicken and increase cumin to 1 teaspoon. Cook 8 ounces 85 percent lean ground beef and ¼ teaspoon salt in 10-inch nonstick skillet over medium heat until no longer pink, 3 to 5 minutes. Add scallions, garlic, cumin, and remaining ½ teaspoon salt and proceed with stirring in tomatoes.

Chicken and Potato Empanadas

Jamaican Beef Patties

jamaican beef patties

makes 4 patties • **total time** 2¼ hours, plus 1 hour chilling

dough

- ⅓ cup sour cream, chilled
- 1 large egg yolk, lightly beaten
- 1 tablespoon water
- 1½ cups (7½ ounces) all-purpose flour
- 1½ teaspoons sugar
- ½ teaspoon table salt
- ½ teaspoon ground turmeric
- 8 tablespoons unsalted butter, cut into ½-inch pieces and chilled

filling

- 1½ teaspoons plus ½ cup water, divided, plus extra as needed
- ½ teaspoon table salt
- ⅛ teaspoon baking soda
- ½ pound 85 percent lean ground beef
- 1 tablespoon vegetable oil
- 6 scallions, chopped fine
- 2 garlic cloves, minced
- ½ habanero chile, stemmed, seeded, and minced
- ½ teaspoon dried thyme
- ½ teaspoon curry powder
- ½ teaspoon ground allspice
- ⅛ teaspoon pepper
- ¼ cup panko bread crumbs

why this recipe works Jamaican beef patties are probably one of the most satisfying snacks in pocket form. This recipe is inspired by the patties made at Kingston Tropical Bakery in the Bronx. Jamaican patties' signature pastry is flaky and golden-colored, so we add turmeric to a food-processor butter pie dough. Where typical pie dough recipes call for ice water to bring them together, we swap in cold sour cream and an egg yolk for an ultratender dough that doesn't crack during rolling and shaping. For the filling, we treat the ground beef with a touch of baking soda to soften its pebbly toughness and add ¼ cup of panko bread crumbs, which break down almost to a velvety gravy that clings to the beef. For a heady spice profile, we season the beef with a typical blend of Jamaican aromatics: scallions, garlic, curry powder, allspice, and habanero chile (which is more widely available than Scotch bonnet). These patties are easy to put together and can be stored in the freezer to bake off when you're looking for a bit of afternoon spice.

1 For the dough: Whisk sour cream, egg yolk, and water together in small bowl. Process flour, sugar, salt, and turmeric in food processor until combined, about 3 seconds. Scatter butter over top and pulse until butter is no larger than size of peas, about 10 pulses. Add half of sour cream mixture and pulse until combined, about 5 pulses. Add remaining sour cream mixture and pulse until dough begins to form, about 15 pulses.

2 Turn dough onto sheet of plastic wrap and shape into 6-inch square, smoothing any cracks. Wrap tightly and refrigerate for at least 1 hour or up to 2 days.

3 For the filling: Combine 1½ teaspoons water, salt, and baking soda in large bowl. Add beef and mix until thoroughly combined; let sit for 10 minutes.

4 Heat oil in 12-inch nonstick skillet over medium-high heat until just smoking. Add beef mixture and cook, breaking up meat with wooden spoon, until beginning to brown, 5 to 7 minutes. Add scallions, garlic, habanero, thyme, curry powder, allspice, and pepper and cook, stirring frequently, until scallions are softened, about 3 minutes.

freeze and bake

After sealing patties in step 8, place all or a portion of patties on parchment-lined baking sheet and freeze until firm; transfer patties to zipper-lock bag and store in freezer for up to 1 month. Do not thaw before baking; bake for 35 to 40 minutes.

bake in your air fryer

Place up to 2 patties in air-fryer basket. Place basket in air fryer, set temperature to 300 degrees, and bake until patties are puffed and lightly browned, 30 to 40 minutes from fresh or 50 to 60 minutes from frozen, flipping patties with 10 minutes remaining.

5 Stir in panko and remaining ½ cup water and bring to simmer. Reduce heat to low and cook, stirring occasionally, until sauce thickens and coats beef, 8 to 10 minutes. Off heat, mash beef mixture with potato masher until fine-textured and panko is fully incorporated, about 2 minutes. Transfer to bowl and let cool completely. (Filling can be covered and refrigerated for up to 24 hours.)

6 Adjust oven rack to upper-middle position and heat oven to 375 degrees. Line rimmed baking sheet with parchment paper. Cut dough into 2 equal pieces (about 7½ ounces each); cover with plastic. Working with 1 piece, sprinkle dough with flour and roll into rough 11 by 9-inch rectangle (about ⅛ inch thick) on lightly floured counter, with long side parallel to counter edge, reflouring counter and dough as needed.

7 Place two ⅓-cup mounds of filling on bottom half of dough, about 4 inches apart and about 2 inches from bottom edge of dough. Flatten mounds to roughly 3-inch rounds. Lightly brush bottom half of dough with water. Fold top half of dough over filling, pressing along sides, bottom edge, and between filling to adhere.

8 Cut between mounds and trim edges to form two 5 by 4-inch rectangles. Using floured tines of fork, crimp edges to seal, then transfer to prepared sheet. Repeat with remaining dough and filling. Bake patties until puffed and lightly browned, about 30 minutes. Let patties cool on wire rack for 15 minutes. Serve warm or at room temperature.

ham and cheddar hand pies

makes 2 hand pies • **total time** 1¼ hours

8 ounces Basic Pizza Dough (page 334), room temperature

1 tablespoon yellow mustard, divided

4 ounces thinly sliced deli ham

2 ounces thinly sliced deli cheddar

1 large egg, lightly beaten with 1 tablespoon water

1 teaspoon sesame seeds, divided

---

bake in your air fryer

Place hand pies in air-fryer basket and tent with greased foil. Place basket in air fryer, set temperature to 300 degrees, and bake for 20 to 25 minutes.

why this recipe works Our Ham and Cheddar Hand Pies are a homemade interpretation of the iconic handheld Hot Pockets, with the ease of a ham and cheese sandwich. We achieve a sturdy crust that safely encases the filling by using pizza dough (you can use homemade or store-bought). You can bake these in the oven, but we really love popping them in the air fryer whenever we have a craving. Either way, the pockets' savory ham matched with gooey sharp cheese and zesty yellow mustard, plus their simple assembly, will have you making them more often than you might expect. Topping with sesame seeds before baking gives the pastries the slight nuttiness of a fresh deli roll. Let the dough sit at room temperature while preparing the remaining ingredients and heating the oven; otherwise, it will be difficult to stretch.

1 Adjust oven rack to middle position and heat oven to 400 degrees. Line rimmed baking sheet with aluminum foil and spray with vegetable oil spray. On a lightly floured counter, press and roll dough into 10 by 7½-inch rectangle, about ¼ inch thick, with long side parallel to counter edge. Using pizza wheel or knife, cut dough rectangle in half crosswise.

2 Spread 1½ teaspoons mustard over middle third of each dough rectangle, leaving top and bottom thirds empty. Layer ham and cheddar evenly on top of mustard, leaving ¼-inch border on sides. Working with 1 dough rectangle at a time, brush top and bottom portions of dough with some of egg wash. Fold bottom third of dough over filling, followed by top third, like business letter, to form approximate 5 by 2½-inch rectangle. Pinch seam and ends firmly to seal. Transfer hand pie to prepared sheet, seam side down, and tuck short ends underneath.

3 Cut three 1-inch slits on top of each hand pie (do not cut through filling). Brush tops with remaining egg wash and sprinkle with sesame seeds. Cover loosely with greased aluminum foil and bake for 15 minutes. Remove foil and continue to bake until crust is golden and center registers 200 degrees, 20 to 25 minutes, rotating sheet halfway through baking. Let hand pies cool on wire rack for 5 minutes. Serve warm or at room temperature.

salami, capicola, and provolone stromboli

serves 2 • **total time** 1 hour

8	ounces Basic Pizza Dough (page 334), room temperature
2	ounces thinly sliced deli salami
2	ounces thinly sliced deli capicola
2	ounces thinly sliced deli provolone cheese
¼	cup jarred roasted red peppers, rinsed, patted dry, and sliced thin
¼	cup grated Parmesan cheese
1	large egg, lightly beaten with 1 tablespoon water
1	teaspoon sesame seeds

why this recipe works When you want a hot lunch or supper for two without a lot of fuss, think stromboli. For our take on this American cousin to the calzone, we take the classic components of an Italian cold-cut sandwich, roll them in a spiral of pizza dough, and bake it all up to crusty, golden-brown perfection. The bold no-prep filling includes salami and capicola for a balance of saltiness and mild heat, provolone cheese for creaminess, and jarred roasted red peppers for sweet brightness. You can use homemade or store-bought dough. Let the dough sit at room temperature while preparing the remaining ingredients and heating the oven; otherwise, it will be difficult to stretch. Serve with your favorite tomato sauce for dipping, if you like.

1   Adjust oven rack to middle position and heat oven to 400 degrees. Spray rimmed baking sheet with vegetable oil spray.

2   On lightly floured counter, press and roll dough into 10 by 7½-inch rectangle, about ¼ inch thick, with long side parallel to counter edge. Lay salami, capicola, and provolone over dough, leaving ¾-inch border at edge. Top with red peppers and Parmesan. Brush edges with some of egg wash. Starting from long side, roll dough tightly into long cylinder, then pinch seam and ends to seal. Transfer stromboli to prepared sheet, seam side down, and tuck short ends underneath.

3   Brush top of stromboli with remaining egg wash. Using sharp knife, make 3 evenly spaced ¼-inch-deep slashes, 2 inches long, on top of stromboli. Sprinkle with sesame seeds. Cover loosely with greased aluminum foil and bake for 15 minutes. Remove foil and continue to bake until crust is golden and center registers 200 degrees, 20 to 25 minutes, rotating sheet halfway through baking. Let stromboli cool on wire rack for 5 minutes. Slice in half and serve warm or at room temperature.

spinach calzones

serves 2 • **total time** 1 hour

5 ounces frozen chopped spinach, thawed and thoroughly squeezed dry

4 ounces (½ cup) whole-milk ricotta cheese

2 ounces mozzarella cheese, shredded (½ cup)

¼ cup grated Parmesan cheese

1 tablespoon extra-virgin olive oil

1 large egg yolk, plus 1 large egg lightly beaten with 1 tablespoon water, divided

1 garlic clove, minced

¼ teaspoon table salt

   Pinch pepper

   Pinch dried oregano

   Pinch red pepper flakes (optional)

8 ounces Basic Pizza Dough (page 334), room temperature

why this recipe works With pizza dough on hand you can whip up just two calzones that'll put takeout versions to shame. A no-cook filling of thawed frozen spinach and a trio of cheeses—creamy ricotta, easy-melting mozzarella, and nutty Parmesan—keep the process streamlined. An egg yolk thickens the filling, and garlic and pepper flakes give it a kick. After just 15 minutes in a hot oven, the calzones emerge golden brown, crisp-crusted, and delicious. You can use homemade or store-bought dough. Let the dough sit at room temperature while preparing the remaining ingredients and heating the oven; otherwise, it will be difficult to stretch. If you want to bake this in a toaster oven, note that most don't go higher than 450 degrees; heat the toaster oven to 450 degrees and bake for 20 to 25 minutes (or desired level of golden brown). Serve with your favorite tomato sauce.

1 Adjust oven rack to middle position and heat oven to 475 degrees. Line rimmed baking sheet with aluminum foil and spray with vegetable oil spray. Combine spinach, ricotta, mozzarella, Parmesan, oil, egg yolk, garlic, salt, pepper, oregano, and pepper flakes, if using, in bowl.

2 Divide pizza dough into 2 equal pieces. Press and roll each piece into 8-inch round on lightly floured counter. Spread half of spinach mixture on bottom half of each dough round, leaving 1-inch border around edges. Brush edges with some of egg wash. Fold top half of dough over bottom half, leaving ½-inch border of bottom layer uncovered. Press edges of dough together and crimp to seal.

3 Transfer calzones to prepared sheet and brush tops with remaining egg wash. Using sharp knife, make 2 evenly spaces slashes, 1 inch long, in top layer of dough on each calzone. Bake until golden brown, about 15 minutes, rotating sheet halfway through baking. Let calzones cool on wire rack for 5 minutes before slicing and serving.

buffalo chicken calzones

serves 2 • **total time** 1 hour

1 cup shredded rotisserie chicken

4 ounces mozzarella cheese, shredded (1 cup)

1½ ounces blue cheese, crumbled (⅓ cup)

3 tablespoons Frank's RedHot Original Cayenne Pepper Sauce

¼ teaspoon pepper

8 ounces Basic Pizza Dough (page 334), room temperature

1 large egg lightly beaten with 1 tablespoon water

why this recipe works The irresistible flavors of Buffalo wings in the easy-to-eat form of a calzone? Yes, please. Multipurpose rotisserie chicken is the convenient starting point for a quickly assembled filling. A generous glug of hot sauce adds a lip-smacking bite, while crumbled blue cheese enlivens the mildness of mozzarella. You can use homemade or store-bought dough. Let the dough sit at room temperature while preparing the remaining ingredients and heating the oven; otherwise, it will be difficult to stretch. If you want to bake this in a toaster oven, note that most don't go higher than 450 degrees; heat the toaster oven to 450 degrees and bake for 20 to 25 minutes (or desired level of golden brown).

1   Adjust oven rack to middle position and heat oven to 475 degrees. Line rimmed baking sheet with aluminum foil and spray with vegetable oil spray. Combine chicken, mozzarella, blue cheese, hot sauce, and pepper in bowl.

2   Divide pizza dough into 2 equal pieces. Press and roll each piece into 8-inch round on lightly floured counter. Spread half of chicken mixture on bottom half of each dough round, leaving 1-inch border around edges. Brush edges with some of egg wash. Fold top half of dough over bottom half, leaving ½-inch border of bottom layer uncovered. Press edges of dough together and crimp to seal.

3   Transfer calzones to prepared sheet and brush tops with remaining egg wash. Using sharp knife, make 2 evenly spaced slashes, 1 inch long, in top layer of dough on each calzone. Bake until crust is golden brown, about 15 minutes. Let calzones cool on wire rack for 5 minutes. Serve.

cardamom-orange morning buns

makes 6 buns • **total time** 1¾ hours, plus 1½ to 2 hours rising

dough

1½	cups (7½ ounces) all-purpose flour
1½	teaspoons granulated sugar
1⅛	teaspoons instant or rapid-rise yeast
¾	teaspoon table salt
12	tablespoons unsalted butter, cut into ¼-inch-thick slices and chilled
½	cup sour cream, chilled
2	tablespoons orange juice, chilled
1½	tablespoons ice water

filling

½	cup packed (3½ ounces) light brown sugar
1	teaspoon grated orange zest
¾	teaspoon ground cardamom
½	teaspoon vanilla extract

pan swap

Recipe can be made in a 6- or 12-cup muffin tin or in six 4-ounce ramekins placed on a rimmed baking sheet.

why this recipe works Stunning morning buns feature a sweet spiced filling swirled through a golden brown layered pastry, which is often croissant dough. These buns are still stunning, browned, and layered, but they use an easier dough, something called quick puff pastry, which isn't laminated. You roll butter slices into a yeasted flour mixture (we do it in a zipper-lock bag to keep things neat) to create pockets of flakiness. Rolling the resulting dough into a rectangle, then into a cylinder, and gently patting it flat is a simple process that forms even more layers. Instead of cinnamon sugar, we combine light brown sugar, orange zest, cardamom, and vanilla for a filling with subtle floral notes and a rich molasses flavor. If you're having folks over, you can bake the six buns, but the proofed dough freezes well, and you can thaw and bake off at another time. If the dough becomes too soft to work with at any point, refrigerate it until it's firm enough to easily handle.

1 **For the dough:** Combine flour, granulated sugar, yeast, and salt in 1-gallon zipper-lock bag. Add butter, seal, and shake to coat. Press out air and reseal. Roll over bag several times with rolling pin, shaking bag after each roll, until butter is pressed into large flakes.

2 Transfer mixture to large bowl and stir in sour cream, orange juice, and ice water with wooden spoon or rubber spatula until combined. Transfer dough to lightly floured counter and knead by hand to form smooth, round ball, about 30 seconds.

3 Press and roll dough into 10 by 6-inch rectangle, with short side parallel to counter edge. Roll up dough away from you into firm cylinder, keeping roll taut by tucking it under itself as you go. With seam side down, gently flatten cylinder into 6 by 2-inch rectangle. Transfer to parchment paper–lined rimmed baking sheet, cover loosely with greased plastic wrap, and freeze for 15 minutes.

4 **For the filling:** Combine all ingredients in bowl. Line 6 cups of muffin tin with paper or foil liners and spray with vegetable oil spray. Transfer dough to lightly floured counter and roll into 10 by 8-inch rectangle, with long side parallel to counter edge. Sprinkle with sugar mixture, leaving ½-inch border around edges, and press lightly to adhere.

5 Roll dough away from you into firm cylinder, keeping roll taut by tucking it under itself as you go. Pinch seam closed, then reshape cylinder to be 10 inches in length with uniform thickness. Using serrated knife, trim ½ inch dough from each end; discard. Cut cylinder into 6 pieces and place cut side up in prepared muffin cups. Cover loosely with greased plastic and let rise until doubled in size, 1½ to 2 hours.

6 Adjust oven rack to middle position and heat oven to 425 degrees. Bake until buns begin to rise, about 5 minutes, then reduce oven temperature to 325 degrees. Continue to bake until buns are deep golden brown, 30 to 40 minutes, rotating muffin tin halfway through baking. Let buns cool in muffin tin for 10 minutes, then transfer to wire rack and discard liners. Serve warm.

---

freeze and bake

In step 5, transfer all or a portion of cut, unproofed buns in their liners to a baking sheet and freeze until firm, about 30 minutes. Transfer buns (with liners) to zipper-lock bag and freeze for up to 2 months. Return buns to muffin tin or ramekins and let sit at room temperature for at least 10 or up to 12 hours before baking.

---

bake in your air fryer

Place up to 4 buns in lined 4-cup muffin tin or four 4-ounce ramekins. Place muffin tin, or ramekins spaced evenly apart, in air-fryer basket. Place basket in air fryer and set temperature to 325 degrees. Bake until buns are deep golden brown, 30 to 40 minutes.

croissants

makes 7 croissants • **total time** 1¾ hours, plus 9¼ hours resting, chilling, rising, and cooling

2⅓ cups (11⅔ ounces) King Arthur all-purpose flour

2 tablespoons sugar

2 teaspoons instant or rapid-rise yeast

1 teaspoon table salt

15 tablespoons unsalted European-style butter, divided

1 cup whole milk

1 large egg, lightly beaten with 1 tablespoons water, or 2 tablespoons heavy cream

why this recipe works Breaking into a just-baked croissant, with flakes flying and butter moistening each bite, is a distinct joy, especially if it's a pastry you made yourself. Homemade croissants are a true labor of love, and for the small-batch baker, we wanted to make sure that the buttery, flaky reward was well worth the effort. Our recipe makes seven croissants, just enough to bake off a few right away, then store the rest in your freezer to bake another day. To achieve this storied pastry's signature layers, we wrap a yeasted dough around a thin block of butter, then roll and fold it repeatedly (a process known as lamination with each repetition called a "turn") to form paper-thin layers of dough and butter. Using the freezer to superchill the dough throughout the lamination process ensures that the butter and dough are of similar texture when rolling and folding, preventing the butter from cracking or melting into the dough. We strongly encourage using high-protein all-purpose flour, such as King Arthur, and European-style butter (we like Plugrà). If the dough retracts, softens, or is no longer cool to the touch at any point, wrap it in plastic and freeze for 15 minutes. Do not make these in a room that is warmer than 80 degrees. The croissants take at least 10 hours to make from start to finish, but the process can be spread over two days. We developed this recipe using a 4.5-quart stand mixer; if using a larger mixer you may need to increase mixing times.

1 Dough: Whisk flour, sugar, yeast, and salt together in bowl of stand mixer. Melt 2 tablespoons butter in small saucepan over low heat. (Refrigerate remaining 13 tablespoons butter.) Remove saucepan from heat and immediately stir in milk (temperature of mixture should be lower than 90 degrees). Fit stand mixer with dough hook, add milk mixture to flour mixture, and mix on low speed until cohesive dough forms, about 2 minutes. Increase speed to medium-low and knead for 1 minute (dough will be stretchy, not smooth, and very sticky). Remove bowl from mixer and cover with plastic wrap. Let dough rest at room temperature for 30 minutes.

2 Transfer dough to large sheet of plastic wrap on counter and shape into 7 by 5-inch rectangle about 1 inch thick. Wrap dough tightly with plastic and refrigerate for 2 hours.

3 Butter block: Meanwhile, cut 12 by 16-inch sheet of parchment paper. Fold in half to create 8 by 12-inch rectangle. Measure 3 inches in from each short side and fold toward center. Orient rectangle with open side away from you. Measure 2 inches from top then fold open side down to form 6-inch square packet with enclosed sides. Crease folds firmly.

4 Place reserved 13 tablespoons cold butter side by side directly on counter. Beat with rolling pin for about 60 seconds, until butter is just pliable but not warm, then fold butter in on itself using bench scraper to form rough 4-inch square. Unfold parchment envelope. Using bench scraper, transfer butter to center of parchment, refolding at creases to enclose. Turn packet over so that flaps are underneath and gently roll until butter fills parchment square, taking care to achieve even thickness. Refrigerate for 45 minutes.

5 **Laminate:** Transfer dough from refrigerator to freezer for 15 minutes. Set butter block aside on counter just before rolling out dough. Working on lightly floured counter, roll dough into 13 by 6-inch rectangle, then place dough so that long side is parallel to counter edge. (If dough starts to crack on sides, let sit at room temperature for 5 minutes).

6 Unwrap butter and place in center of dough (if butter doesn't hold its shape as a block, return to refrigerator for 5 minutes before proceeding). Fold sides of dough over butter so they meet in center. Pinch and press seam together with your fingertips. Pinch each open end of packet to seal dough around butter.

7 **First turn:** Roll dough into 18 by 6-inch rectangle with short side parallel to counter edge. Starting at bottom of dough, fold into thirds like business letter to form approximate 6-inch square. Turn dough 90 degrees counterclockwise.

(continued)

8   **Second turn:** Roll dough into 18 by 6-inch rectangle with short side parallel to counter edge and fold into thirds. Wrap dough tightly with plastic and return to freezer for 15 minutes.

9   **Third turn:** Transfer dough to lightly floured counter so that top flap opens on right (folded edge will be on left side). Roll dough into 18 by 6-inch rectangle with short side parallel to counter edge and fold into thirds. Wrap dough with plastic and refrigerate for 2 hours or up to 24 hours.

10   **Shape:** Transfer dough to freezer for 15 minutes. Working on lightly floured counter, roll dough into 14 by 10-inch rectangle with long side parallel to counter edge. (Let dough warm slightly if it starts to crack on sides.) Using ruler, mark dough at 3½-inch intervals along bottom edge (you should have 3 marks). Using ruler, mark dough 1¾ inches in from top left corner of dough. From there, continue to mark dough along top edge at 3½-inch intervals (you should have 4 marks).

11   Connect bottom left corner of dough to leftmost mark along top edge with ruler, then use sharp pizza wheel or knife to cut dough from corner to mark, using ruler to ensure straight cuts. Continue connecting marks and cutting dough to create 7 triangles of similar size and 2 scrap end pieces. Discard scraps or bake separately (see tips).

12   **Roll:** Working with 1 triangle at a time (keep remaining triangles covered with plastic), cut ½-inch slit in center of short side of triangle. Grasp triangle by 2 corners on either side of slit and stretch gently to widen base of triangle so that slit forms a "v." Then, grasping base of triangle with your hand gently pull length of triangle with your other hand, stretching and extending dough (triangle will now be roughly 12 to 13 inches long). Position triangle on counter so point is facing you. Fold down dough at base of triangle on both sides of slit, then gently roll folded dough halfway toward point. Gently grasp point with your hand and stretch again. Resume rolling, tucking point underneath.

13   **Proof:** Line 2 rimmed baking sheets with parchment paper. Place number of croissants you want to bake (up to 5 croissants) on 1 prepared sheet at least 2½ inches apart. Lightly wrap with plastic. Place remaining croissants on second prepared sheet.

Wrap second sheet with plastic and freeze until firm, about 2 hours; transfer to zipper-lock bag and freeze for up to 2 months. (Or you can proof and bake all 7 croissants using the 2 rimmed baking sheets.) Let first sheet stand at room temperature until croissants are puffy, jiggle when shaken, and are nearly doubled in size, 3 to 4 hours. (To thaw and proof frozen croissants, remove from freezer and let sit, covered with plastic, at room temperature for 7 to 10 hours, until croissants are puffy, jiggle when shaken, and are nearly doubled in size.)

14   **Bake:** Adjust oven rack to upper-middle position and heat oven to 400 degrees. Brush croissants with egg wash and bake until deep golden brown, 17 to 20 minutes, rotating sheet halfway through baking. Transfer sheet to wire rack and let cool for 15 minutes. Serve warm or at room temperature.

croissant tips

- Use a ruler that's longer than 12 inches.

- Use your bench scraper and ruler to help ensure straight sides and corners; don't worry too much about perfectly squared-off edges.

- If your dough tears while you're rolling it out, lightly dust with flour. Chill the dough if it's warm; let it rest at room temperature if it's too cold.

- The ideal temperature for proofing croissants is 75 degrees; if you have an oven thermometer with an air probe, you can proof croissants in an off oven with the light on; turn off the light if it approaches 80 degrees. You can also place an 8-inch square baking dish with 2 cups of boiling water on the bottom rack of an off oven, and proof the croissants on the middle rack, again monitoring temperature.

- Frozen croissants will defrost and proof in roughly 7 to 8 hours; if ambient temperature is cooler than 70 degrees, you may need to increase the proofing time to up to 10 hours.

making the butter packet

1 Fold parchment in half to create 12 by 8-inch rectangle.

2 Measure 3 inches in from each short side and fold sides toward center.

3 Measure 2 inches from top, then fold open side down to form 6-inch square packet.

shaping the croissants

1 Measure in 1¾ inches from top left, then measure out 3½-inch intervals along top edge.

2 Cut dough from mark to mark to create 7 triangles.

3 Cut ½-inch slit in center of short side of each triangle. Grasp triangle by 2 corners on either side of slit and stretch gently.

4 Grasp base of triangle and gently pull length of triangle, stretching and extending dough.

5 Fold down dough at base of triangle on both sides of slit, then roll dough halfway toward point.

6 Gently grasp point and stretch again. Resume rolling, tucking point underneath.

pain au chocolat

makes 8 pastries • **total time** 1¾ hours, plus 9¼ hours resting, chilling, rising, and cooling

1 recipe Croissants (page 228), prepared through step 9

3 ounces milk chocolate, sliced into eight ½-inch wide bars

why this recipe works The only thing possibly more satisfying than a warm, flaky, buttery homemade croissant is one filled with chocolate. We start with the same fool-proof lamination method we use in our plain croissants, but cut the dough into eight rectangles. You can choose to bake eight pastries now, or save some in your freezer for later. Instead of the traditional French batons of chocolate (which can be hard to find, and generally come in large quantities), we carefully cut a bar of chocolate into thin slices to create homemade batons. Placing one at each end of the rectangle before rolling provides plenty of chocolate in each bite, without weighing down the delicate layers of dough. We had the best success using 5½ by 3-inch chocolate bars that were approximately ¼ inch thick. A serrated knife makes easy work of cutting the chocolate into bars. It's okay if the chocolate bars crack while slicing, simply piece them together while arranging on dough in step 3. If the dough retracts, softens, or is no longer cool to the touch at any point, wrap it in plastic and freeze for 15 minutes. Do not make these in a room that is warmer than 80 degrees. The pain au chocolat take at least 10 hours to make from start to finish, but the process can be spread over two days.

1 Transfer dough to freezer for 15 minutes. Working on lightly floured counter, roll dough into 14 by 10-inch rectangle with long side parallel to counter edge. (Let dough warm slightly if it starts to crack on sides.) Using ruler, mark dough at 3½-inch intervals along top and bottom edges (you should have 6 total marks).

2 Using ruler placed parallel with short side of dough, connect top and bottom marks, then use sharp pizza wheel or knife to cut dough into four 10 by 3½-inch strips. Using pizza wheel, cut each dough strip crosswise into 5 by 3½-inch rectangles. (You will have 8 rectangles.)

(continued)

3 Position 1 rectangle on counter with short side parallel to counter edge. (Keep remaining rectangles covered with plastic.) Place 1 bar of chocolate ½ inch from bottom edge and second bar of chocolate ½ inch from top edge. Fold bottom edge of dough over chocolate, and gently press seam together; repeat at top edge. Roll top and bottom folds toward each other to touch in center, then place, rolled side down, on counter, lightly pressing on top of pastry to flatten. Repeat with remaining dough rectangles and chocolate.

4 Line 2 rimmed baking sheets with parchment paper. Place number of pastries you want to bake (up to 5 pastries) on 1 prepared sheet at least 2½ inches apart. Lightly wrap with plastic. Place remaining pastries on second prepared sheet. Wrap second sheet with plastic and freeze until firm, about 2 hours; transfer to zipper-lock bag and freeze for up to 2 months. (Or you can proof and bake all 8 pastries using the 2 rimmed baking sheets.) Let first sheet stand at room temperature until pastries are puffy, jiggle when shaken, and are nearly doubled in size, 3 to 4 hours. (To thaw and proof frozen pain au chocolat, remove from freezer and let sit, covered with plastic, at room temperature for 7 to 10 hours, until pastries are puffy, jiggle when shaken, and are nearly doubled in size.)

5 Adjust oven rack to upper-middle position and heat oven to 400 degrees. Brush pain au chocolat with egg wash. Bake until deep golden brown, 17 to 20 minutes, rotating sheet halfway through baking. Transfer sheet to wire rack and let cool for 15 minutes. Serve warm or at room temperature.

shaping pain au chocolat

1 Mark dough at 3½-inch intervals along top and bottom edges.

2 Cut dough from mark to mark to create 4 strips, then cut each strip in half to create 8 rectangles.

3 Place 1 bar of chocolate ½ inch from bottom edge and second bar of chocolate ½ inch from top edge.

4 Fold bottom edge of dough over chocolate and gently press seam together; repeat at top edge.

5 Roll top and bottom folds toward each other to touch in center.

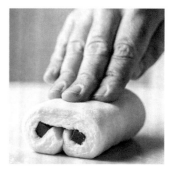

6 Place pastry rolled side down on counter and lightly press on top to flatten.

prosciutto and gruyère croissants

makes 7 croissants • **total time** 1¾ hours, plus 9¼ hours resting, chilling, rising, and cooling

1 recipe Croissants (page 228), prepared through step 11

7 thin slices prosciutto (3½ ounces)

4 ounces Gruyère, shredded (1¼ cups), divided

why this recipe works Ham and cheese is a classic croissant filling, so we wanted to wrap our savory croissant dough around salty, delicate prosciutto and nutty Gruyère. Starting with our small-batch croissant dough, we shape these similarly to our plain croissants (see page 228), but on each triangle of dough we layer shredded cheese and a thin slice of prosciutto—enough to be indulgent without over-burdening the gossamer layers of dough. If the dough retracts, softens, or is no longer cool to the touch at any point, wrap it in plastic and freeze for 15 minutes. Do not make these in a room that is warmer than 80 degrees. The croissants take at least 10 hours to make from start to finish, but the process can be spread over two days.

1   Working with 1 triangle at a time (keep remaining triangles covered with plastic), cut ½-inch slit in center of short side of triangle. Grasp triangle by 2 corners on either side of slit and stretch gently to widen base of triangle so that slit forms a "v." Then, grasping base of triangle with one hand, gently pull length of triangle with other hand, stretching and extending dough (triangle will now be roughly 12 to 13 inches long).

2   Position triangle on counter so point is facing you. Starting ½ inch from top edge, place 1 slice prosciutto along length of triangle, then mound scant 2 tablespoons Gruyère on top of prosciutto at wide end of triangle. Fold down dough at base of triangle on both sides of slit, then gently roll halfway toward point, encasing filling. Gently grasp point with 1 hand and stretch again. Resume rolling, tucking point underneath. Repeat with remaining triangles, prosciutto, and ¾ cup Gruyère.

3   Line 2 rimmed baking sheets with parchment paper. Place number of croissants you want to bake (up to 5 croissants) on 1 prepared sheet at least 2½ inches apart. Place remaining croissants on second prepared sheet. Wrap second sheet with plastic and freeze until firm, about 2 hours; transfer to zipper-lock bag and freeze for up to 2 months. (Or you can proof and bake all 7 croissants using the 2 rimmed baking sheets.) Let the first sheet stand at room temperature until croissants are puffy, jiggle when shaken, and are nearly doubled in size, 3 to 4 hours. (To thaw and proof frozen croissants, remove from freezer and let sit, covered with plastic, at room temperature for 7 to 10 hours, until croissants are puffy, jiggle when shaken, and are nearly doubled in size.)

4 Adjust oven rack to upper-middle position and heat oven to 400 degrees. Brush croissants with egg wash then sprinkle each with remaining Gruyère. Bake until deep golden brown, 17 to 20 minutes, rotating sheet halfway through baking. Transfer sheet to wire rack and let cool for 15 minutes. Serve warm or at room temperature.

chapter six
biscuits, scones, and muffins

easiest-ever drop biscuits

makes 4 biscuits • **total time** 30 minutes

⅔ cup (3⅓ ounces) all-purpose flour

¾ teaspoon baking powder

¼ teaspoon baking soda

⅛ teaspoon sugar

⅛ teaspoon table salt

⅓ cup buttermilk

3 tablespoons unsalted butter, melted, divided

---

bake in your air fryer

Line air-fryer basket with aluminum foil, crimping edges. Space biscuits at least ½ inch apart in prepared basket. (Depending on size of air fryer, you may need to bake biscuits in batches.) Place basket in air fryer, set temperature to 325 degrees, and bake for 12 to 15 minutes.

why this recipe works You don't need to rationalize baking for just yourself (or a friend or two) when baked goods come together as quickly as these mix, scoop, and drop biscuits do. Simple to make yet extraordinarily good, they're just as rich and tender as roll-and-cut biscuits. For a buttery tang, we use buttermilk, a move that also encourages a crisp crust and fluffy interior. Stirring melted butter into the buttermilk creates clumps in the batter that may look problematic but—surprisingly—produce better biscuits. The water in the clumps of butter turns to steam in the oven, creating additional height. A combination of baking powder and baking soda produces even more rise for four superlight biscuits. You can eat these rich, fluffy biscuits at room temperature, but we don't think they'll last that long. If you have one, a spring-loaded ice cream scoop makes portioning the biscuits particularly easy.

1 Adjust oven rack to middle position and heat oven to 450 degrees. Line rimmed baking sheet with parchment paper. Whisk flour, baking powder, baking soda, sugar, and salt together in medium bowl. In separate bowl, stir buttermilk and 2 tablespoons melted butter together (butter will form small clumps). Using wooden spoon or rubber spatula, stir buttermilk mixture into flour mixture until just incorporated and dough pulls away from sides of bowl.

2 Using greased ¼-cup dry measure, drop 4 level scoops of dough about 1½ inches apart onto prepared sheet. Bake until biscuit tops are golden brown, 12 to 15 minutes, rotating sheet halfway through baking.

3 Brush biscuits with remaining 1 tablespoon melted butter, transfer to wire rack, and let cool for 5 minutes. Serve warm or at room temperature.

variations

easiest-ever cinnamon-sugar drop biscuits

Combine ½ cup sugar and 1 teaspoon ground cinnamon in small bowl; set aside. Increase melted butter to 6 tablespoons. Let biscuits cool on wire rack for 5 minutes, then brush with remaining 4 tablespoons melted butter. Working with 1 biscuit at a time, coat in sugar-cinnamon mixture.

easiest-ever herb drop biscuits

Whisk 2 teaspoons minced fresh tender herbs (basil, chives, cilantro, dill, parsley, or tarragon) or 1 teaspoon minced fresh hardy herbs (sage, thyme, or rosemary) into flour mixture before adding buttermilk mixture.

easiest-ever pepper-bacon drop biscuits

Cook 2 slices finely chopped bacon in 10-inch skillet over medium heat until crispy, 5 to 7 minutes. Using slotted spoon, transfer to paper towel–lined plate and let cool slightly. Stir bacon and ¼ teaspoon coarsely ground pepper into flour mixture before adding buttermilk mixture.

cream biscuits

makes 6 biscuits • **total time** 45 minutes

2 cups (10 ounces) all-purpose flour

2 teaspoons sugar

2 teaspoons baking powder

½ teaspoon table salt

1½ cups heavy cream

freeze and bake

At end of step 3, place rounds on parchment paper–lined baking sheet and freeze until firm; transfer biscuits to zipper-lock bag and store in freezer for up to 1 month. Bake for 20 to 25 minutes; do not thaw before baking.

bake in your air fryer

Line air-fryer basket with aluminum foil, crimping edges. Place desired number of biscuits in prepared basket. Place basket in air fryer and set temperature to 325 degrees. Bake until biscuit tops are golden brown, 20 to 25 minutes from fresh or 25 to 30 minutes from frozen.

why this recipe works Cream biscuits have unique appeal: They're almost as rich as butter-laced biscuits, but the liquid ingredient gives them a lighter, fluffier interior texture. As a bonus, stirring the heavy cream into the dry ingredients before patting the dough out means you can make uniformly round stamped biscuits without a rolling pin. We love to split these and smear them with butter and jam for a comforting treat. They also serve as a nice side for soup or stew, or a base for cured meats and cheeses. Stretch a batch to do both things by freezing some of the dough rounds and baking them at a later time.

1 Adjust oven rack to upper-middle position and heat oven to 400 degrees. Line rimmed baking sheet with parchment paper. Whisk flour, sugar, baking powder, and salt together in large bowl. Using wooden spoon or rubber spatula, stir cream into flour mixture until very shaggy dough forms (some bits of dry flour will remain; do not overmix).

2 Turn dough onto lightly floured counter and, using your lightly floured hands, gently knead until dough comes together, about 30 seconds. Press and roll dough into rough ¾-inch-thick round.

3 Using 2½-inch round biscuit cutter dipped in flour, stamp out 4 biscuits, making sure not to twist cutter while pressing down and dipping cutter in flour after each cut. Gather remaining dough scraps, reroll into ¾-inch-thick round, and stamp out remaining 2 biscuits.

4 Transfer biscuits to prepared sheet, spaced at least 1½ inches apart. Bake until tops are golden brown, 15 to 20 minutes, rotating sheet halfway through baking. Let biscuits cool on wire rack for 5 minutes. Serve warm or at room temperature.

sun-dried tomato and za'atar biscuits

makes 4 biscuits • **total time** 40 minutes

1	cup (5 ounces) all-purpose flour
1	teaspoon baking powder
	Pinch baking soda
½	teaspoon sugar
¼	teaspoon table salt
⅛	teaspoon pepper
⅔	cup heavy cream
1	garlic clove, minced
⅓	cup oil-packed sun-dried tomatoes, rinsed, patted dry, and chopped fine
2	teaspoons za'atar

bake in your air fryer

Line air-fryer basket with aluminum foil, crimping edges. Space biscuits at least ½ inch apart in prepared basket. (Depending on size of air fryer, you may need to bake biscuits in batches.) Place basket in air fryer, set temperature to 325 degrees, and bake for 14 to 19 minutes.

why this recipe works The ease of preparing scoop-and-drop biscuits makes these savory treats the perfect canvas for experimenting with lots of different flavor combinations. Here, the biscuits are emboldened with piquant pantry ingredients: sun-dried tomatoes, garlic, and za'atar. Our trick for getting garlic flavor throughout—without studding the biscuits with pungent pieces—is to use the microwave to infuse the recipe's heavy cream with minced garlic. We prefer our homemade za'atar (see page 317), but you can use store-bought if you prefer. We recommend a brand without added salt; if you can't find it, reduce the salt in the flour mixture to ⅛ teaspoon.

1 Adjust oven rack to upper-middle position and heat oven to 450 degrees. Line rimmed baking sheet with parchment paper. Whisk flour, baking powder, baking soda, sugar, salt, and pepper together in medium bowl. Microwave cream and garlic in separate bowl until just warmed (100 degrees), 60 to 90 seconds, stirring halfway through microwaving. Using wooden spoon or rubber spatula, stir cream mixture and tomatoes into flour mixture until just incorporated and dough pulls away from sides of bowl.

2 Using greased ⅓-cup dry measure, drop 4 level scoops of dough about 1½ inches apart onto prepared sheet. Sprinkle biscuits with za'atar and bake until biscuit tops are golden brown, 14 to 19 minutes, rotating sheet halfway through baking. Let biscuits cool on wire rack for 5 minutes. Serve warm or at room temperature.

flaky whole-wheat buttermilk biscuits

makes 6 biscuits • **total time** 1 hour, plus 30 minutes chilling

1 cup (5½ ounces) bread flour

1 cup (5½ ounces) whole-wheat flour

4 teaspoons sugar

4 teaspoons baking powder

¼ teaspoon baking soda

1 teaspoon table salt

12 tablespoons unsalted butter (1½ sticks), cut into 3 pieces and frozen for 30 minutes

¾ cup plus 2 tablespoons buttermilk

why this recipe works Sure, drop biscuits and cream biscuits satisfy with a certain amount of ease, but we wanted to develop tall, tender biscuits, stacked with flakes upon flakes, that were practical to make in a modest quantity. And we wanted them to feature nutty whole-wheat flour for wholesome, hearty flavor. Baking the biscuits fresh is a treat, but creating those flakes can take some effort. So we developed the recipe so that the cut-up biscuit dough can be put in the freezer, then later baked from frozen, making it easy to prep the biscuits one day and bake another for a cozy breakfast plate or unexpected dinner company. Or bake off one or two at a time when you crave comfort. In hot or humid environments, chill the flour mixture, grater, and work bowls before use. The dough will start out very crumbly and dry in pockets, but will be smooth by the end of the folding process; do not add extra buttermilk. Flour the counter and the top of the dough as needed to prevent sticking, but be careful not to incorporate large pockets of flour into the dough when folding.

1 Line rimmed baking sheet with parchment paper. Whisk bread flour, whole-wheat flour, sugar, baking powder, baking soda, and salt together in large bowl. Coat butter pieces in flour mixture, then grate 3 tablespoons from each piece on large holes of box grater directly into flour mixture. Gently toss to combine. Set aside remaining 3 tablespoons butter.

2 Using wooden spoon or rubber spatula, fold buttermilk into flour mixture until just combined (dough will look dry). Turn dough onto liberally floured counter. Dust surface of dough with flour and, using your floured hands, press dough into rough 6-inch square.

(continued)

freeze and bake

At end of step 5, return all or a portion of biscuits to parchment-lined sheet and freeze until firm; transfer frozen biscuits to zipper-lock bag and store in freezer for up to 1 month. Bake for 25 to 30 minutes; do not thaw before baking.

bake in your air fryer

Line air-fryer basket with aluminum foil, crimping edges. Place desired number of biscuits in prepared basket. Place basket in air fryer and set temperature to 325 degrees. Bake until biscuit tops are golden brown, 20 to 25 minutes from fresh or 25 to 30 minutes from frozen.

3 Roll dough into 10 by 8-inch rectangle with short side parallel to counter edge. Starting at bottom of dough, fold into thirds like a business letter, using bench scraper or metal spatula to release dough from counter. Press top of dough firmly to seal folds. Turn dough 90 degrees clockwise. Repeat rolling into 10 by 8-inch rectangle, folding into thirds, and turning clockwise 3 more times, for total of 4 sets of folds.

4 After last set of folds, fold dough in half, pressing top of dough firmly to seal folds. Roll dough into 7-inch square, about ¾ inch thick. Transfer dough to prepared sheet, cover with plastic wrap, and refrigerate for 30 minutes.

5 Transfer dough to lightly floured cutting board. Using floured sharp chef's knife, trim ¼ inch of dough from each side of square and discard. Cut square in half, then cut each half crosswise into thirds, flouring knife after each cut. Melt reserved butter and brush over tops of biscuits; you may not need all of butter.

6 Adjust oven rack to upper-middle position and heat oven to 400 degrees. Place biscuits on parchment-lined sheet, spaced at least 1½ inches apart, and bake until tops are golden brown, 20 to 25 minutes, rotating sheet halfway through baking. Let biscuits cool on wire rack for 5 minutes. Serve warm or at room temperature.

variation

flaky buttermilk biscuits

Substitute 2 cups (10 ounces) all-purpose flour for bread flour and whole-wheat flour.

shaping flaky buttermilk biscuits

1 Roll dough into 10 by 8-inch rectangle, then fold into thirds like a business letter.

2 Turn dough 90 degrees clockwise. Repeat rolling into rectangle, folding into thirds, and turning clockwise 3 times.

3 Fold dough in half, then roll into 7-inch square. Refrigerate for 30 minutes.

4 Using floured knife, trim edges of square. Cut square in half, then cut each half crosswise into thirds.

british-style currant scones

makes 6 scones • **total time** 45 minutes

- 1½ cups (7½ ounces) all-purpose flour
- 2 tablespoons plus 1 teaspoon sugar
- 1 tablespoon baking powder
- ¼ teaspoon table salt
- 4 tablespoons unsalted butter, cut into ½-inch pieces and softened
- ⅓ cup dried currants
- ½ cup milk
- 1 large egg

---

bake in your air fryer

Line air-fryer basket with aluminum foil, crimping edges. Space scones at least ½ inch apart in prepared basket. (Depending on size of air fryer, you may need to bake scones in batches.) Place basket in air fryer, set temperature to 300 degrees, and bake for 15 to 18 minutes.

why this recipe works Traditional currant scones are meant to be fluffy, tender, and only modestly rich—as such, they are best eaten fresh. This recipe allows you to bake up just six for a teatime treat. If you have a couple leftover, you can freeze them, then refresh for 15 minutes in a 300-degree oven. To make the lightest, fluffiest scones, we add more than the usual amount of leavening: 1 teaspoon of baking powder per ½ cup of flour. Rather than leaving pieces of cold butter in the dough, as we do for other scones and biscuits, we work in softened butter until it's fully integrated. This protects some of the flour granules from moisture, which in turn limits gluten development to keep the crumb tender and cakey. Milk of any fat level can be used. The dough will be quite soft and wet; dust your work surface and your hands liberally with flour. For a tall, even rise, use a sharp-edged biscuit cutter and push straight down; do not twist the cutter. Serve with jam as well as salted butter or clotted cream.

1 Adjust oven rack to upper-middle position and heat oven to 500 degrees. Line rimmed baking sheet with parchment paper. Whisk flour, sugar, baking powder, and salt in medium bowl until combined. Add butter and rub into flour mixture until fully incorporated and mixture looks like very fine crumbs with no visible butter. Stir in currants.

2 Whisk milk and egg together in second bowl. Set aside 1 tablespoon milk mixture. Add remaining milk mixture to flour mixture and, using rubber spatula, fold together until almost no dry bits of flour remain.

3 Transfer dough to well-floured counter and gather into ball. Using your floured hands, knead until surface is smooth and free of cracks, 25 to 30 times. Press gently to form disk. Pat disk into 6-inch round, about 1 inch thick. Using floured 2½-inch round cutter, stamp out 4 rounds, recoating cutter with flour if it begins to stick. Arrange scones on prepared sheet. Gather dough scraps, form into ball, and knead gently until surface is smooth. Pat dough to 1-inch thickness and stamp out 1 round. Repeat patting and cutting to create sixth round. Discard remaining dough.

4 Brush tops of scones with reserved milk mixture. Reduce oven temperature to 425 degrees and bake scones until risen and golden brown, 10 to 12 minutes, rotating sheet halfway through baking. Transfer scones to wire rack and let cool for at least 10 minutes. Serve scones warm or at room temperature.

maple-pecan scones with maple glaze

makes 4 scones • **total time** 45 minutes, plus 25 minutes cooling and resting

1	cup (5 ounces) all-purpose flour
1½	teaspoons baking powder
¼	teaspoon table salt
3	tablespoons unsalted butter, cut into ¼-inch pieces and chilled
¼	cup pecans, toasted and chopped
2½	tablespoons maple syrup, divided
½	cup heavy cream
3	tablespoons confectioners' sugar

bake in your air fryer

Line air-fryer basket with aluminum foil, crimping edges. Space scones at least ½ inch apart in prepared basket. (Depending on size of air fryer, you may need to bake scones in batches.) Place basket in air fryer, set temperature to 300 degrees, and bake for 18 to 23 minutes.

why this recipe works Maple syrup elevates just about any breakfast food from good to irresistible, including these nutty American-style scones, rich with butter and pecans. We add syrup to the dough for a maple bass note and then take it higher with a simple maple glaze. Toasting mild pecans bumps up their flavor so it rings through; don't skip this step.

1 Adjust oven rack to middle position and heat oven to 375 degrees. Line rimmed baking sheet with parchment paper.

2 Process flour, baking powder, and salt in food processor until combined, about 5 seconds. Scatter butter over top and pulse until mixture resembles coarse cornmeal with some slightly larger butter lumps, about 6 pulses. Transfer mixture to medium bowl and stir in pecans. Whisk 1½ tablespoons maple syrup into cream until syrup has dissolved. Using wooden spoon or rubber spatula, stir cream into flour mixture until shaggy dough forms (some bits of dry flour will remain; do not overmix).

3 Turn dough onto lightly floured counter and, using your lightly floured hands, gently knead until dough comes together, 5 to 10 seconds. Press dough into 5-inch round, about ¾ inch thick, sealing any cracked edges. Cut dough into 4 wedges and transfer scones to prepared sheet, spaced at least 1½ inches apart.

4 Bake until edges of scones are golden brown, 18 to 23 minutes, rotating sheet halfway through baking. Transfer scones to wire rack set over sheet of parchment paper (to catch glaze) and let cool for 20 minutes. Meanwhile, whisk confectioners' sugar and remaining 1 tablespoon maple syrup together in bowl. Drizzle glaze over scones and let set for 5 minutes before serving.

blue cheese–apple rye scones

makes 4 scones • **total time** 45 minutes, plus 30 minutes chilling

½ cup (2¾ ounces) bread flour

½ cup (2¾ ounces) rye flour

1 tablespoon sugar

¾ teaspoon baking powder

½ teaspoon table salt

4 tablespoons unsalted butter, cut into ½-inch pieces and chilled, plus 1 tablespoon melted

2 ounces firm blue cheese, crumbled (½ cup)

3 tablespoons chopped dried apples

1¾ teaspoons minced fresh thyme, divided

⅓ cup whole milk

1 large egg

2 teaspoons honey

bake in your air fryer

Line air-fryer basket with aluminum foil, crimping edges. Space scones at least ½ inch apart in prepared basket. (Depending on size of air fryer, you may need to bake scones in batches.) Place basket in air fryer, set temperature to 325 degrees, and bake for 15 to 20 minutes.

why this recipe works These handheld scones boast a bold combination of blue cheese and apples that will wake you up on the morning commute, or pick you up in the afternoon alongside a hot beverage. In addition to the butter, the blue cheese provides fat—with a whole lot of flavor—for really rich scones. This was a great place for us to use rye flour, a nutty, malt-forward flour we love that pairs well with fruity flavors, like the dried apples in these scones. We went with dried apples because they pack concentrated flavor without contributing unpredictable amounts of moisture to the dough like fresh fruit can. The scones can be shaped up to 24 hours before baking, so you can easily bake when it's convenient for optimal freshness. You can use light or dark rye flour in this recipe.

1 Line rimmed baking sheet with parchment paper. Process bread flour, rye flour, sugar, baking powder, and salt in food processor until combined, about 5 seconds. Scatter chilled butter over top and pulse until butter is reduced to pea-size pieces, 10 to 12 pulses. Transfer mixture to medium bowl and stir in blue cheese, apples, and ¾ teaspoon thyme. Whisk milk and egg in separate bowl until fully combined. Using wooden spoon or rubber spatula, stir milk mixture into flour mixture until shaggy dough forms (some bits of dry flour will remain; do not overmix).

2 Turn dough onto liberally floured counter and, using your lightly floured hands, gently knead until dough just comes together, 5 to 10 seconds. Using your floured hands and bench scraper, shape dough into 6 by 3-inch rectangle with long side parallel to counter edge, dusting with extra flour if dough begins to stick. Using sharp, floured chef's knife, cut dough in half crosswise to form 2 squares. Dip knife in flour again and cut each square diagonally into 2 triangles (you should have 4 scones total). Transfer scones to prepared sheet, spaced at least 1½ inches apart. Cover with plastic wrap and refrigerate for at least 30 minutes or up to 24 hours.

3 Adjust oven rack to middle position and heat oven to 425 degrees. Combine honey, melted butter, and remaining 1 teaspoon thyme in small bowl. Bake scones until golden brown, 15 to 20 minutes, rotating sheet halfway through baking.

4 Brush scones with butter mixture, transfer to wire rack, and let cool for 5 minutes. Serve warm or at room temperature.

lemon blueberry muffins

makes 4 muffins • **total time** 1 hour

¾ cup (3¾ ounces) all-purpose flour

1½ teaspoons baking powder

Pinch baking soda

⅛ teaspoon table salt

⅔ cup sour cream

½ cup (3½ ounces) granulated sugar

2 tablespoons unsalted butter, melted

1 teaspoon grated lemon zest plus 1 teaspoon juice

2½ ounces (½ cup) fresh or frozen blueberries

1 tablespoon turbinado sugar (optional)

pan swap
Recipe can be made in a 4-cup, 6-cup, or 12-cup muffin tin, or in four 4-ounce ramekins placed on a rimmed baking sheet.

bake in your air fryer
Place 4-cup muffin tin, or ramekins spaced evenly apart, in air-fryer basket. Place basket in air fryer, set temperature to 300 degrees, and bake for 25 to 30 minutes.

why this recipe works Blueberry muffins are a delightful classic, but the longer they sit around, the less appetizing they become. This recipe produces the perfect number of muffins for enjoying fresh and warm right out of the oven, with only a couple left over for the next day. In scaling down to four muffins, we found it irksome to measure out a small amount of an egg, so we omitted it and let the sour cream in the recipe do more work to add fat and moisture for a tender crumb. Adding lemon zest to the batter contributes vibrant citrus flavor while enhancing the sweetness of the berries; the generous sour cream enhances that lemon tang. Even though you're baking just four muffins, there's no need to fuss over what size muffin tin you use, or in what cups to deposit the batter. They'll bake the same no matter. We sprinkle the batter with turbinado sugar before baking, which gently caramelizes into a sweet, crackling shell as the muffins bake. Do not thaw frozen blueberries before adding them to batter.

1 Adjust oven rack to middle position and heat oven to 400 degrees. Spray 4 cups of muffin tin with vegetable oil spray. Whisk flour, baking powder, baking soda, and salt together in medium bowl. Whisk sour cream, granulated sugar, melted butter, and lemon zest and juice in separate bowl until well combined.

2 Using rubber spatula, fold sour cream mixture into flour mixture until just combined. Gently fold in blueberries. Divide batter evenly among prepared muffin cups and sprinkle tops with turbinado sugar, if using.

3 Bake until muffins are golden brown and toothpick inserted in center comes out with few crumbs attached, 20 to 25 minutes, rotating muffin tin halfway through baking. Let muffins cool in muffin tin on wire rack for 10 minutes. Transfer muffins to rack and let cool for 5 minutes before serving.

whole-wheat apple-spice muffins

makes 4 muffins • **total time** 1¼ hours

2   tablespoons packed dark brown
    sugar, divided

¼   teaspoon plus pinch five-spice
    powder, divided

¼   cup vegetable oil, divided

1   Granny Smith, Empire, or
    Braeburn apple, peeled, cored,
    and cut into ¼-inch pieces (1 cup)

6   tablespoons (2 ounces)
    whole-wheat flour

6   tablespoons (1¾ ounces)
    all-purpose flour

¾   teaspoon baking powder

    Pinch baking soda

½   teaspoon table salt

⅓   cup (2⅓ ounces) granulated sugar

1   large egg

⅓   cup apple cider

½   teaspoon vanilla extract

2   tablespoons crystallized ginger,
    chopped

---

pan swap

Recipe can be made in a 4-cup, 6-cup, or 12-cup muffin tin, or in four 4-ounce ramekins placed on a rimmed baking sheet.

---

bake in your air fryer

Place 4-cup muffin tin, or ramekins spaced evenly apart, in air-fryer basket. Place basket in air fryer, set temperature to 300 degrees, and bake for 18 to 23 minutes.

why this recipe works   Apples and cinnamon are a treasured pairing, but we love how the more unexpected addition of intensely aromatic five-spice powder enhances the flavor profile of tart apples in these delightful muffins. With just one cut-up apple, simply browned in a small skillet, the muffins have plenty of natural sweetness. Toasty whole-wheat flour brings warmth that complements the spice, and the flavor is enhanced with spicy crystallized ginger that's folded into the batter, and a spiced sugar topping. These moist muffins still taste great the next day.

1   Adjust oven rack to upper-middle position and heat oven to 400 degrees. Spray 4 cups of muffin tin with vegetable oil spray. Combine 4 teaspoons brown sugar and pinch five-spice powder in small bowl; set aside.

2   Heat 1 tablespoon oil in 10-inch skillet over medium-high heat until shimmering. Add apple, remaining 2 teaspoons brown sugar, and ⅛ teaspoon five-spice powder and cook, stirring often, until apple pieces are softened and lightly browned, 7 to 9 minutes. Let apple mixture cool for 10 minutes.

3   Whisk whole-wheat flour, all-purpose flour, baking powder, baking soda, salt, and remaining ⅛ teaspoon five-spice powder together in medium bowl. Whisk granulated sugar, egg, cider, vanilla, and remaining 3 tablespoons oil in separate bowl until well combined. Using rubber spatula, fold apple mixture, sugar mixture, and ginger into flour mixture until just combined. (Batter will be slightly loose.) Divide batter evenly among prepared muffin cups and sprinkle with reserved sugar-spice mixture.

4   Bake until muffins are golden brown and toothpick inserted in center comes out with few crumbs attached, 18 to 23 minutes, rotating muffin tin halfway through baking. Let muffins cool in muffin tin on wire rack for 10 minutes. Transfer muffins to rack and let cool for 5 minutes before serving.

from-the-freezer cranberry-cardamom muffins

makes 6 muffins • **total time** 1½ hours, plus 3 hours freezing

1¼   cups (6¼ ounces) all-purpose flour

1½   teaspoons baking powder

¼   teaspoon baking soda

½   teaspoon ground cardamom

¼   teaspoon table salt

1   large egg

¼   cup vegetable oil

½   cup plus 2 tablespoons buttermilk

½   cup (3½ ounces) granulated sugar

1   teaspoon grated lemon zest

3   ounces (¾ cup) fresh or frozen cranberries, chopped coarse

1   tablespoon turbinado sugar

why this recipe works The freezer has been our friend throughout this collection, but it might be most helpful for making breakfast happen in a small household. What's more convenient than having a supply of portioned muffin batter for an impromptu morning bake? Fully baked then frozen muffins require careful refreshing before serving; our batter is engineered to bake up tall and fluffy directly from the freezer. The buttermilk-based batter is flavorful but neutral enough to let two confident flavors, cranberries and cardamom, shine. The key is to use plenty of leavener—a whopping 1½ teaspoons of baking powder plus ¼ teaspoon of soda—to maximize the frozen batter's rise and color development in the oven. Partially freezing the batter portions in the (lined) tin set their shape enough for them to be transferred and stored in a zipper-lock bag. And if you want a selection of ready-to-bake muffins in your freezer at all times, we've provided variety with a couple of additional mix-in options. Muffins are intended to be baked from frozen. Do not thaw frozen cranberries before chopping.

1   Line 6 cups of muffin tin with paper or foil liners. Whisk flour, baking powder, baking soda, cardamom, and salt together in medium bowl. Whisk egg and oil in medium bowl until thoroughly combined. Whisk in buttermilk, granulated sugar, and lemon zest until combined.

2   Gently whisk one-third of flour mixture into egg mixture until no lumps remain. Whisk in half of remaining flour mixture until smooth. Using rubber spatula, gently fold in remaining flour mixture until few streaks of flour remain. Stir in cranberries until evenly distributed and no dry streaks of flour remain.

3   Divide batter evenly among prepared muffin cups and sprinkle with turbinado sugar. Cover muffin tin with plastic wrap, transfer to freezer, and freeze until batter is solid, at least 3 hours. Transfer frozen batter portions with liners to zipper-lock bag. (If liners freeze to tin, place muffin tin in rimmed baking sheet filled with ⅛ inch warm water for 1 minute. Twist and lift to release, then transfer to bag for freezing.) Freeze batter portions for up to 2 months.

4 Adjust oven rack to middle position and heat oven to 350 degrees. Arrange desired number of frozen batter portions in muffin tin and bake until muffins have risen and are lightly browned and toothpick inserted into center comes out clean, 33 to 38 minutes. Let muffins cool in muffin tin on wire rack for 10 minutes. Transfer muffins to rack and let cool for 5 minutes before serving.

variations

from-the-freezer chocolate–crystallized ginger muffins

Omit lemon zest. Substitute ground ginger for cardamom and ½ cup bittersweet chocolate chips for cranberries. Add 1 tablespoon minced crystallized ginger to batter with chocolate chips.

from-the-freezer raspberry-almond muffins

Omit cardamom. Add ¼ teaspoon almond extract with lemon zest. Substitute 1 cup whole frozen raspberries for cranberries.

---

pan swap

Recipe can be made in a 6- or 12-cup muffin tin, or in six 4-ounce ramekins placed on a rimmed baking sheet.

---

bake in your air fryer

Place up to 4 frozen batter portions in 4-cup muffin tin or 4 ramekins. Place muffin tin, or ramekins spaced evenly apart, in air-fryer basket. Place basket in air fryer, set temperature to 275 degrees, and bake for 35 to 40 minutes.

corn muffins

makes 4 muffins • **total time** 50 minutes

⅔ cup (3⅓ ounces) all-purpose flour

⅓ cup (1⅔ ounces) stone-ground cornmeal

½ teaspoon baking powder

½ teaspoon baking soda

¼ teaspoon table salt

⅓ cup sour cream

¼ cup (1¾ ounces) sugar

1 large egg

3 tablespoons unsalted butter, melted

2 tablespoons whole milk

---

pan swap

Recipe can be made in a 4-cup, 6-cup, or 12-cup muffin tin, or in four 4-ounce ramekins placed on a rimmed baking sheet.

---

bake in your air fryer

Place 4-cup muffin tin, or ramekins spaced evenly apart, in air-fryer basket. Place basket in air fryer, set temperature to 300 degrees, and bake for 12 to 17 minutes.

why this recipe works A corn muffin should taste like corn, but not overpoweringly so, and should be moist with a tender crumb and crunchy top. We wanted a recipe that struck just the right balance in both texture and flavor. The cornmeal itself proved to be an important factor. Degerminated cornmeal—that is, cornmeal that has been stripped of its germ and bran before milling—just didn't have enough corn flavor. A fine-ground whole-grain meal gave us the flavor and texture we were after. Butter, milk, and sour cream provide moisture and richness plus acidity, which has a tenderizing effect. The muffins get a crunchy browned top in a 400-degree oven.

1 Adjust oven rack to middle position and heat oven to 400 degrees. Spray 4 cups of muffin tin with vegetable oil spray. Whisk flour, cornmeal, baking powder, baking soda, and salt together in medium bowl. Whisk sour cream, sugar, egg, melted butter, and milk in separate bowl until well combined.

2 Using rubber spatula, fold sour cream mixture into flour mixture until just combined. (Batter will be lumpy with a few spots of dry flour; do not overmix.) Divide batter evenly among prepared muffin cups.

3 Bake until muffins are golden brown and toothpick inserted in center comes out clean, 12 to 17 minutes, rotating muffin tin halfway through baking. Let muffins cool in muffin tin on wire rack for 10 minutes. Transfer muffins to rack and let cool for 5 minutes before serving.

variations

apricot-orange corn muffins

Add ¼ cup finely chopped dried apricots and ¼ teaspoon finely grated orange zest to sour cream mixture.

cheddar-scallion corn muffins

Reduce sugar to 2 tablespoons. Add 2 thinly sliced scallions and ½ cup shredded cheddar cheese to sour cream mixture. Sprinkle muffins with additional 2 tablespoons shredded cheddar cheese before baking.

bacon-cheddar muffins

makes 4 muffins • **total time** 1 hour

3 slices bacon

1 large egg, separated

1 teaspoon water

1 cup (5 ounces) all-purpose flour

1 teaspoon baking powder

¼ teaspoon table salt

⅛ teaspoon pepper

⅛ teaspoon smoked paprika

2 scallions, sliced thin

1½ ounces cheddar cheese, cut into ¼-inch pieces (⅓ cup)

6 tablespoons whole milk

¼ cup sour cream

1 tablespoon unsalted butter, melted

---

pan swap

Recipe can be made in a 4-cup, 6-cup, or 12-cup muffin tin, or in four 4-ounce ramekins placed on a rimmed baking sheet.

---

bake in your air fryer

Place 4-cup muffin tin, or ramekins spaced evenly apart, in air-fryer basket. Place basket in air fryer, set temperature to 300 degrees, and bake for 15 to 20 minutes.

why this recipe works These savory, cheesy, hearty-crumbed muffins are a complete breakfast in a portable package for anytime eating. For ease of assembly, we love using the microwave for hands-off cooking of the bacon. The thick batter is easy to portion into muffin cups. Best of all, these muffins are still delicious the next day. A fun variation packs all the flavors of delivery pizza into a handheld delight, using pepperoni slices in place of bacon and sun-dried tomatoes for concentrated flavor (pizza for breakfast anyone?). For on-the-go mornings, using an air fryer, if available, is a smart way to bake off these muffins right on your counter.

1 Adjust oven rack to middle position and heat oven to 375 degrees. Spray 4 cups of muffin tin with vegetable oil spray. Place bacon between 2 layers of paper towels on plate and microwave until bacon is crispy, 4 to 6 minutes. Pat bacon dry with clean paper towels, then crumble into fine ¼-inch pieces; set aside.

2 Beat egg white and water together in small bowl and set aside. Whisk flour, baking powder, salt, pepper, and paprika together in medium bowl. Using rubber spatula, stir in scallions, cheddar, and reserved bacon until coated with flour mixture. Whisk milk, sour cream, melted butter, and egg yolk in separate bowl until well combined. Fold milk mixture into flour mixture until just combined (batter will be heavy and thick). Divide batter evenly among prepared muffin cups and brush with reserved egg white.

3 Bake until muffins are light golden brown and toothpick inserted in center comes out clean, 15 to 20 minutes, rotating muffin tin halfway through baking. Let muffins cool in muffin tin on wire rack for 10 minutes. Transfer muffins to rack and let cool for 5 minutes before serving.

variation

pepperoni pizza muffins

Substitute 3 ounces pepperoni, cut into ¼-inch pieces, for bacon; 2 tablespoons chopped sun-dried tomatoes for scallions; and mozzarella for cheddar.

chapter seven
breads and rolls

garlic and herb breadsticks

makes 8 breadsticks • **total time** 40 minutes

8 ounces pizza dough, room temperature

1 teaspoon minced fresh thyme or ¼ teaspoon dried

1 teaspoon dried oregano

½ teaspoon granulated garlic

½ teaspoon kosher salt

⅛ teaspoon coarsely ground pepper

1 tablespoon unsalted butter, melted

variations

fennel–black pepper breadsticks

Omit thyme and garlic. Substitute 1 teaspoon cracked fennel seeds for oregano. Increase pepper to ¼ teaspoon.

spicy parmesan breadsticks

Omit thyme and oregano and reduce salt to ¼ teaspoon. Add ¼ cup finely grated Parmesan cheese and ¼ teaspoon red pepper flakes to granulated garlic mixture.

why this recipe works Whether you use them to sop up soup, dip in tomato sauce, or rush to grab one (or several) to eat right off the sheet, these breadsticks are as quick and easy to make as they are to eat. Make them whenever you want a small-batch snack of the warm and soft variety. Using store-bought pizza dough gets the sticks in and out of the oven in a flash, but you can also use our homemade Basic Pizza Dough on page 334. Sprinkling the dough generously with granulated garlic, fresh thyme, dried oregano, salt, and pepper packs lots of flavor into this modest-size batch of breadsticks. Wait to make the thyme mixture until just before you're ready to sprinkle it; otherwise, the moisture from the fresh thyme can cause it to clump. If you're in the mood for some heat, try the spicy Parmesan version. Or enjoy aromatic fennel–black pepper breadsticks.

1 Adjust oven rack to middle position and heat oven to 450 degrees. Line rimmed baking sheet with parchment paper. Stretch and roll dough into 8 by 5-inch rectangle on lightly floured counter. Transfer dough to prepared sheet and reshape as needed.

2 Combine thyme, oregano, granulated garlic, salt, and pepper in bowl. Brush top of dough with melted butter and sprinkle with herb mixture. Using bench scraper or chef's knife, cut dough crosswise at 1-inch intervals to create eight 5-inch breadsticks; do not separate breadsticks.

3 Bake breadsticks until golden brown, 10 to 12 minutes. Transfer sheet to wire rack and let cool for 5 minutes. Pull breadsticks apart at seams and serve warm.

individual honey-thyme monkey breads

makes 4 breads • **total time** 50 minutes

2 tablespoons unsalted butter, melted, divided

2 tablespoons honey, divided

1 tablespoon minced fresh thyme

¼ teaspoon table salt

¼ teaspoon pepper

12 ounces refrigerated canned biscuit dough, separated into individual biscuits

---

pan swap

This recipe can be made in a 4-cup, 6-cup, or 12-cup muffin tin, or in four 4- to 8-ounce ramekins placed on a rimmed baking sheet.

---

bake in your air fryer

Place 4-cup muffin tin, or ramekins spaced evenly apart, in air-fryer basket. Place basket in air fryer, set temperature to 300 degrees, and bake for 20 to 22 minutes.

why this recipe works Monkey bread—the fun pull-apart pastry made of small pieces of dough dunked in butter and sugar and baked in a Bundt pan—is made to serve a crowd. But even more fun is having an interactive treat all for oneself. A can of refrigerated biscuit dough yields the right amount to make a smaller batch of four monkey breads in a muffin tin. For a savory-sweet spin on the traditional ingredients, we use honey and fresh thyme, which make these perfect at any meal, or as an anytime snack. We also include a more traditional version, with brown sugar and pumpkin spice, as well as a supersavory version with poppy seeds, Parmesan, and minced dried onion. We developed this recipe using one 12-ounce canister of biscuit dough. If your biscuits come in a slightly larger canister, simply add the extra dough pieces in step 2 and create a fifth monkey bread; increase the flavorings accordingly.

1 Adjust oven rack to middle position and heat oven to 375 degrees. Spray 4 cups of muffin tin with vegetable oil spray. Combine 1 tablespoon melted butter, 1 tablespoon honey, thyme, salt, and pepper in medium bowl.

2 Cut each biscuit into 8 pieces. Add biscuit pieces to butter mixture and toss to coat, separating any pieces that stick together. Divide biscuit pieces evenly among prepared muffin cups, gently pressing biscuit pieces into cup. Bake monkey breads until tops are golden brown, 15 to 17 minutes.

3 Combine remaining 1 tablespoon melted butter and remaining 1 tablespoon honey in small bowl. Let monkey breads cool in muffin tin on wire rack for 10 minutes. Transfer monkey breads to wire rack, drizzle with butter mixture, and serve warm.

individual onion, poppy seed, and parmesan monkey breads

Omit honey and thyme and reduce salt to ⅛ teaspoon. Increase butter in step 1 to 2 tablespoons and add 2 tablespoons minced dried onion and 1 tablespoon poppy seeds to butter mixture. After tossing biscuit pieces with butter mixture, add ½ cup finely grated Parmesan cheese and toss to coat.

individual pumpkin spice monkey breads

Omit honey, thyme, and pepper and reduce salt to ⅛ teaspoon. Increase butter in step 1 to 2 tablespoons and add 3 tablespoons packed brown sugar and 1 teaspoon pumpkin pie spice.

popovers

makes 6 popovers • **total time** 1 hour

1¼ cups (6¾ ounces) bread flour

¾ teaspoon table salt

1½ cups warm 2 percent low-fat milk (110 degrees)

3 large eggs

---

pan swap

Recipe works best in a 6-cup popover pan, but you can substitute a 12-cup muffin tin, distributing batter evenly among 12 cups; start checking for doneness after 25 minutes.

why this recipe works Bronzed and crisp on the outside, lush and custardy on the inside, popovers are a tempting treat, but one that you might be tempted to reserve for company. But thanks to their short ingredient list and speedy prep, you can easily whip up this small batch anytime. A few tricks keep this recipe fuss-free and failproof: Bread flour gives the batter extra gluten-forming proteins so that it's stretchy enough to accommodate the expanding steam—that's what creates that magical "pop." Warm milk jump-starts the rise. And we grease the pan very lightly, which allows the batter to climb up the sides of the cups. Baking at a moderately hot 400 degrees means we don't need to adjust the oven temperature partway through, a common popover step. This batter comes together quickly, so start heating the oven before gathering your ingredients and equipment. Whole or skim milk can be used in place of the low-fat milk. Do not open the oven during the first 30 minutes of baking; if possible, use the oven window and light to monitor the popovers. Serve with salted butter.

1 Adjust oven rack to middle position and heat oven to 400 degrees. Spray cups of popover pan with vegetable oil spray. Using paper towel, wipe out cups, leaving thin film of oil on bottom and sides.

2 Whisk flour and salt together in 8-cup liquid measuring cup or medium bowl. Add milk and eggs and whisk until mostly smooth (some small lumps are OK). Distribute batter evenly among prepared cups in popover pan. Bake until popovers are lofty and deep golden brown all over, 40 to 45 minutes. Serve hot. (Leftover popovers can be stored in zipper-lock bag at room temperature for up to 2 days; reheat directly on middle rack of 300-degree oven for 5 minutes.)

fresh-corn cornbread

makes 1 small loaf • **total time** 55 minutes, plus 20 minutes cooling

⅔ cup (3⅓ ounces) coarse-ground cornmeal

½ cup (2½ ounces) all-purpose flour

1 tablespoon sugar

¾ teaspoon baking powder

⅛ teaspoon baking soda

½ teaspoon table salt

1–2 ears corn, kernels cut from cobs (1 cup)

3 tablespoons unsalted butter, cut into 3 pieces, divided

½ cup buttermilk

1 large egg, lightly beaten

---

pan swap

We prefer to use a well-seasoned cast-iron skillet, but you can use any ovensafe 8-inch skillet. Alternatively, you can use a 6-inch cake pan; in step 3, add 1 tablespoon of butter to the pan and place it in the oven until butter melts, about 2 minutes.

why this recipe works Serving warm cornbread from a small cast-iron skillet is an inviting treat for two (or a few), made even more inviting when the bread is bursting with corn flavor. We like to add fresh corn for flavor that stands out, but instead of tossing kernels into the batter, which can create unpleasant gummy pockets, we fold in a puree of fresh corn. We found that using a coarse-ground cornmeal not only bolsters that full flavor but also provides a heartier crumb. Just a little sugar in the batter keeps the bread moist. Frozen corn will also work here; add 2 tablespoons water to the blender with the corn.

1 Adjust oven rack to middle position and heat oven to 400 degrees. Whisk cornmeal, flour, sugar, baking powder, baking soda, and salt together in medium bowl; set aside.

2 Process corn in blender until smooth, about 2 minutes, scraping down sides of blender jar as needed. Transfer to small saucepan and cook over medium heat, stirring constantly, until very thick, deep yellow, and reduced to ¼ cup, 5 to 8 minutes. Off heat, whisk in 2 tablespoons butter until melted. Whisk in buttermilk and egg until combined. Using rubber spatula, gently fold corn mixture into cornmeal mixture until just combined.

3 Melt remaining 1 tablespoon butter in 8-inch cast-iron skillet over medium heat. Scrape batter into hot skillet and carefully spread into even layer. Transfer skillet to oven and bake until cornbread is golden brown and toothpick inserted in center comes out clean, 20 to 25 minutes.

4 Let cornbread cool in skillet on wire rack for 5 minutes. Being careful of hot skillet handle, remove cornbread from skillet, return to rack, and let cool for 20 minutes. Cut into wedges and serve.

cheese bread with feta and nigella

makes 1 mini loaf • **total time** 1 hour, plus 25 minutes cooling

¾ cup (3¾ ounces) plus
   2 tablespoons all-purpose flour

1 teaspoon baking powder

¾ teaspoon nigella seeds, divided

¼ teaspoon table salt

¼ teaspoon dried mint

   Pinch pepper

3 ounces feta cheese, crumbled
   (¾ cup)

1 scallion, minced

¼ cup milk

3 tablespoons sour cream

1 large egg

1 tablespoon unsalted butter,
   melted

---

pan swap

Recipe can be made using 4 cups of
a muffin tin or four 4-ounce ramekins
placed on a rimmed baking sheet; bake
for 25 to 30 minutes.

---

bake in your air fryer

Place loaf pan, 4-cup muffin tin, or
ramekins, spaced evenly apart, in air-fryer
basket. Place basket in air fryer, set
temperature to 300 degrees, and bake
for 40 to 45 minutes for loaf or 30 to
35 minutes for muffins.

why this recipe works Quick breads are a perfect way to have a baked treat without yeast, kneading, or putting in a whole lot of time or work. And they work equally well in a mini-loaf pan, muffin tin, or ramekins (or even mini Bundt pans if you want). This savory quick bread starts with a whisk-and-stir batter leavened with baking powder and made tender with sour cream. Adding a generous amount of crumbled feta cheese gives the bread more satisfying richness and inserts brininess and tang into every bite. Dried mint is a fitting pairing and provides fresh flavor. We also stir in nigella seeds, tiny black seeds that have an allium-like flavor and are traditional in many breads of the Mediterranean and Asia. To enhance nigella's flavor, we add minced scallion. Eat this bread slightly warm to enjoy the still-soft crumbles of cheese.

1 Adjust oven rack to middle position and heat oven to 375 degrees. Spray 5½ by 3-inch loaf pan with vegetable oil spray. Whisk flour, baking powder, ½ teaspoon nigella seeds, salt, mint, and pepper together in medium bowl. Fold in feta and scallion until cheese is coated with flour mixture. In separate bowl, whisk milk, sour cream, egg, and melted butter until smooth. Using rubber spatula, fold milk mixture into flour mixture until just combined. (Batter will be heavy and thick; do not overmix.)

2 Scrape batter into prepared pan. Smooth top and sprinkle with remaining ¼ teaspoon nigella seeds. Bake until loaf is golden brown and toothpick inserted in center comes out with few moist crumbs attached, 35 to 40 minutes.

3 Let loaf cool in pan on wire rack for 5 minutes. Remove loaf from pan and let cool on rack for 25 minutes. Serve.

banana bread

makes 1 mini loaf • **total time** 50 minutes, plus 25 minutes cooling

½ cup (2¾ ounces) bread flour

1 teaspoon baking powder

⅛ teaspoon baking soda

⅛ teaspoon table salt

1–2 very ripe bananas, peeled and mashed coarse (½ cup)

1 large egg white

¼ cup (1¾ ounces) sugar

2 tablespoons vegetable oil

¾ teaspoon vanilla extract

¼ cup chopped toasted walnuts or pecans

---

pan swap

Recipe can be made using 4 cups of a muffin tin or four 4-ounce ramekins placed on a rimmed baking sheet; bake for 15 to 20 minutes.

---

bake in your air fryer

Place loaf pan, 4-cup muffin tin, or ramekins, spaced evenly apart, in air-fryer basket. Place basket in air fryer, set temperature to 300 degrees, and bake for 30 to 35 minutes for loaf or 15 to 20 minutes for muffins.

why this recipe works Lots of banana bread recipes are touted as a way to "use up" languishing bananas, but when do you actually have a bunch of ripe bananas? Our small-batch recipe makes one small loaf that is full of banana flavor from just 1 or 2 bananas. To prevent the bananas from weighing down the crumb and making the bread dense or gummy, we use bread flour instead of all-purpose flour; its higher protein content not only makes it more absorbent but also provides extra structure so our bread has a uniformly light crumb. Using a full teaspoon of baking powder ensures our mini loaf gets nice height in the oven. Try our date variation that's bold with warm spices and toffee-like dates, or indulge in our chocolate variation.

1 Adjust oven rack to middle position and heat oven to 375 degrees. Spray 5½ by 3-inch loaf pan with vegetable oil spray. Whisk flour, baking powder, baking soda, and salt together in bowl. In medium bowl, whisk bananas, egg white, sugar, oil, and vanilla until combined. Whisk flour mixture into banana mixture until just combined. Stir in walnuts.

2 Scrape batter into prepared pan and smooth top. Bake until loaf is dark golden brown and toothpick inserted in center comes out with few moist crumbs attached, 25 to 30 minutes.

3 Let loaf cool in pan for 5 minutes. Remove loaf from pan and let cool on rack for 25 minutes. Serve.

variations

chocolate banana bread

Add ¾ ounce grated bittersweet chocolate to flour mixture.

date banana bread

Add ¼ teaspoon ground allspice and ⅛ teaspoon ground cardamom to flour mixture. Reduce walnuts to 2 tablespoons and add 2 tablespoons chopped dates to batter with nuts.

zucchini bread

makes 1 mini loaf • **total time** 1 hour, plus 25 minutes cooling

½ zucchini (4 ounces)

½ cup (2¾ ounces) bread flour

½ teaspoon baking powder

⅛ teaspoon baking soda

¼ teaspoon ground cinnamon

¼ teaspoon ground allspice

⅛ teaspoon table salt

½ cup (3½ ounces) sugar

1 large egg

1 tablespoon unsalted butter, melted

1 tablespoon plain yogurt

1 teaspoon lemon juice

¼ cup chopped toasted walnuts or pecans

---

pan swap
Recipe can be made using 4 cups of a muffin tin or four 4-ounce ramekins placed on a rimmed baking sheet; bake for 20 to 25 minutes.

---

bake in your air fryer
Place loaf pan, 4-cup muffin tin, or ramekins, spaced evenly apart, in air-fryer basket. Place basket in air fryer, set temperature to 300 degrees, and bake for about 35 minutes for loaf or 20 to 25 minutes for muffins.

why this recipe works No matter the size of the loaf, most zucchini breads face a common downfall: a dense, soggy texture. So although this recipe uses just half a squash, we carefully squeeze it dry in a dish towel to get rid of excess moisture. The bonus is that this step also intensifies the zucchini flavor for a better-tasting bread. Another fighter: bread flour. Using it instead of all-purpose flour gives the loaf a better gluten structure and therefore a taller rise and lighter crumb. A tablespoon of butter adds richness, and modest amounts of cinnamon and allspice perk up the flavor without taking over. Yogurt and lemon juice add tang. Finally, for nutty flavor in every bite, we stir toasted chopped nuts into the batter.

1 Adjust oven rack to middle position and heat oven to 375 degrees. Spray 5½ by 3-inch loaf pan with vegetable oil spray. Shred zucchini on large holes of box grater. Squeeze shredded zucchini in clean dish towel or several layers of paper towels until very dry.

2 Whisk flour, baking powder, baking soda, cinnamon, allspice, and salt together in bowl. In medium bowl, whisk sugar, egg, melted butter, yogurt, and lemon juice together until smooth. Stir in shredded zucchini until combined, then stir in flour mixture until just combined. Stir in walnuts.

3 Scrape batter into prepared pan and smooth top. Bake until loaf is golden brown and toothpick inserted into center comes out clean, 30 to 35 minutes.

4 Let loaf cool in pan for 5 minutes. Remove loaf from pan and let cool on rack for 25 minutes. Serve.

cocoa zucchini bread with cherries

Substitute ¾ teaspoon unsweetened cocoa powder for cinnamon and pinch ground clove for allspice. Substitute chopped dried cherries for walnuts.

orange zucchini bread with pistachios

Substitute ¾ teaspoon grated orange zest for cinnamon and ground cardamom for allspice. Substitute pistachios for walnuts.

brown soda bread

makes 1 small loaf • **total time** 1 hour, plus 30 minutes cooling

1 cup (5 ounces) all-purpose flour

¾ cup (4⅛ ounces) whole-wheat flour

¼ cup toasted wheat germ

1½ tablespoons sugar

¾ teaspoon table salt

½ teaspoon baking powder

½ teaspoon baking soda

¾ cup plus 2 tablespoons buttermilk

1½ tablespoons unsalted butter, melted, divided

variations

brown soda bread with currants and caraway

Stir ½ cup dried currants and 1½ teaspoons caraway seeds into flour mixture before stirring in buttermilk mixture.

brown soda bread with walnuts and cacao nibs

Stir ½ cup chopped toasted walnuts and 3 tablespoons cacao nibs into flour mixture before stirring in buttermilk mixture.

why this recipe works Brown soda bread might not be the most commonly made quick bread. We think that should change. Still warm from the oven and slathered with butter, it's a welcome start to the day, or a mid-afternoon snack that is perfect alongside a cup of tea. To make a small-scale brown soda bread with good wheaty flavor—and without a gummy, dense texture—we found the right ratio of whole-wheat to all-purpose flour. Toasted wheat germ bumps up the sweet, nutty flavor of the whole wheat and adds texture. Baking powder, in addition to the traditional baking soda, guarantees a hearty—not heavy—loaf. Our bread has a touch of sugar and a few tablespoons of butter so it's both wholesome and delicious. We brush a portion of the melted butter on the loaf after baking to give it a rich crust.

1 Adjust oven rack to middle position and heat oven to 375 degrees. Line rimmed baking sheet with parchment paper. Whisk all-purpose flour, whole-wheat flour, wheat germ, sugar, salt, baking powder, and baking soda together in medium bowl. Combine buttermilk and 1 tablespoon melted butter in 1-cup liquid measuring cup. Using wooden spoon or rubber spatula, stir buttermilk mixture into flour mixture until dough just comes together.

2 Turn dough onto lightly floured counter and, using your lightly floured hands, gently knead until dough comes together, about 30 seconds. Pat dough into 5-inch round and transfer to prepared sheet. Using sharp serrated knife, make ¼-inch-deep cross about 3 inches long on top of loaf. Bake until skewer inserted in center comes out clean and loaf registers 195 degrees, 35 to 40 minutes, rotating sheet halfway through baking.

3 Brush loaf with remaining ½ tablespoon melted butter, transfer to wire rack, and let cool for 30 minutes. Serve warm or at room temperature.

no-knead mini country boule

makes 1 mini loaf • **total time** 1¼ hours, plus 12 hours rising and cooling

1 cup (5½ ounces) King Arthur bread flour

½ cup (2¾ ounces) whole-wheat or spelt flour

¾ teaspoon table salt

⅛ teaspoon instant or rapid-rise yeast

½ cup water, room temperature

¼ cup mild-flavored lager, room temperature

1½ teaspoons distilled white vinegar

why this recipe works You may have never considered making a bakery-style rustic bread—one with a deep golden, crackly crust and chewy crumb—at home for just a couple people. But the no-knead method is ideal for preparing a small-scale boule. No-knead breads, including this one, rely on a very wet dough, a long rest, and some structure-building folds to slowly develop a strong gluten network—one that can support a dramatic open crumb initiated by baking the bread in the humid environment of a preheated Dutch oven. Adding whole-wheat flour ups this loaf's rustic appeal, providing nutty flavor and hearty texture. We prefer King Arthur brand bread flour in this recipe; the dough will be slightly stickier if you use a lower-protein bread flour. While we prefer the flavor that beer adds, you can substitute an equal amount of water. You will need a Dutch oven with a bottom diameter of at least 8 inches for this recipe.

1 Whisk bread flour, whole-wheat flour, salt, and yeast together in large bowl. Using rubber spatula, fold water, beer, and vinegar into flour mixture, scraping up dry flour from bottom of bowl and pressing on dough, until all flour is incorporated (dough will be shaggy).

2 Cover bowl tightly with plastic wrap and let sit at room temperature for at least 8 hours or up to 18 hours.

3 Using greased bowl scraper or your wet fingertips, fold dough over itself by lifting and folding edge of dough toward middle and pressing to seal. Turn bowl 90 degrees and fold dough again; repeat turning bowl and folding dough 4 more times (for a total of 6 folds). Flip dough seam side down in bowl, cover with plastic, and let rest for 15 minutes.

4 Lay 18 by 12-inch sheet of parchment paper on counter and lightly spray with vegetable oil spray. Transfer dough seam side up onto lightly floured counter and pat into rough 6-inch circle using your lightly floured hands. Using bowl scraper or your floured finger-tips, lift and fold edge of dough toward center, pressing to seal. Repeat 5 more times (for a total of 6 folds), evenly spacing folds around circumference of dough. Press down on dough to seal, then use bench scraper to gently flip dough seam side down.

(continued)

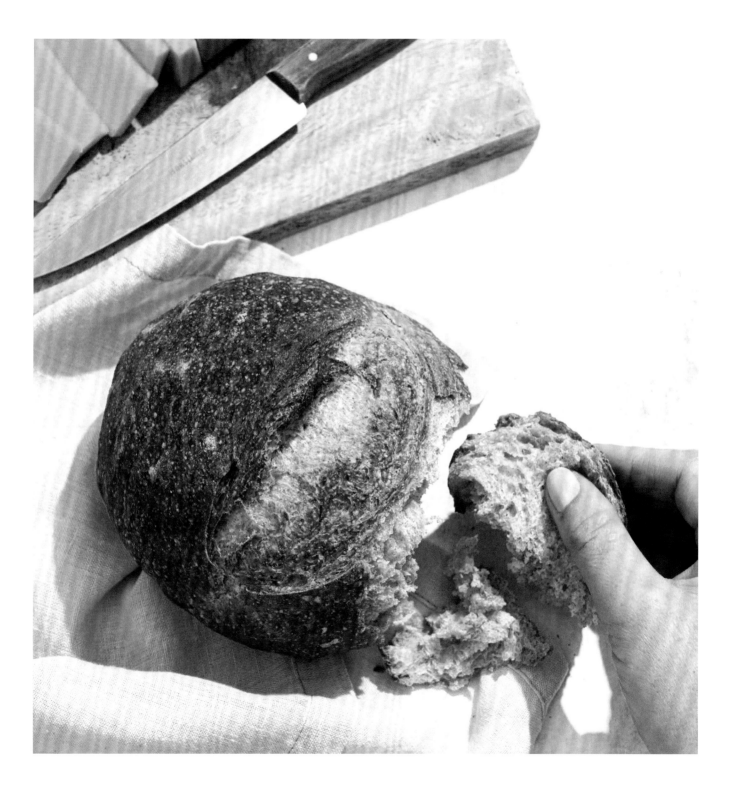

5   Using both hands, cup side of dough furthest away from you and pull dough toward you, keeping your pinky fingers and side of palm in contact with counter and applying slight pressure to dough as it drags to create tension. (If dough slides across surface of counter without rolling, remove excess flour. If dough sticks to counter or your hands, lightly sprinkle counter or hands with flour.) Rotate dough ball 90 degrees, reposition dough ball at top of counter, and repeat pulling dough until taut round ball forms, at least 4 more times. Using your floured hands or bench scraper, transfer dough seam side down to center of prepared parchment.

6   Cover dough with inverted large bowl. Let rise until dough has doubled in size and dough springs back minimally when poked gently with your finger, 1 to 2 hours.

7   Thirty minutes before baking, adjust oven rack to middle position, place Dutch oven with lid on rack and heat oven to 475 degrees. Using sharp knife or single-edge razor blade, make one 4-inch-long, $\frac{1}{2}$-inch-deep slash with swift, fluid motion along top of loaf. Working quickly, carefully remove hot pot from oven and, using parchment as sling, gently transfer parchment and loaf to hot pot. Reinforce scores on top of loaf, if needed, then cover pot and return to oven.

8   Reduce oven temperature to 425 degrees and bake loaf for 20 minutes. Remove lid and continue to bake until loaf is deep golden brown and registers at least 205 degrees, 10 to 15 minutes. Using parchment sling, carefully remove loaf from hot pot and transfer to wire rack; discard parchment. Let cool completely, about 3 hours, before slicing.

shaping a boule

1 Pat dough into rough 6-inch circle.

2 Lift and fold edges of dough toward center, pressing to seal. Flip dough seam side down.

3 Cup dough and pull toward you, keeping your pinky fingers and side of palm in contact with counter.

4 Rotate dough ball 90 degrees and repeat pulling dough until taut round ball forms, at least 4 more times.

from-the-freezer dinner rolls

makes 8 rolls • **total time** 1½ hours, plus 3¼ hours rising, cooling, and freezing

flour paste

¼ cup water

1½ tablespoons bread flour

dough

½ cup milk, chilled

1⅓ cups (7⅓ ounces) bread flour

1 teaspoon instant or rapid-rise yeast

1 tablespoon sugar

½ teaspoon table salt

1 tablespoon unsalted butter, softened

Vegetable oil spray

---

bake in your air fryer

Space desired number of frozen rolls at least 1 inch apart in air-fryer basket. Place basket in air fryer, set temperature to 325 degrees, and bake for 12 to 14 minutes.

why this recipe works Parbaked buns that can go from the freezer to the oven to the plate in less than 15 minutes are a convenient solution for serving a few hot and fresh rolls for dinner. To create a tender, pillowy roll, we start the dough with a cooked flour paste called tangzhong. This helps pack in extra moisture so the rolls withstand their freezer stay. We bake the rolls at 300 degrees, just until they rise and set but are still pale. We cool and freeze the parbaked rolls on their baking sheet, then store in a zipper-lock bag in the freezer for up to six weeks. Just before dinner, bake the desired number of frozen rolls in a very hot oven (or toaster oven), and voilà—freshly baked rolls in the number you need in just 10 minutes. We strongly recommend weighing the flour for this recipe. The par-baked rolls are delicate, so don't handle them until they're fully frozen.

1 **For the flour paste:** Whisk water and flour in small bowl until no lumps remain. Microwave, whisking every 20 seconds, until mixture thickens to stiff, pasty consistency, 40 to 60 seconds.

2 **For the dough:** Whisk flour paste and milk in bowl of stand mixer until combined. Add flour and yeast. Fit mixer with dough hook and mix on low speed until all flour is moistened, about 2 minutes. Let rest for 15 minutes.

3 Add sugar and salt and knead on medium-low speed for 5 minutes. With mixer running, add butter and mix until dough is smooth and elastic, about 5 minutes.

4 Transfer dough to lightly floured counter and knead by hand to form ball. Place dough seam side down in lightly greased large bowl or container. Lightly spray surface of dough with oil spray and cover tightly with plastic wrap. Let rise until doubled in volume, about 1 hour.

5 Line rimmed baking sheet with parchment paper. Press down on dough to deflate. Transfer dough to clean counter and pat into 4 by 2-inch rectangle of even thickness. Cut dough into 8 equal pieces (4 rows by 2 rows) and cover loosely with greased plastic. Working with 1 piece of dough at a time (keep remaining pieces covered), form into rough ball by stretching dough around your thumb and pinching edges together so that top is smooth. Place ball seam side down on counter and, using your cupped hand, drag in small circles until dough feels taut and round. Arrange dough balls seam side down on prepared sheet, spaced at least 1½ inches apart. Cover loosely with greased plastic and let rise until almost doubled in size, 45 minutes to 1 hour.

6 Adjust oven rack to middle position and heat oven to 300 degrees. Bake rolls until risen and register 170 to 175 degrees, 12 to 14 minutes (rolls will have little to no color).

7 Transfer sheet to wire rack and let cool completely, 30 to 45 minutes (rolls will wrinkle slightly). Transfer sheet to freezer and freeze rolls until solid, about 1 hour. Transfer rolls to zipper-lock bag and freeze for up to 6 weeks.

8 Adjust oven rack to middle position and heat oven to 425 degrees. Arrange desired number of frozen rolls on parchment-lined baking sheet, spaced at least 1½ inches apart, and bake until deep golden brown, 8 to 10 minutes. Transfer rolls to wire rack and let cool for at least 5 minutes before serving.

shaping dinner rolls

1 Stretch dough around your thumb and pinch edges together to form rough ball.

2 Using your cupped hand, drag ball in small circles on counter until dough feels taut and round.

From-the-Freezer Dinner Rolls

No-Knead Whole-Wheat Dinner Rolls

no-knead whole-wheat dinner rolls

makes 4 rolls • **total time** 1¼ hours, plus 10 hours rising and cooling

1 cup (5½ ounces) King Arthur bread flour

½ cup (2¾ ounces) whole-wheat flour

¾ teaspoon table salt

⅛ teaspoon instant or rapid-rise yeast

½ cup water, room temperature

¼ cup mild-flavored lager, room temperature

1½ teaspoons distilled white vinegar

why this recipe works We adapted our no-knead bread method to make four perfect rustic rolls with earthy, nutty flavor from whole-wheat flour. While handling wet dough (characteristic of rustic and no-knead breads) can be a challenge, the small size of these rolls makes them easier to master than a large loaf. After you've tried the original, switch things up with our flavor variations by adding olives and herbs, or dried fruit and nuts. We prefer King Arthur brand bread flour in this recipe; the dough will be slightly stickier if you use a lower-protein bread flour. While we prefer the flavor that beer adds, you can substitute an equal amount of water. You will need a Dutch oven with a bottom diameter of at least 8 inches for this recipe.

1   Whisk bread flour, whole-wheat flour, salt, and yeast together in large bowl. Using rubber spatula, fold water, beer, and vinegar into flour mixture, scraping up dry flour from bottom of bowl and pressing on dough, until all flour is incorporated (dough will be shaggy).

2   Cover bowl tightly with plastic wrap and let sit at room temperature for at least 8 hours or up to 18 hours.

3   Using greased bowl scraper or your wet fingertips, fold dough over itself by lifting and folding edge of dough toward middle and pressing to seal. Turn bowl 90 degrees and fold dough again; repeat turning bowl and folding dough 4 more times (for a total of 6 folds). Flip dough seam side down in bowl, cover with plastic, and let rest for 15 minutes.

4   Lay 18 by 12-inch sheet of parchment paper on counter and, using marker, draw 7-inch circle in center of parchment. Flip parchment ink side down and spray lightly with vegetable oil spray.

variations

no-knead spelt, olive, and herb dinner rolls

Substitute 1 cup (5½ ounces) spelt flour for whole-wheat flour. Sprinkle 2 tablespoons chopped pitted brine-cured olives and ¼ teaspoon minced fresh rosemary, oregano, or thyme over dough before folding in step 3. Fold 4 times, then sprinkle additional 2 tablespoons chopped olives and additional ¼ teaspoon minced fresh rosemary, oregano, or thyme over dough and continue with remaining 4 folds.

no-knead whole-wheat fruit and nut rolls

Sprinkle 2 tablespoons chopped raisins, dried cherries, or dried cranberries and 2 tablespoons finely chopped toasted nuts over dough before folding in step 3. Fold 4 times, then sprinkle additional 2 tablespoons chopped dried fruit and 2 tablespoons finely chopped toasted nuts over dough and continue with remaining 4 folds.

5 Transfer dough seam side up to lightly floured counter and pat into rough 4-inch square using your lightly floured hands. Cut dough into 4 equal pieces and cover loosely with greased plastic. Working with 1 piece of dough at a time (keep remaining pieces covered), pat dough into 3-inch disk. Working around circumference of dough, fold edges of dough toward center until ball forms. Place ball seam side down on counter and, using your cupped hand, drag in small circles until dough feels taut and round. (Tackiness of dough against counter and circular motion should work dough into smooth, even ball, but if dough sticks to your hands, lightly dust top of dough with flour.)

6 Arrange dough balls evenly within circle on prepared parchment and cover with inverted large bowl. Let rise until dough has doubled in size and springs back minimally when poked gently with your finger, 1 to 2 hours.

7 Thirty minutes before baking, adjust oven rack to middle position, place Dutch oven with lid on rack, and heat oven to 475 degrees. Using sharp knife or single-edge razor blade, make one 1½-inch-long, ½-inch-deep slash with swift, fluid motion along top of each roll. Working quickly, carefully remove hot pot from oven and, using parchment as sling, gently transfer parchment and rolls to hot pot. Reinforce scores on top of rolls, if needed, then cover pot and return to oven.

8 Reduce oven temperature to 425 degrees and bake rolls for 20 minutes. Remove lid and continue to bake until rolls are deep golden brown and register at least 205 degrees, 10 to 15 minutes. Using parchment sling, carefully remove rolls from hot pot and transfer to wire rack; discard parchment. Let rolls cool completely, about 1 hour. Serve.

shaping no-knead dinner rolls

1 Pat dough into 3-inch disk.

2 Fold edges of dough toward center until ball forms.

3 Using your cupped hand, drag ball in small circles on counter until dough feels taut and round.

brioche hamburger buns

makes 4 buns • **total time** 1¼ hours, plus 2¾ hours rising and cooling

- 1¼ cups (6¾ ounces) bread flour
- 1 teaspoon instant or rapid-rise yeast
- ⅓ cup water, room temperature
- 2 large eggs, divided, 1 lightly beaten
- 4 teaspoons sugar
- ¾ teaspoon table salt
- 4 tablespoons unsalted butter, cut into 4 pieces and softened
- ½ teaspoon sesame seeds (optional)

why this recipe works If you frequently find yourself with more buns than burgers due to standard package sizes, give this small batch of brioche burger buns a go. They're the quintessential bun: perfectly glossy and amber-colored, with a soft, feathery interior that's just rich enough. To support the additions of butter to the dough and encourage the buns to rise tall, we use bread flour to create a strong gluten network. Letting the dough rest before adding the sugar and salt also helps the flour fully hydrate, a necessary step for maximum gluten formation. Simply cupping and rolling portions of the risen dough against the counter pulls the dough into taut balls that, when pressed with the bottom of a measuring cup, bake into the perfect-size hamburger buns. An equal weight of all-purpose flour can be substituted for the bread flour, but the buns won't be as tall.

1 Whisk flour and yeast together in bowl of stand mixer, then add water and unbeaten egg. Fit mixer with dough hook and mix on low speed until all flour is moistened, about 2 minutes. Let rest for 15 minutes.

2 Add sugar and salt and knead on medium-low speed until incorporated, about 2 minutes. Increase speed to medium and, with mixer running, add butter 1 piece at a time, allowing each piece to incorporate before adding next, about 3 minutes total, scraping down bowl and dough hook as needed. Continue to knead on medium speed until dough is elastic and pulls away cleanly from sides of bowl, about 15 minutes. Transfer dough to greased large bowl or container. Cover tightly with plastic wrap and let rise until doubled in volume, 1 to 1 ½ hours.

3 Line rimmed baking sheet with parchment paper. Transfer dough to clean counter and pat into rough 4-inch square. Cut dough into 4 equal pieces and cover loosely with greased plastic. Working with 1 piece of dough at a time (keep remaining pieces covered), form into rough ball by stretching dough around your thumb and pinching edges together so that top is smooth. Place ball seam side down on counter and, using your cupped hand, drag in small circles until dough feels taut and round. Arrange dough balls seam side down on prepared sheet, spaced at least 1½ inches apart. Using greased bottom of dry measuring cup, press dough balls to 3-inch diameter, about ¾ inch thick. Pop any air bubbles in dough balls with tip of paring knife. Cover loosely with greased plastic and let rise until almost doubled in size, about 1 hour.

4 Adjust oven rack to middle position and heat oven to 350 degrees. Brush tops and sides of dough balls with beaten egg (you do not need to use all of it) and sprinkle tops with sesame seeds, if using. Bake until buns are deep golden brown and register 205 to 210 degrees, 18 to 20 minutes, rotating sheet halfway through baking. Transfer sheet to wire rack and let cool completely, about 45 minutes. Serve.

bolos lêvedos

makes 4 muffins • **total time** 1¼ hours, plus 2¼ hours rising and cooling

flour paste

⅓   cup water

2   tablespoons all-purpose flour

dough

3   tablespoons whole milk

1   large egg

2   tablespoons unsalted butter, cut into 2 pieces and softened

1½ cups (7½ ounces) all-purpose flour plus extra for shaping

½   teaspoon instant or rapid-rise yeast

¼   cup (1¾ ounces) sugar

½   teaspoon table salt

½   teaspoon vegetable oil

---

bake in your air fryer

After step 6, place browned muffins, spaced evenly apart, in air-fryer basket. (Depending on size of air fryer, you may need to bake muffins in batches.) Place basket in air fryer, set temperature to 275 degrees, and bake for 8 to 10 minutes.

why this recipe works These Portuguese "cakes" (bolos means "cakes" and lêvedos means "leavened"), originally from the Azores, may bring to mind an English muffin, but they're richer, finely textured, and slightly sweet. They're also versatile, traditionally served for breakfast in their home country; on our shores, they've also been repurposed as hamburger buns. To make them extra tender, we incorporate tangzhong, a flour paste, which also keeps the baked buns fresh for longer, so you don't have to worry about having a few left over—what's lunch today is breakfast tomorrow. To achieve the characteristic color and shape, we brown our cakes in a skillet and finish cooking them in the oven. For a delicious breakfast, split the bolos in half and toast, then slather with butter, or fill them with your favorite sandwich fixings for lunch or dinner.

1   **For the flour paste:** Whisk water and flour in small bowl until no lumps remain. Microwave, whisking every 20 seconds, until mixture thickens to stiff, pasty consistency, 40 to 60 seconds.

2   **For the dough:** Whisk flour paste and milk in bowl of stand mixer until combined. Whisk in egg and butter until fully incorporated. Add flour and yeast. Fit mixer with dough hook and mix on low speed until all flour is moistened, about 2 minutes. Let rest for 15 minutes.

3   Add sugar and salt and knead on low speed until incorporated, about 1 minute. Increase speed to medium and knead until dough is elastic and pulls away from sides of bowl but still sticks to bottom (dough will be sticky), about 8 minutes. Transfer dough to greased large bowl or container. Cover tightly with plastic wrap and let rise until doubled in volume, 1 to 1½ hours.

4   Transfer dough to clean counter and pat into rough 4-inch square. Cut dough into 4 equal pieces (about 4 ounces each) and cover loosely with greased plastic. Working with 1 piece of dough at a time (keep remaining pieces covered), form into rough ball by stretching dough around your thumb and pinching edges together so that top is smooth. Place ball seam side down on counter and, using your cupped hand, drag in small circles until dough feels taut and round. Cover balls loosely with greased plastic and let rest for 15 minutes.

5   Line rimmed baking sheet with parchment paper. Sprinkle ¼ cup flour on counter. Working with 1 dough ball at a time, turn dough ball in flour and press with your hand to flatten into 3½- to 4-inch diameter. Transfer dough disks to prepared sheet, spaced at least 1½ inches apart. Lay second sheet of parchment over dough disks, then place second rimmed baking sheet on top to keep disks flat during second rise. Let rise for 30 minutes.

6   Adjust oven rack to middle position and heat oven to 350 degrees. Heat oil in 12-inch nonstick skillet over medium-low heat until shimmering. Using paper towels, carefully wipe out oil from skillet. Transfer dough disks to skillet and cook until deeply browned, 2 to 4 minutes per side. Return toasted disks to sheet.

7   Bake until muffins register 190 degrees, 8 to 10 minutes. Transfer muffins to wire rack and let cool for 30 minutes. Serve.

from-the-freezer cinnamon buns

makes 6 buns • **total time** 1¾ hours, plus 1 hour 40 minutes rising and freezing

flour paste

- ⅓ cup water
- 2 tablespoons bread flour

dough

- ⅓ cup milk
- 1 large egg yolk
- 1½ cups (8¼ ounces) bread flour
- 1 teaspoon instant or rapid-rise yeast
- 1½ tablespoons granulated sugar
- ¾ teaspoon table salt
- 3 tablespoons unsalted butter, softened
- Vegetable oil spray

filling

- ¾ cup packed (5¼ ounces) light brown sugar
- 2¼ teaspoons ground cinnamon
- ⅛ teaspoon table salt
- 2 tablespoons unsalted butter, melted

why this recipe works It's a familiar scene: a casserole of fused pillowy warm cinnamon buns, brilliantly frosted and ready for lots of hungry guests to pull apart. It's hard to beat fresh-from-the-oven buns, but what about when you don't have a host of hungry guests? That's what led us to develop cinnamon buns that you could store in the freezer and then bake when you need them. We shape and fill individual pieces of dough and freeze them until they're solid. When it's time to bake, we fashion aluminum foil cups to hold the frozen buns so we can bake off just the number we want. (For a bakery look, you can make a parchment-paper cup to fit inside the foil; remove the foil cups before serving to reveal the parchment wrapping.) We developed this recipe using a 4.5-quart tilt-head stand mixer; we recommend using a mixer with a capacity of 5 quarts or less. If you use a larger stand mixer, note that kneading times will be longer and may not follow given visual cues. You can bake the cinnamon buns without freezing if you prefer: Place all the buns in the foil cups as instructed in step 7, cover loosely with greased plastic, and let rise until puffy, 40 minutes to 1 hour. Proceed with baking as instructed, reducing the bake time to 25 to 30 minutes. Drizzle or frost with Sour Cream Glaze (recipe follows).

1   **For the flour paste:** Whisk water and flour in small bowl until no lumps remain. Microwave, whisking every 20 seconds, until mixture thickens to stiff, pasty consistency, 40 to 60 seconds.

2   **For the dough:** Whisk flour paste and milk in bowl of stand mixer until smooth. Add egg yolk and whisk until incorporated. Add flour and yeast. Fit mixer with dough hook and mix on low speed until all flour is moistened, about 2 minutes. Let rest for 15 minutes.

3   Add granulated sugar and salt and knead on medium speed for 5 minutes. With mixer running, add butter and mix until butter is incorporated and dough clears sides of bowl (dough will stick to bottom of bowl), 5 to 7 minutes, scraping down dough hook and sides of bowl halfway through mixing.

(continued)

sour cream glaze

makes *about 2 tablespoons (enough for 2 buns)*
total time *5 minutes*

This recipe can be easily doubled (or tripled).

- 6 tablespoons (1½ ounces) confectioners' sugar
- 1 tablespoon sour cream
- ¼ teaspoon vanilla extract

Whisk all ingredients together in bowl. Spoon over warm buns.

4 Transfer dough to clean counter and knead by hand to form ball. Place dough seam side down in lightly greased large bowl or container. Lightly spray surface of dough with oil spray and cover tightly with plastic wrap. Let rise until just doubled in volume, 40 minutes to 1 hour.

5 **For the filling:** Combine brown sugar, cinnamon, and salt in bowl. Transfer dough to lightly floured counter; press gently but firmly to expel air. Working from center toward edge, pat and roll dough to form 12-inch square. Brush melted butter evenly over dough, leaving 1-inch border along top edge. Sprinkle cinnamon sugar over butter, then smooth into even layer with your hand and gently press mixture into dough to adhere.

6 Roll dough away from you into tight cylinder; pinch seam to seal. Roll cylinder seam side down; using serrated knife, cut into 6 equal pieces. Transfer buns cut side down to parchment-lined rimmed baking sheet and cover with plastic; freeze buns until solid, at least 1 hour. Transfer buns to zipper-lock bag and store in freezer for up to 1 month.

7 Adjust oven rack to middle position and heat oven to 350 degrees. Cut one 6-inch square of aluminum foil for each cinnamon bun you plan on baking. Working with 1 square at a time, press into cup of standard muffin tin, creasing foil to form cup that holds its shape when removed from tin. Spray interiors of foil cups with oil spray and place on parchment-lined sheet, spacing at least 2 inches apart. Place 1 frozen bun in each foil cup and bake until golden brown and center of dough registers at least 200 degrees, 34 to 38 minutes.

8 Transfer sheet to wire rack and let buns cool for 5 minutes. Remove foil from buns and serve warm.

preparing cinnamon buns for the oven

1 Cut one 6-inch square of aluminum foil for each cinnamon bun you plan on baking.

2 Press desired number of foil squares into muffin tin, creasing foil to create cups that hold their shape.

3 Remove foil cups from muffin tin, spray interiors with oil spray, and space 2 inches apart on parchment-lined sheet.

4 Place 1 frozen bun in each foil cup and bake.

chapter eight
flatbreads and pizzas

flour tortillas

makes 6 tortillas • **total time** 40 minutes, plus 30 minutes chilling

1	cup (5 ounces) all-purpose flour
¾	teaspoon table salt
2½	tablespoons vegetable shortening, cut into ½-inch pieces
6	tablespoons warm tap water
1	teaspoon vegetable oil

pan swap

Recipe can be made using a carbon-steel or cast-iron skillet; be sure to adjust heat as needed to prevent scorching.

why this recipe works Store-bought tortillas are often packaged in bags of a dozen (or more), which can make it hard to use them up when you're cooking for two. When you make your own, you've got a small batch of fresh tortillas that taste worlds better than store-bought. And it's easy to do: The dough for these flour tortillas comes together quickly, and resting it makes it a cinch to roll out. Each tortilla takes just a couple minutes to cook in a hot skillet. Lard can be substituted for the shortening, if desired.

1   Combine flour and salt in medium bowl. Using your fingers, rub shortening into flour mixture until mixture resembles coarse meal. Stir in warm water until combined.

2   Transfer dough to counter and knead briefly to form smooth, cohesive ball. Divide dough into 6 equal portions, about 2 tablespoons each; roll each into smooth 1-inch ball between your hands. Transfer to plate, cover with plastic wrap, and refrigerate until dough is firm, at least 30 minutes or up to 2 days.

3   Cut six 6-inch squares of parchment paper. Roll 1 dough ball into 6-inch round on lightly floured counter. Transfer to parchment square and set aside. Repeat with remaining dough balls, stacking tortillas on top of each other with parchment squares between.

4   Heat oil in 12-inch nonstick skillet over medium heat until shimmering. Wipe out skillet with paper towels, leaving thin film of oil on bottom. Place 1 tortilla in skillet and cook until surface begins to bubble and bottom is spotty brown, about 1 minute. (If not browned after 1 minute, turn up heat slightly. If browning too quickly, reduce heat.) Flip and cook until spotty brown on second side, 30 to 45 seconds. Transfer to plate and cover with clean dish towel. Repeat with remaining tortillas. (Cooled tortillas can be layered between parchment paper, covered with plastic wrap, and refrigerated for up to 3 days. To serve, discard plastic, cover tortillas with clean dish towel, and microwave at 50 percent power until heated through, about 20 seconds.)

corn tortillas

makes 6 tortillas · **total time** 40 minutes

1 cup (4 ounces) masa harina

½ teaspoon table salt

⅔–1 cup warm water

1 tablespoon vegetable oil, divided

---

pan swap

Recipe can be made using a carbon-steel or cast-iron skillet; adjust heat as needed to prevent scorching.

why this recipe works You don't need a tortilla press to make these scaled-down, no-fuss corn tortillas, so you can easily make just enough for one meal whenever tacos beckon. Once the masa dough is the right consistency, just roll it into balls and press them with your hands. Any slight irregularities are part of the charm of fresh homemade corn tortillas—along with their superior flavor. Pressing the tortillas with a spatula as they cook encourages them to puff, which gives them a light, fluffy texture.

1   Whisk masa harina and salt together in medium bowl. Stir in ⅔ cup warm water and 2 teaspoons oil with rubber spatula until combined. Using your hands, knead dough in bowl until it is soft and tacky and has texture of Play-Doh. If necessary, add up to ⅓ cup more warm water, 1 tablespoon at a time, until proper texture is achieved. (You can test for proper hydration by gently flattening a golf ball–size piece of dough with your hands. If many large cracks form around edges, it is too dry.)

2   Divide dough into 6 equal portions, about a scant 3 tablespoons (1¾ ounces) each. Roll each portion into smooth ball between your hands. Transfer dough balls to plate and keep covered with damp paper towel.

3   Using your damp hands and working with 1 dough ball at a time, press dough ball between your palms into 3-inch disk; transfer to parchment paper. Press top of dough disk with your hand to flatten further while cupping circumference of dough disk with your other hand to prevent cracking. Rotate parchment as you press to create even, 5-inch-wide disk (it doesn't have to be perfectly round).

4   Heat remaining 1 teaspoon oil in 10-inch nonstick skillet over medium-high heat until just smoking. Wipe out skillet with paper towels, leaving thin film of oil on bottom. Carefully peel parchment away from dough disk and transfer tortilla to skillet. Cook until bottom begins to brown at edges, about 90 seconds.

5   Using thin spatula, flip tortilla and cook until second side is browned at edges, about 1 minute. Flip tortilla again and press firmly with spatula all over to encourage puffing, about 30 seconds. Transfer to tortilla warmer or wrap in damp dish towel to keep warm. Repeat with remaining dough balls, making sure to moisten your hands as needed to prevent dough from cracking and adjusting heat or removing skillet from heat as needed between tortillas. Serve. (Cooled tortillas can be layered between parchment paper, covered with plastic wrap, and refrigerated for up to 3 days. To serve, discard plastic, dip each tortilla in water, and reheat over medium heat in a dry nonstick skillet for about 30 seconds per side.)

chapatis

makes 4 chapatis • **total time** 40 minutes, plus 30 minutes resting

¾ cup (4⅛ ounces) whole-wheat flour

¾ cup (3¾ ounces) all-purpose flour

1 teaspoon table salt

½ cup warm water (110 degrees)

3 tablespoons plus 2 teaspoons vegetable oil, divided

---

pan swap

Recipe can be made using a carbon-steel skillet or nonstick skillet; adjust heat as needed to prevent scorching. For a nonstick skillet, in step 4, heat the ½ teaspoon oil over medium heat until shimmering, then wipe out skillet.

why this recipe works Chapatis are wheaty, unleavened Indian flatbreads often used as utensils for scooping up a number of sumptuous dishes. They're delicious fresh, so we like to make just four at a time. A finely ground hard wheat flour called atta is traditionally the ingredient of choice for chapatis. On its own, relatively coarse American whole-wheat flour doesn't make the best substitute, but combined with an equal amount of all-purpose flour yields tender, elastic, wheaty chapatis. A well-seasoned cast-iron skillet stands in nicely for the tava pan, but you can use another nonstick skillet.

1 Whisk whole-wheat flour, all-purpose flour, and salt together in bowl. Stir in water and 3 tablespoons oil until cohesive dough forms. Transfer dough to lightly floured counter and knead by hand to form smooth ball, about 1 minute.

2 Divide dough into 4 pieces and cover with plastic wrap. Working with 1 piece at a time (keep remaining pieces covered), form into ball by stretching dough around your thumbs and pinching edges together so that top is smooth. Place ball seam side down on clean counter and shape into smooth, taut ball. Place on plate seam side down. Cover with plastic wrap and let sit for 30 minutes. (Dough balls can be refrigerated for up to 3 days.)

3 Line rimmed baking sheet with parchment paper. Roll 1 dough ball into 9-inch round on lightly floured counter (keep remaining pieces covered). Transfer to prepared sheet and top with additional sheet of parchment. Repeat with remaining dough balls.

4 Heat 12-inch cast-iron skillet over medium heat for 3 minutes. Add ½ teaspoon oil to skillet, then use paper towels to carefully wipe out skillet, leaving thin film of oil on bottom; skillet should be just smoking.

5 Place 1 dough round in hot skillet and cook until dough is bubbly and bottom is browned in spots, about 2 minutes. Flip dough and press firmly with spatula all over to encourage puffing, cooking until puffed and second side is spotty brown, 1 to 2 minutes. Transfer to clean plate and cover with dish towel to keep warm. Repeat with remaining dough rounds and oil. Serve. (Cooled chapatis can be layered between parchment paper, stored in a zipper-lock bag, and refrigerated for up to 3 days or frozen for up to 3 months. To serve, stack chapatis on plate, cover with damp dish towel, and microwave until warm, 60 to 90 seconds.)

pan-grilled flatbreads

makes 4 flatbreads • **total time** 1¼ hours, plus 1½ to 2 hours rising

2½ cups (13¾ ounces) bread flour

¼ cup (1⅓ ounces) whole-wheat flour

2¼ teaspoons instant or rapid-rise yeast

1½ teaspoons table salt

1 cup water, room temperature

¼ cup plain whole-milk yogurt, room temperature

2 tablespoons extra-virgin olive oil, divided

2 teaspoons sugar

1½ tablespoons unsalted butter, melted, divided

Flake sea salt

---

pan swap

Recipe can be made using a carbon-steel skillet or nonstick skillet; adjust heat as needed to prevent scorching.

why this recipe works Inspired by the soft pillowy texture of naan, these flavorful, rustic, tender-chewy all-purpose flatbreads are easy enough to cook while dinner is in the works. To keep the flatbreads supple and prevent a tough crust, we mist each side with water, then cover the pan to trap steam and moisture. Brushing the finished breads with butter and sprinkling with sea salt adds flavor. We developed this recipe using a 4.5-quart stand mixer; if using a larger mixer you may need to increase mixing times. For efficiency, stretch the next ball of dough while each flatbread is cooking.

1 Whisk bread flour, whole-wheat flour, yeast, and table salt together in bowl of stand mixer. Whisk water, yogurt, 1 tablespoon oil, and sugar in 4-cup liquid measuring cup until sugar has dissolved. Using dough hook on low speed, slowly add water mixture to flour mixture and mix until cohesive dough starts to form and no dry flour remains, about 2 minutes, scraping down bowl as needed. Increase speed to medium-low and knead until dough is smooth and elastic and clears sides of bowl but sticks to bottom, about 8 minutes. Transfer dough to lightly floured counter and knead by hand to form smooth, round ball, about 30 seconds.

2 Place dough seam side down in lightly greased large bowl or container, cover with plastic wrap, and let rise until doubled in volume, 1½ to 2 hours.

3 Adjust oven rack to middle position and heat oven to 200 degrees. Transfer dough to clean counter, divide into quarters, and cover loosely with greased plastic. Working with 1 piece of dough at a time (keep remaining pieces covered), form into rough ball by stretching dough around your thumb and pinching edges together so that top is smooth. Place ball seam side down on clean counter and, using your cupped hand, drag in small circles until dough feels taut and round. Let balls rest, covered, for 10 minutes.

4 Heat remaining 1 tablespoon oil in 12-inch cast-iron skillet over medium heat for 5 minutes. Meanwhile, press and roll 1 dough ball into 9-inch round of even thickness, sprinkling dough and counter with flour as needed to prevent sticking. Using fork, poke entire surface of round 20 to 25 times.

5 Using paper towels, carefully wipe out skillet, leaving thin film of oil on bottom and sides. Mist top of dough with water. Place dough moistened side down in skillet, then mist top of dough with water. Cover and cook until flatbread is lightly puffed and bottom is spotty brown, 2 to 4 minutes. Flip flatbread, cover, and continue to cook until spotty brown on second side, 2 to 4 minutes. (If large air pockets form, gently poke with fork to deflate.)

6　Brush 1 side of flatbread with about 1 teaspoon melted butter and sprinkle with sea salt. Serve immediately or transfer to ovensafe plate, cover loosely with aluminum foil, and keep warm in oven. Repeat with remaining dough balls, melted butter, and sea salt. Serve.

variations

pan-grilled garlic-cilantro flatbreads

Microwave 3 thinly sliced garlic cloves with 1 tablespoon oil until garlic is golden and crisp, 2 to 3 minutes, stirring halfway through microwaving. Using fork, remove garlic and reserve garlic and oil. Whisk crispy garlic into flour mixture in step 1 and garlic oil into yogurt mixture. Increase butter to 4 tablespoons and add 2 minced garlic cloves and ½ teaspoon garlic powder before melting. Sprinkle each flatbread with 1 tablespoon minced fresh cilantro along with sea salt.

pan-grilled honey-chile flatbreads

Increase butter to 4 tablespoons and add 1 tablespoon honey, 2 teaspoons minced serrano chile, and 2 teaspoons grated fresh ginger before melting.

scallion pancakes

serves 2 • **total time** 35 minutes, plus 30 minutes resting

¾ cup (¾ ounces) plus 1½ teaspoons all-purpose flour, divided

6 tablespoons boiling water

1½ teaspoons plus 2 tablespoons vegetable oil, divided

1½ teaspoons toasted sesame oil

½ teaspoon kosher salt

2 scallions, sliced thin

Soy sauce

---

pan swap

Recipe can be made using a carbon-steel or nonstick skillet; adjust the heat as needed to prevent scorching. For a nonstick skillet, in step 5, heat 1 tablespoon vegetable oil over medium heat in skillet until shimmering.

why this recipe works Savory, deep golden-brown, crispy, flaky, and delicately chewy all at once, Chinese scallion pancakes are a treat you want to eat right from the pan. The shaping might look complex, but it's really just a few steps to savory pancakes whenever the craving strikes: First, use boiling water; it decreases the elasticity of the dough, which allows you to roll out a nice, thin pancake. Next, for the hallmark flaky shards, roll a thin round of dough into a cylinder, coil the cylinder into a spiral, and then roll it out into a round again—instant layers. Finally, cover the pan for the first few minutes to aid in even cooking and then uncover it so the pancake develops a gorgeously brown, crisp exterior. For an accurate measurement of boiling water, bring a kettle of water to a boil and then measure out the desired amount.

1 Using wooden spoon, mix ¾ cup flour and boiling water in medium bowl to form rough dough. Once cool enough to handle, transfer dough to lightly floured counter and knead until tacky (but not sticky) ball forms, about 4 minutes (dough will not be perfectly smooth). Cover loosely with plastic wrap and let rest for 30 minutes.

2 Meanwhile, stir together remaining 1½ teaspoons flour, 1½ teaspoons vegetable oil, and sesame oil. Set aside.

3 Roll dough into 12-inch round on lightly floured counter. Drizzle with reserved oil-flour mixture and use pastry brush to brush evenly over entire surface. Sprinkle with salt and scallions. Roll dough away from you into cylinder. Coil cylinder into spiral, tuck end underneath, and flatten spiral with your palm.

4 Roll spiral into 9-inch round, then cut ½-inch slit in center of pancake. Cover with plastic. (Pancake can be wrapped tightly in plastic wrap and refrigerated for up to 24 hours.)

(continued)

5   Place 10-inch cast-iron skillet over low heat and preheat for 10 minutes. Place 1 tablespoon vegetable oil in skillet and increase heat to medium. Place pancake in skillet (oil should sizzle). Cover and cook, shaking skillet occasionally, until pancake is slightly puffy and golden brown on underside, 1 to 1½ minutes. (If underside is not browned after 1 minute, turn heat up slightly. If it is browning too quickly, turn heat down slightly.)

6   Drizzle remaining 1 tablespoon vegetable oil over pancake, then use pastry brush to brush over entire surface. Carefully flip pancake. Cover and cook, shaking skillet occasionally, until second side is golden brown, 1 to 1½ minutes. Uncover skillet and continue to cook until bottom is deep golden brown and crispy, 30 to 60 seconds longer. Flip and cook until deep golden brown and crispy, 30 to 60 seconds. Cut pancake into 8 wedges and serve with soy sauce.

shaping scallion pancakes

1 Roll scallion-sprinkled dough round into cylinder.

2 Coil cylinder, tucking end underneath, then flatten.

3 Roll out flattened spiral into 9-inch round; cut ½-inch slit in center of pancake.

mana'eesh za'atar

makes 2 flatbreads • **total time** 50 minutes, plus 2 to 2½ hours rising

dough

1¼	cups (6¼ ounces) all-purpose flour
¾	teaspoon instant or rapid-rise yeast
½	teaspoon table salt
7	tablespoons cold water
1	tablespoon extra-virgin olive oil

topping

1½	tablespoons za'atar (page 317)
3	tablespoons plus 1 teaspoon extra-virgin olive oil

why this recipe works Mana'eesh za'atar are Levantine street-food flatbreads that are absolutely lavished with the zesty herb-and-spice blend and shiny from the region's treasured olive oil. Ripping into a warm man'oushe is a treat, and this small-batch recipe allows you to easily create that experience for just the two of you, especially if you make the dough a day ahead. We prefer our homemade za'atar, but you can use store-bought if you prefer; we recommend a blend without added salt if you can find it.

1 For the dough: Process flour, yeast, and salt in food processor until combined, about 2 seconds. Combine cold water and oil in liquid measuring cup. With processor running, slowly add water mixture and process until dough forms sticky ball that clears sides of bowl, about 90 seconds. Transfer dough to clean counter and knead by hand to form smooth, round ball, about 30 seconds.

2 Place dough seam side down in lightly greased large bowl or container, cover bowl with plastic wrap, and let dough rise until almost doubled in volume, 2 to 2½ hours. (Alternatively, dough can be refrigerated for up to 24 hours.)

3 One hour before baking, adjust oven rack to middle position, set baking stone on rack, and heat oven to 500 degrees. Divide dough into 2 equal pieces on clean counter. Working with 1 piece of dough at a time (keep remaining piece covered), form into rough ball by stretching dough around your thumb and pinching edges together so that top is smooth. Place ball seam side down on clean counter and, using your cupped hand, drag in small circles until dough feels taut and round. Cover loosely with plastic and let rest for 15 minutes.

4 For the topping: Combine za'atar and oil in bowl; set aside. Coat 1 dough ball lightly with flour and, using your fingertips, flatten into 6- to 7-inch disk on lightly floured counter. Using rolling pin, roll into 9- to 10-inch round. Transfer round to well-floured baking peel or overturned large baking sheet, then spread one-half of topping over surface of dough with back of spoon, stopping ½ inch from edge. Firmly tap dough all over with your fingertips, about 6 times.

(continued)

5 Slide dough round carefully onto stone in oven and bake until lightly bubbled and brown on top, about 5 minutes. Using baking peel, transfer man'oushe to wire rack. Repeat with remaining dough and topping. Serve.

variations

tomato mana'eesh

Omit topping. Toss 8 ounces quartered cherry tomatoes and 1 teaspoon table salt in colander set over bowl. Let drain for 15 minutes. Discard liquid. Combine drained tomatoes, 1 thinly sliced small shallot, 1½ tablespoons extra-virgin olive oil, 1 teaspoon minced fresh thyme, and ⅛ teaspoon table salt in bowl. After rolling out and tapping dough in step 5, distribute one-half of tomato mixture over each dough round, stopping ½ inch from edge. Proceed with step 6.

cheese mana'eesh

Omit topping. Combine 1 cup shredded whole-milk block mozzarella cheese and ⅓ cup crumbled feta in small bowl. After rolling out and tapping dough in step 5, sprinkle one-half cheese mixture evenly over each dough round, followed by ½ teaspoon nigella seeds, stopping ½ inch from edge. Proceed with step 6.

za'atar

makes *about ⅓ cup*
total time *5 minutes*

- 2   tablespoons dried thyme
- 1   tablespoon dried oregano
- 1½ tablespoons sumac
- 1   tablespoon sesame seeds, toasted
- ¼   teaspoon table salt

Process thyme and oregano in spice grinder or mortar and pestle until finely ground and powdery. Transfer to bowl and stir in sumac, sesame seeds, and salt. (Za'atar can be stored at room temperature in airtight container for up to 1 year.)

lahmajun

serves 2 • **total time** 1 hour, plus 17 hours chilling and resting

dough

1⅔	cups (8⅓ ounces) King Arthur All-Purpose Flour
⅛	teaspoon instant or rapid-rise yeast
½	cup plus 2 tablespoons ice water
1½	teaspoons vegetable oil
¾	teaspoon table salt
	Vegetable oil spray

topping

½	red bell pepper, stemmed, seeded, and cut into 1-inch pieces
1	shallot, quartered
1	tablespoon chopped fresh parsley
1	tablespoon mild biber salçasi
2	teaspoons tomato paste
1	small garlic clove, peeled
½	teaspoon ground allspice
½	teaspoon paprika
¼	teaspoon ground cumin
¼	teaspoon table salt
	Pinch pepper
	Pinch cayenne pepper
3	ounces ground lamb, broken into small pieces
	Lemon wedges

why this recipe works These thin, crispy, savory meat-and-vegetable-topped Armenian flatbreads can be sprayed with lemon juice and eaten like pizza—or why not turn them into sandwiches by rolling them around a salad of fresh or pickled vegetables? Making just two at a time is no hassle as the whole thing, both dough and lamb topping, comes together quickly in the food processor; plus the dough requires 16 hours to ferment in the fridge so it's ready for shaping for dinner the next day. Biber salçası is a Turkish red pepper paste made from sweet or a combination of sweet and hot peppers. Be sure to use the mild variety; if it's unavailable, increase the tomato paste in the topping to 1 table-spoon and increase the paprika to 2 teaspoons. Eat the lahmajun out of hand, whether whole, cut into halves or quarters, folded in half, or rolled into a cylinder. We prefer King Arthur brand bread flour in this recipe (the higher protein flour gives the flatbreads the perfect balance of crispness and tenderness), but you can substitute another brand if it's unavailable. If desired, omit the lemon wedges and serve with Cucumber-Tomato Salad (recipe follows). If serving with the salad, use a slotted spoon to distribute 1 cup of salad evenly along the center third of each lahmajun. Fold the outer thirds of the lahmajun over the filling. Turn the rolled lahmajun seam side down and cut in half.

1 **For the dough:** Process flour and yeast in food processor until combined, about 2 seconds. With processor running, slowly add ice water; process until dough is just combined and no dry flour remains, about 10 seconds. Let dough rest for 10 minutes.

2 Add oil and salt and process until dough forms shaggy ball, 30 to 60 seconds. Transfer dough to lightly oiled counter and knead until uniform, about 1 minute (texture will remain slightly rough). Divide dough into 2 equal pieces. Working with 1 piece of dough at a time (keep remaining piece covered), form into rough ball by stretching dough around your thumb and pinching edges together so that top is smooth. Place ball seam side down on clean counter and, using your cupped hand, drag in small circles until dough feels taut and round. Transfer, seam side down, to rimmed baking sheet coated with oil spray. Spray tops of balls lightly with oil spray. Cover tightly with plastic wrap and refrigerate for at least 16 hours or up to 2 days.

(continued)

cucumber-tomato salad

makes 2 cups
total time 25 minutes

This salad is best eaten within 1 hour of being dressed. You can substitute two Persian cucumbers for the ½ English cucumber.

- ½ English cucumber, quartered lengthwise and cut into ¼-inch pieces
- 1 tomato, cored and cut into ¼-inch pieces
-    Table salt for salting tomatoes
- ¼ cup pitted green olives, chopped coarse
- 2 tablespoons shredded fresh mint
- 1 tablespoon extra-virgin olive oil
- 1 tablespoon lemon juice
- ¼ teaspoon pepper

Toss cucumber, tomato, and ¼ teaspoon salt together in colander set over bowl. Let drain for 15 minutes, then discard liquid. Toss drained cucumber-tomato mixture, olives, mint, oil, lemon juice, and pepper together in bowl.

3 For the topping: In now-empty processor, process bell pepper, shallot, parsley, biber salçasi, tomato paste, garlic, allspice, paprika, cumin, salt, pepper, and cayenne until smooth, scraping down sides of bowl as needed, about 15 seconds. Add lamb and pulse to combine, 8 to 10 pulses. Transfer to bowl, cover, and refrigerate until needed. (Topping can be refrigerated for up to 24 hours).

4 One hour before baking, remove dough from refrigerator and let sit at room temperature until slightly puffy and no longer cool to touch. Meanwhile, adjust oven rack to upper-middle position (rack should be 4 to 5 inches from broiler element), set baking stone on rack, and heat oven to 500 degrees.

5 Place 1 dough ball on clean counter and dust top lightly with flour. Using heel of your hand, press dough ball into 5-inch disk. Using rolling pin, gently roll into 12-inch round of even thickness. (Use tackiness of dough on counter to aid with rolling; if dough becomes misshapen, periodically peel round from counter, reposition, and continue to roll.) Dust top of round lightly but evenly with flour and, starting at 1 edge, peel dough off counter and flip, floured side down, onto floured baking peel or overturned large baking sheet (dough will spring back to about 11 inches in diameter). Place half of topping in center of dough. Cover dough with large sheet of plastic and, using your fingertips and knuckles, gently spread filling evenly across dough, leaving ⅛-inch border. Starting at 1 edge, peel away plastic, leaving topping in place (reserve plastic for topping remaining lahmajun).

6 Carefully slide lahmajun onto stone and bake until bottom crust is browned, edges are lightly browned, and topping is steaming, 4 to 6 minutes.

7 Transfer baked lahmajun to wire rack. Repeat rolling, topping, and baking remaining dough ball. Serve with lemon wedges.

focaccia

serves 4 • **total time** 1¼ hours, plus 2 to 2½ hours rising

2 cups (10 ounces) all-purpose flour

1 teaspoon sugar

1 teaspoon instant or rapid-rise yeast

1 cup plus 2 tablespoons water, room temperature

1 teaspoon table salt

¼ cup extra-virgin olive oil, divided

¼ teaspoon flake sea salt

why this recipe works Focaccia, beloved for its crispy crust; pillowy, open crumb; and fruity, olive oil–laden flavor, is equally at home by itself or sandwiching a mound of Italian meats and cheeses. But it's typically a large-scale bread baked in a large baking sheet or a couple cake pans. Given its great reward-to-effort ratio, we wanted to make small-scale focaccia possible. A very high hydration dough—90 percent—promotes the characteristic chewy interior. Such wet doughs better resemble pancake batter than a workable dough, so we formulated the recipe so the dough doesn't have to be touched until its final shaping. This made using a stand mixer essential; however, a dough hook was inefficient at working such a small batch of dough. We switched to a paddle to engage the dough and promote long strands of gluten that create the beautiful airy interior. We found that by liberally oiling the bowl we let the dough rise in, we could simply tip the dough straight into our baking sheet. We developed this recipe using a 4.5-quart stand mixer; note that kneading times will be longer and may not follow given visual cues. We like to cut the bread into small squares for mopping up more olive oil.

1 Whisk flour, sugar, and yeast together in bowl of stand mixer. Using paddle on low speed, slowly add water to flour mixture and mix until no dry flour remains, about 45 seconds, scraping down bowl as needed. Let sit for 10 minutes.

2 Add table salt and mix on medium-high speed until dough masses around paddle and clears sides and bottom of bowl, 2 to 4 minutes. Reduce speed to medium and mix until dough is very shiny and smooth, about 5 minutes.

3 Spray large bowl with vegetable oil spray, then brush bottom and sides of bowl with 1 tablespoon oil. Transfer dough to prepared bowl and flip to coat dough with oil. Cover bowl with plastic wrap. Let dough rise at room temperature until bubbly and tripled in volume, 2 to 2½ hours. (Alternatively, dough can be refrigerated for up to 24 hours. Let dough sit at room temperature until bubbly and tripled in volume, 2 to 2½ hours before proceeding with recipe.)

(continued)

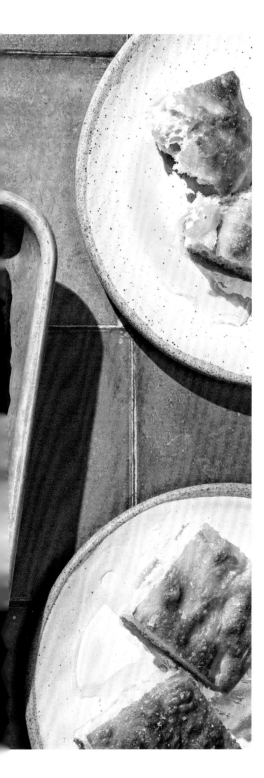

4   Adjust oven rack to middle position and heat oven to 450 degrees. Spray 13 by 9-inch rimmed baking sheet with vegetable oil spray, then brush bottom and sides of sheet with 2 tablespoons oil.

5   Slowly tilt bowl so that dough slides out of bowl and onto prepared sheet (side of dough that was in contact with bowl should be in contact with sheet). Gently pat and stretch dough out to corners of sheet (dough will snap back). Let rest for 5 minutes, then stretch dough out again to corners of sheet. Let dough sit for 10 minutes.

6   Press your fingertips into dough about 30 times to deflate dough. Pop any bubbles larger than 1 inch with fork. Drizzle dough with remaining 1 tablespoon oil and sprinkle with sea salt. Bake until focaccia is deep golden brown, 20 to 25 minutes.

7   Transfer sheet to wire rack and let cool for 5 minutes. Transfer focaccia to wire rack and let cool for 10 minutes. Serve warm or at room temperature.

variations

anchovy and chive focaccia

Omit flake sea salt. After pressing dough with your fingers in step 6, arrange 12 anchovies evenly over top of dough. (A 2-ounce can of anchovies will yield 12 anchovies.) Brush cooled focaccia with 1 teaspoon extra-virgin olive oil and sprinkle with 2 teaspoons minced chives.

grape, fennel, and charred shallot focaccia

Slice 1 shallot ¼ inch thick and toss with 1 teaspoon extra-virgin olive oil. After deflating dough with your fingers in step 6, sprinkle with 1 teaspoon cracked, toasted fennel seeds. Arrange 1 cup red grapes over top of focaccia, pressing grapes into dough, then sprinkle sliced shallots over top before baking.

pear and bacon flatbread

serves 2 • **total time** 45 minutes

3 slices bacon

¼ cup apricot jam

4 teaspoons extra-virgin olive oil, divided

2 teaspoons Dijon mustard

⅛ teaspoon table salt, divided

⅛ teaspoon pepper, divided

1 small ripe but firm Bartlett pear, peeled, halved, cored, and cut into ½-inch pieces

1 shallot, chopped fine

8 ounces Basic Pizza Dough (page 334), room temperature

4 ounces goat cheese, crumbled (1 cup)

why this recipe works Flatbreads are a blank canvas for imaginative dinners—and ones that you can get on the table in 45 minutes at that. Top premade pizza dough (you can use dough you've made yourself or store-bought) with Dijon-boosted apricot jam, crispy bacon, honey-flavored pears, and some tangy goat cheese for a surprising sweet-savory supper for two that just needs a salad to complete it. If the dough springs back in step 3, let it rest for a few minutes before trying to roll it again. You could also shape the dough into one 11-inch flatbread; follow preheating, shaping, and baking instructions in our Mushroom-Miso Flatbread recipe on page 326.

1　Adjust oven rack to middle position and heat oven to 500 degrees. Spray rimmed baking sheet with vegetable oil spray. Place bacon between 2 layers of paper towels on plate and microwave until bacon is crispy and golden brown, 4 to 6 minutes. Discard paper towels then blot bacon with clean paper towels to absorb excess oil. Crumble bacon into ¼-inch pieces.

2　Combine apricot jam, 1 tablespoon oil, mustard, pinch salt, and pinch pepper in bowl. In separate bowl, toss crumbled bacon, pear, shallot, remaining 1 teaspoon oil, remaining pinch salt, and remaining pinch pepper until well combined.

3　Divide dough into 2 equal pieces. Press and roll each piece into 7 by 5-inch rectangle on lightly floured counter. Transfer dough to prepared sheet and restretch to 7 by 5-inch rectangles if needed. Brush each dough rectangle with jam mixture, leaving ½-inch border. Sprinkle evenly with pear mixture.

4　Bake until crust is golden, 12 to 14 minutes, rotating sheet halfway through baking. Transfer sheet to wire rack and sprinkle with goat cheese; let cool for 5 minutes. Transfer to cutting board or plates, slice, and serve.

mushroom-miso flatbread

serves 2 • **total time** 45 minutes, plus 1 hour preheating

2 teaspoons white miso

1½ teaspoons unseasoned rice vinegar

1½ teaspoons water, plus more if needed

½ teaspoon sugar

3 garlic cloves, minced, divided

3 tablespoons vegetable oil, divided

12 ounces mushrooms

1 tablespoon soy sauce

8 ounces Basic Pizza Dough (page 334), room temperature

3 ounces block mozzarella cheese, shredded (¾ cup)

1 cup baby arugula

1 teaspoon sesame seeds, toasted

¼ cup bonito flakes (optional)

why this recipe works Mushrooms are front and center in this umami powerhouse of a flatbread. To create extra-savory mushrooms for the topping—and to keep that topping from sogging out the flatbread—we employ a two-step cooking process. An initial covered sear in a skillet encourages the mushrooms to release their excess moisture. Uncovering the skillet browns them nicely. We use just a modest amount of mozzarella to provide some richness and also help the mushrooms stick to the pizza. We finish the flatbread with fresh peppery arugula and a sweet-and-sour miso-based vinaigrette to cut through the savory richness. Use one variety of mushroom or a combination: Stem and halve portobello mushrooms and cut each half crosswise into ½-inch strips. Trim white or cremini mushrooms; quarter them if large or medium, or halve them if small. Tear trimmed oyster mushrooms into 1- to 1½-inch pieces. Stem shiitake mushrooms; quarter large caps and halve small caps. Cut trimmed maitake (hen-of-the-woods) mushrooms into 1- to 1½-inch pieces. You can use homemade or store-bought dough. If the dough springs back in step 4, let it rest for a few minutes before trying to stretch it again. You could also shape the dough into 2 individual flatbreads; follow preheating, shaping, and baking instructions in our Pear and Bacon Flatbread recipe on page 325.

1 One hour before baking, adjust oven rack to lower-middle position, set baking stone on rack, and heat oven to 500 degrees.

2 Whisk miso, vinegar, water, sugar, and ¼ teaspoon minced garlic together in small bowl. Whisking constantly, slowly drizzle in 1 tablespoon oil until emulsified; set aside.

3 Heat remaining 2 tablespoons oil in 12-inch nonstick skillet over medium-high heat until shimmering. Add mushrooms and cook, covered, until they have released their liquid, 3 to 5 minutes. Uncover and cook until mushrooms are dry and starting to brown, 3 to 6 minutes. Stir in remaining minced garlic and cook until fragrant, about 30 seconds. Off heat, add soy sauce, tossing to coat. Set aside off heat.

4 Coat dough ball lightly with flour and, using your fingertips, flatten into 8-inch disk on lightly floured counter. Using hands, gently stretch disk into 10-inch round, working along edges and giving disk quarter turns as you stretch. Transfer dough to well-floured baking peel or overturned large baking sheet and stretch into 11-inch round. Sprinkle with mozzarella, leaving ¼-inch border around edge, then scatter reserved mushrooms over top.

5 Slide flatbread carefully onto stone in oven and bake until crust is golden brown at edges, 8 to 11 minutes, rotating flatbread halfway through. Transfer flatbread to wire rack and let rest for 5 minutes.

6 Meanwhile, stir reserved miso sauce and adjust consistency with additional water, ½ teaspoon at a time, as needed. Top flatbread with arugula and drizzle with miso sauce. Sprinkle with sesame seeds and bonito flakes, if using. Slice and serve.

easy skillet cheese pizza

serves 2 • **total time** 30 minutes

2 tablespoons extra-virgin olive oil

8 ounces Basic Pizza Dough
(page 334), room temperature

½ cup Pizza Sauce (page 335)

4 ounces whole-milk mozzarella
cheese, shredded (1 cup)

2 tablespoons grated Parmesan
cheese

why this recipe works When homemade pizza is this quick—and this good—there's no need for takeout and the inevitable greasy box of leftovers. This is your ideal thin-crust cheese pizza made fast and for just two. Building the small pizza in a skillet is an easy hack that lets you mimic the effect of a pizza oven by jump-starting the crust with a blast of stovetop heat. The pizza is then popped into the oven to cook through, no pizza stone required. If the dough springs back in step 2, let it rest for a few minutes before trying to stretch it again. You can use homemade or store-bought dough and sauce. Feel free to add simple toppings before baking, but keep them light or they may weigh down the thin crust and make it soggy (see page 336).

1 Adjust oven rack to upper-middle position and heat oven to 500 degrees. Brush bottom of 12-inch ovensafe skillet with oil.

2 Coat dough ball lightly with flour and, using your fingertips, flatten into 8-inch disk on lightly floured counter. Using your hands, gently stretch disk into 11-inch round, working along edges and giving disk quarter turns as you stretch. Transfer dough to prepared skillet; reshape as needed. Spread sauce over dough, leaving ½-inch border. Sprinkle mozzarella and Parmesan evenly over sauce.

3 Set skillet over high heat and cook until outside edge of dough is set, pizza is lightly puffed, and bottom crust is spotty brown when gently lifted with spatula, about 3 minutes.

4 Transfer skillet to oven and bake until crust is brown and cheese is golden in spots, 7 to 10 minutes. Using pot holders (skillet handle will be hot), remove skillet from oven and slide pizza onto wire rack. Let pizza cool for 5 minutes before slicing and serving.

cast-iron pan pizza

serves 2 • **total time** 1 hour, plus 14 hours chilling, resting, and rising

1 cup (5½ ounces) bread flour

½ teaspoon table salt

½ teaspoon instant or rapid-rise yeast

½ cup warm water (110 degrees)

Vegetable oil spray

2 tablespoons extra-virgin olive oil

⅓ cup Pizza Sauce (page 335)

6 ounces Monterey Jack cheese, shredded (1½ cups), divided

why this recipe works Pan pizza is a bar favorite—thick, crisp, and cheesy—that's the perfect size for two. It's also easy to make pretty much whenever those qualities appeal since there's no rolling, stretching, or baking stone required. We start with a simple stir-together dough; warm water in the mix jump-starts yeast activity so that the crust's crumb is open and light. Instead of kneading, we let the dough rest overnight in the refrigerator. This prolonged gluten development creates a crust with enough structure to support toppings without being tough. Then comes the pan part: We bake the pie in a generously oiled cast-iron skillet, which "fries" the outside of the crust. For the crispy cheese edge known as frico, we press shredded Monterey Jack cheese around the edge of the dough and up the sides of the skillet. Finishing the pizza on the stove crisps the crust's underside. You can substitute ¾ cup shredded block mozzarella for the Monterey Jack that is sprinkled over the sauce in step 3, if desired. You can use homemade or store-bought sauce.

1 Whisk flour, salt, and yeast together in bowl. Add warm water and mix until most of flour is moistened. Using your hands, knead dough in bowl until dough forms sticky ball, about 1 minute. Spray 9-inch pie plate or cake pan with vegetable oil spray. Transfer dough to prepared plate and press into 6- to 7-inch disk. Spray top of dough with oil spray. Cover tightly with plastic wrap and refrigerate for at least 12 hours or up to 24 hours.

2 Two hours before baking, remove dough from refrigerator and let sit at room temperature for 30 minutes. Coat bottom of 10-inch cast-iron skillet with olive oil. Transfer dough to prepared skillet and use your fingertips to flatten dough until it is ⅛ inch from edge of skillet. Cover tightly with plastic and let rest until slightly puffy, about 1½ hours. Adjust oven rack to lowest position and heat oven to 400 degrees.

3 Spread pizza sauce in thin layer over surface of dough, leaving ½-inch border around edge. Sprinkle ¾ cup Monterey Jack over dough border and press into side of skillet, forming ½- to ¾-inch-tall wall. (Not all cheese will stick to side of skillet.) Evenly sprinkle remaining ¾ cup Monterey Jack over sauce. Bake pizza until cheese at edge of skillet is well browned, 25 to 30 minutes.

4 Transfer skillet to stovetop (skillet handle will be hot) and let sit off heat until sizzling stops, about 3 minutes. Run butter knife around rim of skillet to loosen pizza. Using thin metal spatula, gently lift edge of pizza and peek at underside to assess browning. Cook pizza over medium heat until bottom crust is well browned, 2 to 5 minutes. Using 2 spatulas, transfer pizza to wire rack and let cool for 10 minutes. Slice and serve.

variation

cast-iron pan pizza with pepperoni, pickled peppers, and honey

At the end of step 3, sprinkle just ½ cup Monterey Jack over sauce. Scatter 1 ounce thinly sliced pepperoni and 2 tablespoons thinly sliced jarred hot cherry peppers over top, then sprinkle with remaining ¼ cup Monterey Jack. Just before serving, drizzle baked pizza with 1 teaspoon honey (for a spicy kick, use hot honey).

thin-crust pizza

serves 4 to 6 (makes two 13-inch pizzas) • **total time** 1 hour, plus 25 hours chilling and resting

3 cups (16½ ounces) bread flour

2 teaspoons sugar

½ teaspoon instant or rapid-rise yeast

1⅓ cups ice water

1 tablespoon vegetable oil

1½ teaspoons table salt

1 cup Pizza Sauce (page 335), divided

1 ounce Parmesan cheese, grated (½ cup), divided

8 ounces whole-milk block mozzarella, shredded (2 cups), divided

---

freeze and bake

Refrigerate dough for 24 hours in step 2, then place on parchment-lined baking sheet or plate and cover loosely with plastic wrap. Freeze until firm, about 3 hours or up to overnight. Wrap frozen dough ball in plastic and store in zipper-lock bag in freezer for up to 2 weeks. To use, unwrap ball, place in lightly oiled bowl, cover with plastic, and let sit in refrigerator for 12 to 24 hours before shaping.

why this recipe works For pizza nights when you want to go all out and mimic your favorite parlor pie, we present our thin-crust pizza. A quick mix (in a food processor) and a slow rise of the dough are the key combination for pizza with an easy and authentic-tasting crust. The recipe makes two full-size pizzas that are appropriate for sharing with a couple friends at your next get-together. If you want to make one now and enjoy the other in a week or two, just follow the directions for freezing the dough and halve the sauce and cheese amounts. You can use homemade or store-bought pizza sauce. If making both pizzas, you can shape the second dough round while the first pizza bakes, but don't add the toppings until just before baking.

1 Pulse flour, sugar, and yeast in food processor until combined, about 5 pulses. With processor running, slowly add ice water and process until dough is just combined and no dry flour remains, about 10 seconds. Let dough rest for 10 minutes.

2 Add oil and salt to dough and process until dough forms satiny, sticky ball that clears sides of workbowl, 30 to 60 seconds. Remove dough from bowl; knead briefly on lightly oiled countertop until smooth, about 1 minute. Shape dough into tight ball and place in large, lightly greased bowl. Cover tightly with plastic wrap and refrigerate for at least 24 hours or up to 3 days.

3 One hour before baking pizza, adjust oven rack to second highest position (rack should be 4 to 5 inches below broiler), set pizza stone on rack, and heat oven to 500 degrees. Remove dough from refrigerator and divide in half. Shape each half into smooth, tight ball. Place on lightly oiled baking sheet, spacing them at least 3 inches apart. Cover loosely with plastic wrap coated with vegetable oil spray and let stand for 1 hour.

4 Coat 1 ball of dough generously with flour and place on well-floured counter. Using your fingertips, gently flatten into 8-inch disk, leaving 1 inch of outer edge slightly thicker than center. Using your hands, gently stretch disk into 12-inch round, working along edges and giving disk quarter turns as you stretch. Transfer dough to well-floured peel and stretch into 13-inch round. Spread ½ cup pizza sauce in thin layer over surface of dough, leaving ¼-inch border around edge. Sprinkle ¼ cup Parmesan evenly over sauce, followed by 1 cup mozzarella. Slide pizza carefully onto stone in oven and bake until crust is well browned and cheese is bubbly and beginning to brown, 10 to 12 minutes, rotating pizza halfway through cooking. Remove pizza and place on wire rack for 5 minutes before slicing and serving. Repeat step 4 to shape, top, and bake second pizza.

variations

fontina, arugula, and prosciutto pizza

Toss 2 cups baby arugula or spinach with 4 teaspoons extra-virgin olive oil and salt and pepper to taste. Omit Parmesan and substitute shredded fontina for mozzarella. Immediately after baking, sprinkle 4 ounces thinly sliced prosciutto, cut into ½-inch strips, and dressed arugula over top of pizza.

goat cheese, olive, and garlic pizza

Brush 2 tablespoons garlic oil (store-bought, or use our recipe on page 336) over pizza dough before adding sauce in step 4. Omit Parmesan and reduce mozzarella to 1 cup. Sprinkle 1 cup crumbled goat cheese and ½ cup pitted and halved olives over mozzarella before baking.

ricotta, bacon, and scallion pizza

Mix 1 cup ricotta, 2 thinly sliced scallions, ¼ teaspoon table salt, and ⅛ teaspoon pepper together in bowl. Omit Parmesan and reduce mozzarella to 1 cup. Dollop ricotta mixture, 1 tablespoon at a time, on top of mozzarella, then sprinkle with 4 ounces crispy cooked bacon or pancetta. Sprinkle baked pizza with 1 more sliced scallion before serving.

two's a pizza party

Pizza sounds like a project, but it's actually as practical a dinner for two as it is fun. We make it even more accessible with plenty of options. Make your own pizza dough on pizza day, make it in advance and refrigerate or freeze so it's ready for a weeknight, or simply source from the store or pizzeria. And you can make your own sauces and toppings, or get a little help with premade condiments. If you follow the techniques in this chapter, you'll have a smart, satisfying dinner for two, no matter the ingredients you take to get there. Here are five of our core pizza-making recipes, all of which have storage capabilities.

foundation

basic pizza dough
makes *8 ounces dough*
total time *10 minutes plus 1½ hours rising*

A food processor makes quick work of mixing just the right amount of dough for a personal pizza. You can let the dough rise at room temperature for a same-day pizza or refrigerate it to use the next day.

1	cup (5½ ounces) bread flour, plus extra as needed
¾	teaspoon instant or rapid-rise yeast
½	teaspoon table salt
7	tablespoons warm water (110 degrees)
1½	teaspoons extra-virgin olive oil

1   Process flour, yeast, and salt in food processor until combined, about 2 seconds. Combine warm water and oil in liquid measuring cup. With processor running, slowly add water mixture and process until dough forms sticky ball that clears sides of bowl, 1½ to 2 minutes. (If, after 1 minute, dough is sticky and clings to blade, add extra flour, 1 tablespoon at a time, as needed until it clears sides of bowl.)

2   Transfer dough to lightly floured counter and knead briefly until smooth, about 1 minute. Shape dough into tight ball and place in large greased bowl. Cover tightly with plastic wrap and let rise at room temperature until doubled in volume, 1 to 1½ hours. (Alternatively, you can refrigerate the dough for up to 16 hours. To freeze dough, place refrigerated dough on parchment-lined baking sheet or plate and cover loosely with plastic wrap. Freeze until firm, about 3 hours or up to overnight. Wrap frozen dough ball in plastic and store in zipper-lock bag in freezer for up to 2 weeks. To use, unwrap ball, place in lightly oiled bowl, cover with plastic, and let sit in refrigerator for 12 to 24 hours before shaping.)

basic whole-wheat pizza dough

You can use whole-wheat pizza dough in any of the recipes in this book that call for pizza dough.

Substitute ½ cup (2¾ ounces) whole-wheat flour for ½ cup (2¾ ounces) of the bread flour.

sauce

pizza sauce

makes 2 cups
total time 10 minutes

1	(28-ounce) can whole peeled tomatoes, drained
1	tablespoon extra-virgin olive oil
1	teaspoon red wine vinegar
2	garlic cloves, minced
1	teaspoon table salt
1	teaspoon dried oregano
¼	teaspoon ground black pepper

Process all ingredients in food processor until smooth, about 30 seconds. Transfer to bowl and refrigerate until ready to use. (Sauce can be refrigerated for up to 1 week or frozen for up to 1 month.)

perfect pesto

makes 1¾ cups
total time 30 minutes

If you don't have a scale to measure the Parmesan, the amount of processed Parmesan should be about ½ cup plus 2 tablespoons.

¾	cup extra-virgin olive oil, divided
½	cup pine nuts
4	ounces fresh basil leaves and stems
¾	teaspoon table salt, plus salt for blanching basil
1¼	ounces Parmesan cheese
2	garlic cloves, peeled

1   Combine 1 tablespoon oil and pine nuts in 8-inch skillet. Cook over medium heat, stirring often, until pine nuts are light golden, 3 to 6 minutes. Spread pine nuts out on plate and let cool for 15 minutes.

2   Meanwhile, bring 2 quarts water to boil in medium saucepan. Remove basil stems from leaves; you should have 4 cups leaves (3 ounces by weight). Add basil leaves and 1½ teaspoons salt to boiling water and cook until basil is wilted and bright green, 5 to 10 seconds. Using spider skimmer or slotted spoon, transfer basil directly to salad spinner and spin to remove excess water. Spread basil on clean dish towel to dry. (If you don't have a salad spinner, drain basil on clean dish towel and thoroughly pat dry with paper towels.)

(continued)

3   Process Parmesan in food processor until finely ground, about 30 seconds; transfer to medium bowl. Process pine nuts, basil, salt, garlic, and remaining oil in now-empty processor until smooth, about 1 minute, scraping down sides of bowl as needed. Transfer pesto to bowl with Parmesan and stir to combine. Serve. (Pesto, covered with additional 1 tablespoon extra-virgin olive oil can be refrigerated for up to 2 days or frozen for up to 1 month.)

flourish

garlic oil

makes *about ½ cup*
total time *10 minutes*

We use garlic oil in our recipe for Goat Cheese, Olive, and Garlic Pizza but you can drizzle it on a number of flatbreads or use it as a dip for bread. Extra-virgin olive oil can be substituted for the vegetable oil.

- ½   cup vegetable oil
- 4   garlic cloves, smashed and peeled

Heat oil and garlic in small saucepan over medium-low heat until fragrant and starting to bubble, 3 to 5 minutes. Let cool completely. Strain oil through fine-mesh strainer into airtight container; discard solids. (Garlic oil can be refrigerated for up to 3 days.)

build-your-own pizza

You can add toppings you like—even better if they're ingredients that would otherwise languish in the fridge—to your skillet, sheet-pan, or free-form pizzas. It's wise to choose items that aren't too heavy, and veggies that don't throw off a lot of water so your crust doesn't get bogged down.

Delicate vegetables and herbs: Leafy greens such as baby spinach and herbs like basil are best placed either beneath the cheese to shield them from the intense heat or added raw atop the fully cooked hot pizza.

Hardy vegetables: Aim for a maximum of 6 ounces per 13-inch pie or 3 ounces per 9½-inch pie, spread out in a single layer. Thinly slice and lightly sauté (or microwave for a minute or two along with a little olive oil) sturdy vegetables such as onions, peppers, and mushrooms.

Meats: Plan for 2 to 4 ounces. We prefer to poach meats such as sausage (broken up into ½-inch chunks), pepperoni, or ground beef in ¼ cup water in a wide skillet for 4 to 5 minutes, which helps render the fat while keeping the meat moist. Or you could simply drape paper-thin slices of prosciutto over the top of the finished pizza.

Fruit: You can place sliced peaches, thinly sliced figs, or sliced apples right on top of the pizza before cooking. You can also use dried fruit; we recommend placing them under the cheese so they don't get leathery. Chop larger dried fruits like dried figs.

Chiles: You can add banana pepper rings, Calabrian chiles, or sliced fresh or canned jalapeños right on top of the pizza before cooking.

pepperoni sheet-pan pizza

serves 2 • **total time** 1 hour 20 minutes

8 ounces Basic Pizza Dough (page 334), room temperature

⅔ cup canned crushed tomatoes

1 tablespoon extra-virgin olive oil

1 garlic clove, minced

1 anchovy fillet, minced

¾ teaspoon dried oregano

½ teaspoon sugar

¼ teaspoon red pepper flakes, plus extra for sprinkling

¼ teaspoon table salt

¼ cup grated Parmesan cheese, plus extra for sprinkling

6 ounces whole-milk block mozzarella cheese, shredded (1½ cups)

2 ounces thinly sliced pepperoni

why this recipe works Typically, rectangular pizzas are a delicious choice to feed a crowd, especially when you spread the cheese all the way to the sides of the pan to get those irresistible lacy edges. We keep that cheesy crust but cut the pizza down to size by forming it right in a quarter sheet pan—that means a cheese lace edge on every slice! A short rest of the dough makes the crust puffy and light. A quick tomato sauce boosted with garlic, anchovy, and pepper flakes makes a worthy base for a savory blanket of cheese and pepperoni. We prefer to buy link pepperoni and slice it thin rather than using presliced pepperoni. You can use homemade or store-bought dough. If the dough springs back in step 2, let it rest for a few minutes before trying to stretch it again.

1　One hour before baking, adjust oven rack to lowest position, place pizza stone on rack, and heat oven to 500 degrees.

2　Spray 13 by 9-inch rimmed baking sheet with vegetable oil spray. Transfer dough to sheet and gently stretch to corners of sheet, pressing lightly with your fingertips to deflate dough and carefully lifting corners and edges to pull toward edges of sheet. (It's OK if dough shrinks back slightly from corners of sheet at this point.) Cover loosely with plastic and let rise in warm place until slightly puffed, about 20 minutes.

3　Meanwhile, combine crushed tomatoes, oil, garlic, anchovy, oregano, sugar, pepper flakes, and salt in bowl. (Sauce can be refrigerated for up to 24 hours.)

4　Press dough all the way to edges and corners of sheet. Using your fingertips, pinch edges of dough against sides of sheet to form small lip. Spread sauce into thin layer over surface of dough, leaving ½-inch border. Sprinkle Parmesan evenly over sauce. Sprinkle mozzarella over entire surface of dough, making sure some cheese sits on edges of dough against sheet. Top pizza with pepperoni.

5　Place baking sheet on stone and bake pizza until cheese is bubbly and well browned, about 15 minutes, rotating sheet halfway through baking. Run knife around edge of sheet to loosen pizza and transfer pizza to wire rack. Let cool for 5 minutes. Slice and serve, sprinkled with extra Parmesan and pepper flakes as desired.

caprese sheet-pan pizza

serves 2 • **total time** 1½ hours

tomatoes

5 ounces assorted color cherry tomatoes, sliced ¼ inch thick

¼ teaspoon table salt

¼ teaspoon sugar

1 garlic clove, minced

pizza

8 ounces Basic Pizza Dough (page 334), room temperature

½ cup pesto

5 ounces fresh mozzarella, sliced into ¼-inch-thick rounds

⅛ teaspoon pepper

⅛ teaspoon table salt

¼ cup shaved Parmesan cheese

3 tablespoons torn fresh basil leaves

1 tablespoon balsamic glaze (optional)

why this recipe works Sheet-pan pizza is so easy, so well sized, and so good that we just had to develop a second option. This caprese pizza is fresh and light, with summer caprese toppings brought together by bright basil pesto. The pizza serves two, but we think it's also well suited to one person (late night seconds?). You can use homemade or store-bought dough. We recommend making our Perfect Pesto (page 335), but you can also use store-bought pesto here. If the dough springs back in step 3, let it rest for a few minutes before trying to stretch it again.

1 One hour before baking, adjust oven rack to lowest position, place pizza stone on rack, and heat oven to 500 degrees.

2 **For the tomatoes:** Toss all ingredients together in bowl. Transfer to colander set over bowl; set aside to drain.

3 **For the pizza:** Spray 13 by 9-inch rimmed baking sheet with vegetable oil spray. Transfer dough to sheet and gently stretch to corners of sheet, pressing lightly with your fingertips to deflate dough and carefully lifting corners and edges to pull toward edges of sheet. (It's OK if dough shrinks back slightly from corners of sheet at this point.) Cover loosely with plastic and let rise in warm place until slightly puffed, about 20 minutes.

4 Press dough all the way to edges and corners of sheet. Using your fingertips, pinch edges of dough against sides of sheet to form small lip. Spread pesto into thin layer over surface of dough, leaving ½-inch border. Evenly distribute mozzarella over entire surface of dough, making sure some cheese sits on edges of dough against pan. Sprinkle with reserved drained tomatoes, pepper, and salt.

5 Bake until cheese is bubbly and well browned, about 15 minutes, rotating sheet halfway through baking. Run knife around edge of sheet to loosen pizza and transfer pizza to wire rack. Let cool for 5 minutes. Top pizza with Parmesan and basil leaves. Drizzle with balsamic glaze, if using. Slice and serve.

breakfast pizza

serves 2 • **total time** 45 minutes plus 20 minutes rising

3 tablespoons extra-virgin olive oil, divided, plus extra for drizzling

8 ounces Basic Pizza Dough (page 334), room temperature

4 ounces whole-milk block mozzarella cheese, shredded (1 cup)

¼ cup grated Parmesan cheese

2 ounces (¼ cup) cottage cheese

⅛ teaspoon dried oregano

4 ounces breakfast sausage, casings removed

4 large eggs

⅛ teaspoon table salt

⅛ teaspoon pepper

2 tablespoons minced fresh chives

why this recipe works We've illustrated how easy—advantageous even—it is to feast on pizza in a small household. What if you could get all your breakfast food groups on a crisp crust to bake, slice, and serve in about an hour's time? This recipe creates a shortcut white sauce with a simple spread of seasoned cottage cheese and topping of mozzarella and Parmesan on a parbaked crust. We parbake the crust so it doesn't need much time in the oven once the eggs are added on top; your final cooking time will depend on how you like your eggs. Crumbles of breakfast sausage add satisfying savor and a sprinkling of fresh chive freshens this rich breakfast dish. You can use homemade or store-bought dough. We prefer small-curd (sometimes labeled "country-style") cottage cheese here.

1 Spray 13 by 9-inch rimmed baking sheet with vegetable oil spray then brush bottom with 2 tablespoons oil. Transfer dough to sheet and gently stretch to corners, pressing lightly with your fingertips to deflate dough and carefully lifting corners and edges to pull toward edges of sheet. (It's OK if dough shrinks back slightly from corners of sheet at this point.) Brush dough evenly with 1 teaspoon oil, cover loosely with plastic wrap, and let rise in warm place until slightly puffed, about 20 minutes. Adjust oven rack to lowest position and heat oven to 450 degrees.

2 Press dough all the way to edges and corners of sheet. Using your fingertips, pinch edges of dough against sides of sheet to form small lip. Bake until dough has puffed slightly, 5 to 7 minutes.

3 Combine mozzarella and Parmesan in bowl. Combine cottage cheese, oregano, and remaining 2 teaspoons oil in separate bowl. Remove sheet from oven and, using spatula, press down on any air bubbles. Spread cottage cheese mixture evenly over top, leaving ½-inch border around edges. Pinch sausage into dime-size pieces and arrange evenly over cottage cheese mixture. Sprinkle mozzarella mixture evenly over pizza, leaving ½-inch border. Using back of spoon, create 4 evenly spaced indentations in cheese, each about 3 inches in diameter. Crack 1 egg into each well, then sprinkle with salt and pepper.

4 Bake until crust is golden brown on bottom and eggs are just set, 9 to 10 minutes for slightly runny yolks or 11 to 12 minutes for soft but set yolks. Remove pizza from pan and transfer to wire rack; let rest for 5 minutes. Sprinkle with chives and drizzle with extra oil. Slice and serve.

nutritional information for our recipes

To calculate the nutritional values of our recipes per serving, we used The Food Processor SQL by ESHA Research. When using this program, we entered all the ingredients, using weights for important ingredients such as most vegetables. We also used our preferred brands in these analyses. When the recipe called for seasoning with an unspecified amount of salt and pepper, we added ½ teaspoon of salt and ¼ teaspoon of pepper to the analysis. We did not include additional salt or pepper for food that's "seasoned to taste." If there is a range in the serving size, we used the highest number of servings to calculate the nutritional values.

	CAL	TOTAL FAT (G)	SAT FAT (G)	CHOL (MG)	SODIUM (MG)	TOTAL CARBS (G)	DIETARY FIBER (G)	TOTAL SUGARS (G)	ADDED SUGAR (G)	PROTEIN (G)
Chapter 1. Cookies and Bars										
Chewy Chocolate Chip Cookies	200	9	6	30	110	29	1	21	21	2
Oatmeal Raisin Cookies	190	7	4	45	70	27	1	16	12	3
Soft and Chewy Molasses Spice Cookies	180	8	3.5	30	80	29	0	17	17	2
Chocolate Crinkle Cookies	150	5	3	35	90	25	1	19	18	2
Coffee Toffee Cookies	160	7	4	30	100	22	0	13	13	2
Peanut Butter Sandwich Cookies	230	15	4.5	10	160	23	1	15	14	6
Madeleines	70	4.5	2.5	40	70	7	0	4	4	1
Browned Butter–Cardamom Madeleines	70	4.5	2.5	40	70	7	0	4	4	1
Chocolate-Hazelnut Madeleines	100	6	3.5	40	70	10	0	6	4	1
Lemon Madeleines	70	4.5	2.5	40	70	7	0	4	4	1
Fudgy Brownies	220	10	6	60	85	30	0	23	15	3
Browned Butter Blondies	300	14	6	50	230	41	1	28	27	4
Lemon Bars	260	13	8	120	160	32	0	21	21	3
Ultranutty Pecan Bars	340	25	6	20	105	29	2	15	14	3
Cherry Streusel Bars	240	10	6	25	50	33	1	20	10	2
Chapter 2. Crisps, Crumbles, Custards, and More										
Apple Crisp	730	34	15	60	300	111	11	77	39	5
Individual Blueberry Crumbles with Cornmeal and Lavender	660	24	14	60	80	108	5	63	49	6
Pear Crumble with Miso and Almonds	770	32	18	80	410	113	8	72	37	8
Cherry-Pecan Crumble	480	17	7	30	220	76	5	48	21	7

	CAL	TOTAL FAT (G)	SAT FAT (G)	CHOL (MG)	SODIUM (MG)	TOTAL CARBS (G)	DIETARY FIBER (G)	TOTAL SUGARS (G)	ADDED SUGAR (G)	PROTEIN (G)
Chapter 2. Crisps, Crumbles, Custards, and More (cont.)										
Strawberry-Rhubarb Crumble	620	17	11	45	390	113	3	79	74	5
Apple-Blackberry Betty	610	20	11	45	590	99	5	54	32	7
Peach Cobbler	540	18	11	45	520	90	4	59	35	7
Cherry Cobbler with Spiced Wine	610	11	7	30	450	111	1	48	46	6
Griddled Corn Cakes with Berry Compote and Cream	680	43	24	115	530	63	5	26	19	11
Clafouti	380	14	8	130	150	56	2	43	28	7
German Pancake	710	25	12	415	490	91	0	26	19	26
Apple Topping	190	6	3.5	15	80	35	3	30	13	0
Banana Topping	190	6	3.5	15	80	37	3	26	13	1
Crepes with Sugar and Lemon	160	6	3	60	110	20	0	7	5	5
Crepes with Chocolate and Orange	190	8	4	60	110	26	0	12	7	5
Crepes with Honey and Toasted Almonds	190	9	3	60	260	22	1	8	6	6
Classic Bread Pudding	740	29	17	255	640	103	0	60	38	15
Banana–Peanut Butter Bread Pudding	920	46	20	255	710	107	4	54	39	23
Dirty Chai Bread Pudding	680	29	17	255	640	89	0	45	38	15
Individual Chocolate Soufflés	380	23	12	200	170	41	0	33	14	10
Individual Mocha Soufflés	380	23	12	200	170	42	0	33	14	10
Individual Pavlovas with Berries, Lime, and Basil Topping	550	22	14	70	150	84	6	78	71	7
Individual Pavlovas with Mango, Kiwi, and Mint Topping	590	22	14	70	75	95	3	90	70	7
Strawberry Shortcakes	530	36	23	115	390	46	2	17	9	7
Brown Sugar–Berry Shortcakes	600	37	23	115	400	62	6	31	23	8
Rhubarb Shortcakes	590	36	23	115	400	60	2	32	28	7
Whipped Cream	10	1	0.5	5	0	0	0	0	0	0
Berry Gratins	170	8	4.5	110	85	22	2	19	13	3
Lemon, Blueberry, and Almond Parfaits	730	43	23	170	280	84	3	71	13	8
Guava, Strawberry, and Tahini Parfaits	680	42	25	115	250	73	2	60	53	6
Crème Brûlée	580	50	30	410	120	27	0	26	23	7
Roasted Sesame Crème Brûlée	620	54	31	410	120	29	0	26	23	9
Tea-Infused Crème Brûlée	580	50	30	410	120	27	0	26	23	7
Flan	410	12	6	215	160	64	0	64	19	13

	CAL	TOTAL FAT (G)	SAT FAT (G)	CHOL (MG)	SODIUM (MG)	TOTAL CARBS (G)	DIETARY FIBER (G)	TOTAL SUGARS (G)	ADDED SUGAR (G)	PROTEIN (G)
Chapter 3. Cakes										
Molten Chocolate Microwave Mug Cakes	570	36	20	245	470	59	9	38	25	10
Molten Mocha Microwave Mug Cakes	580	36	20	245	470	61	0	38	25	10
S'mores Molten Microwave Mug Cakes	640	33	19	245	370	75	1	39	26	11
Vanilla Cupcakes	630	39	24	150	210	66	0	48	47	4
Olive Oil Cake	340	16	2.5	50	220	45	0	28	27	4
Coconut Snack Cake	510	30	20	105	400	55	0	34	27	7
Whole-Wheat Carrot Snack Cake	470	25	10	90	440	55	5	34	31	7
Blueberry Buckle	460	18	11	90	200	68	2	39	32	6
Cinnamon Streusel Coffee Cake	580	24	25	110	630	81	1	45	43	8
Pound Cakes	440	25	15	155	240	50	0	33	33	5
Lemon Pound Cakes	440	25	15	155	240	50	1	33	33	5
Ginger Pound Cakes	460	25	15	155	240	54	1	37	33	5
Blueberry Compote	35	0	0	0	35	8	2	6	3	0
Cider-Glazed Apple-Spelt Mini Bundt Cakes	510	16	9	85	410	83	7	47	32	7
Vanilla Cake	1210	75	47	205	380	128	0	105	103	5
Chocolate Cake	1170	68	38	255	610	133	0	109	107	8
Vanilla Frosting	810	58	37	160	75	71	0	70	70	0
Coffee Frosting	810	58	37	160	75	72	0	70	70	0
Coconut Frosting	810	58	37	160	75	71	0	70	70	0
Orange Frosting	810	58	37	160	75	72	0	70	70	0
Raspberry Buttercream	820	58	37	160	75	74	1	71	69	1
Chocolate Ermine Frosting	1530	107	66	215	140	162	0	99	61	8
Cream Cheese Frosting	410	31	18	85	250	32	0	30	28	3
Passion Fruit Curd	370	23	15	45	15	42	0	38	23	2
Financiers	120	8	3	15	40	11	1	9	8	2
Chocolate Chunk Financiers	170	12	5	15	40	16	2	12	8	3
Plum Financiers	120	8	3	15	40	11	1	9	8	2
Raspberry Financiers	120	8	3	15	40	11	1	9	8	2
Chocolate-Raspberry Torte	660	48	23	155	200	61	3	45	17	11
Rustic Peach Cake	300	16	2.5	45	220	37	1	23	19	4
French Apple Cake	470	30	5	50	290	49	0	34	25	5

	CAL	TOTAL FAT (G)	SAT FAT (G)	CHOL (MG)	SODIUM (MG)	TOTAL CARBS (G)	DIETARY FIBER (G)	TOTAL SUGARS (G)	ADDED SUGAR (G)	PROTEIN (G)
Chapter 3. Cakes (cont.)										
Semolina and Ricotta Cake	340	17	10	140	260	33	1	25	21	12
Cranberry Upside-Down Cake	390	17	10	130	160	54	1	38	33	5
Pear-Walnut Upside-Down Cake	490	29	9	75	230	54	3	42	36	5
Individual New York Cheesecakes	950	72	46	425	710	56	0	47	39	16
Basque Cheesecake	520	34	22	240	330	41	0	36	33	10
Chapter 4. Pies and Tarts										
Fried Peach Hand Pies	410	23	7	25	370	46	1	19	12	5
Sweet Cherry Pie	540	28	18	75	340	67	3	31	16	6
Lemon Ricotta Pie	410	26	16	125	250	34	1	16	14	11
Icebox Strawberry Pie	440	26	16	75	210	50	2	27	21	5
Banana Cream Pie	550	34	21	230	270	55	2	30	18	8
Key Lime Pie	340	16	9	130	80	40	0	37	4	6
Classic Cheese Quiche	330	23	14	155	370	20	0	4	2	10
Ham and Swiss Quiche	350	24	14	160	490	20	0	4	2	13
Quiche Lorraine	390	29	15	160	450	21	1	4	2	12
Chocolate-Pecan Slab Pie	800	54	24	150	350	72	4	47	44	9
Triple-Berry Slab Pie with Ginger-Lemon Streusel	460	22	14	60	250	61	4	26	17	5
Foolproof All-Butter Pie Dough	770	50	32	135	580	71	1	9	6	9
Whole-Grain All-Butter Pie Dough	790	51	32	135	580	74	7	8	6	11
Slab Pie Dough	770	50	32	135	580	71	1	9	6	9
Apple Galette	240	9	5	10	125	36	3	20	4	3
Rustic Berry Tart	560	28	18	75	290	71	3	29	19	7
Pineapple, Ginger, and Lime Tarts	670	28	18	75	370	100	4	56	16	7
Pear and Chestnut Tarts	730	49	26	180	350	69	4	28	1	13
Pear and Almond Tarts	730	55	26	180	250	56	5	20	1	14
Tarte Tatin	570	29	18	75	380	74	3	44	35	4
Lemon Tartlets	510	34	19	440	125	40	0	12	10	11
Walnut Tartlets	910	53	23	185	310	98	2	55	54	11

	CAL	TOTAL FAT (G)	SAT FAT (G)	CHOL (MG)	SODIUM (MG)	TOTAL CARBS (G)	DIETARY FIBER (G)	TOTAL SUGARS (G)	ADDED SUGAR (G)	PROTEIN (G)
Chapter 4. Pies and Tarts (cont.)										
Chocolate–Passion Fruit Tartlets	820	57	36	130	180	71	0	39	25	7
Rustic Tart Dough	430	28	18	75	290	38	0	0	0	5
Browned-Butter Tart Shells	360	22	14	60	75	36	0	10	10	4
Browned-Butter Whole-Wheat Tart Shells	370	23	14	60	75	39	4	11	10	5
Chapter 5. Pastries and Pockets										
Easy Apple Turnovers	340	16	8	45	230	51	4	19	7	6
Guava and Cheese Pastelitos	360	21	11	60	270	46	1	17	15	7
Everything Bagel Danish	420	31	18	85	690	31	1	3	0	9
Goat Cheese, Sun-Dried Tomato, and Basil Danish	400	27	14	65	500	29	1	2	0	13
Hortopita	670	44	12	130	1070	49	4	5	0	18
Eggplant and Tomato Phyllo Pie	560	39	9	25	1420	40	4	6	0	13
Apple Strudel	630	21	12	55	430	107	0	41	11	10
Bean and Cheese Pupusas	200	8	3.5	15	490	26	4	1	0	9
Curtido	15	0	0	0	85	3	1	2	0	1
Chicken and Potato Empanadas	230	10	1	25	620	26	1	1	0	8
Beef and Potato Empanadas	240	11	2	20	610	26	1	1	0	8
Jamaican Beef Patties	600	40	21	160	690	41	1	3	2	18
Ham and Cheddar Hand Pies	490	18	8	145	1630	55	0	7	0	28
Salami, Capicola, and Provolone Stromboli	630	28	12	165	2140	56	0	8	0	36
Spinach Calzones	630	31	13	150	1510	61	2	9	0	31
Buffalo Chicken Calzones	700	31	15	115	2100	57	0	9	0	47
Cardamom-Orange Morning Buns	420	26	16	75	310	42	0	20	10	4
Croissants	440	25	16	95	360	42	2	5	4	9
Pain au Chocolat	440	25	16	85	320	43	2	10	3	8
Prosciutto and Gruyère Croissants	530	32	19	125	860	42	2	5	4	18
Chapter 6. Biscuits, Scones, and Muffins										
Easiest-Ever Drop Biscuits	460	10	6	25	270	81	3	1	0	12
Easiest-Ever Cinnamon-Sugar Drop Biscuits	370	21	13	55	270	45	1	26	25	3
Easiest-Ever Herb Drop Biscuits	150	6	3.5	15	270	19	1	1	0	3
Easiest-Ever Pepper-Bacon Drop Biscuits	490	12	6	30	350	81	3	1	0	13

	CAL	TOTAL FAT (G)	SAT FAT (G)	CHOL (MG)	SODIUM (MG)	TOTAL CARBS (G)	DIETARY FIBER (G)	TOTAL SUGARS (G)	ADDED SUGAR (G)	PROTEIN (G)
Chapter 6. Biscuits, Scones, and Muffins (cont.)										
Cream Biscuits	380	0.5	14	70	360	39	1	3	1	7
Sun-Dried Tomato and Za'atar Biscuits	260	16	9	45	330	25	1	2	1	5
Flaky Whole-Wheat Buttermilk Biscuits	380	21	12	50	800	44	3	5	3	8
Flaky Buttermilk Biscuits	360	20	12	50	800	40	0	5	3	6
British-Style Currant Scones	340	19	12	55	250	38	2	10	4	5
Maple-Pecan Scones with Maple Glaze	400	24	13	55	320	43	2	14	13	5
Blue Cheese–Apple Rye Scones	290	17	10	90	590	26	2	4	1	9
Lemon Blueberry Muffins	320	12	7	35	290	51	1	31	28	4
Whole-Wheat Apple-Spice Muffins	350	16	1.5	45	420	51	2	32	21	4
From-the-Freezer Cranberry-Cardamom Muffins	290	10	1	30	320	43	1	20	19	5
From-the-Freezer Chocolate–Crystallized Ginger Muffins	360	15	3.5	30	320	53	2	29	26	6
From-the-Freezer Raspberry-Almond Muffins	290	11	2	30	310	44	2	21	19	5
Corn Muffins	310	14	8	80	380	41	1	13	12	6
Apricot-Orange Corn Muffins	330	14	8	80	380	46	2	18	12	6
Cheddar-Scallion Corn Muffins	360	20	11	95	500	36	2	8	6	10
Bacon-Cheddar Muffins	350	20	9	135	500	29	0	2	0	12
Pepperoni Pizza Muffins	360	21	10	140	710	29	0	2	0	13
Chapter 7. Breads and Rolls										
Garlic and Herb Breadsticks	80	2.5	1	5	240	14	0	2	0	2
Fennel–Black Pepper Breadsticks	80	2.5	1	5	240	14	0	2	0	2
Spicy Parmesan Breadsticks	90	3	1.5	5	250	14	0	2	0	3
Individual Honey-Thyme Monkey Breads	350	17	6	15	1050	44	0	13	8	5
Individual Onion, Poppy Seed, and Parmesan Monkey Breads	400	24	10	30	1160	39	1	6	0	8
Individual Pumpkin Spice Monkey Breads	380	20	8	25	980	45	0	15	10	5
Popovers	180	3.5	1.5	100	350	26	1	3	0	9
Fresh-Corn Cornbread	310	12	6	75	470	44	5	6	3	7
Cheese Bread with Feta and Nigella	190	9	5	65	380	20	0	2	0	7

	CAL	TOTAL FAT (G)	SAT FAT (G)	CHOL (MG)	SODIUM (MG)	TOTAL CARBS (G)	DIETARY FIBER (G)	TOTAL SUGARS (G)	ADDED SUGAR (G)	PROTEIN (G)
Chapter 7. Breads and Rolls (cont.)										
Banana Bread	160	4	0	0	190	28	1	13	10	4
Chocolate Banana Bread	180	5	1	0	190	31	1	15	10	4
Date Banana Bread	160	2	0	0	190	32	2	17	10	4
Zucchini Bread	210	7	2	45	150	33	1	21	20	5
Cocoa Zucchini Bread with Cherries	220	3.5	2	45	150	43	1	27	20	4
Orange Zucchini Bread with Pistachios	210	6	2	45	150	34	1	21	20	5
Brown Soda Bread	350	8	4	15	700	59	5	8	5	11
Brown Soda Bread with Currants and Caraway	400	8	4	15	700	73	6	20	5	12
Brown Soda Bread with Walnuts and Cocoa Nibs	450	18	6	15	700	63	5	8	5	14
No-Knead Mini Country Boule	220	0	0	0	440	43	3	0	0	8
From-the-Freezer Dinner Rolls	130	2.5	1.5	5	150	23	1	2	2	4
No-Knead Whole-Wheat Dinner Rolls	220	0	0	0	440	43	3	0	0	8
No-Knead Spelt, Olive, and Herb Dinner Rolls	310	3	0	0	660	57	6	0	0	10
No-Knead Whole-Wheat Fruit and Nut Rolls	290	4.5	0	0	440	52	4	7	0	9
Brioche Hamburger Buns	340	14	8	125	470	40	2	4	4	10
Bolos Lêvedos	330	8	4.5	65	320	54	0	13	12	8
From-the-Freezer Cinnamon Buns	360	10	6	55	65	60	2	28	27	7
Sour Cream Glaze	100	1.5	1	5	10	23	0	22	22	0
Chapter 8. Flatbreads and Pizzas										
Flour Tortillas	130	5	1.5	0	240	17	0	0	0	2
Corn Tortillas	80	2.5	0	0	260	14	1	0	0	2
Chapatis	300	14	1	0	580	40	3	0	0	7
Pan-Grilled Flatbreads	530	15	5	15	490	85	4	7	6	15
Pan-Grilled Garlic-Cilantro Flatbreads	630	25	10	35	500	86	4	7	6	15
Pan-Grilled Honey-Chile Flatbreads	610	22	10	35	490	89	4	11	10	15
Scallion Pancakes	310	19	1.5	0	500	28	0	1	1	5

	CAL	TOTAL FAT (G)	SAT FAT (G)	CHOL (MG)	SODIUM (MG)	TOTAL CARBS (G)	DIETARY FIBER (G)	TOTAL SUGARS (G)	ADDED SUGAR (G)	PROTEIN (G)
Chapter 8. Flatbreads and Pizzas (cont.)										
Mana'eesh Za'atar	590	31	4.5	0	660	65	1	0	0	10
Tomato Mana'eesh	510	19	2.5	0	1030	75	4	4	0	11
Cheese Mana'eesh	610	25	12	60	1190	71	3	3	0	25
Za'atar	5	0	0	0	35	1	0	0	0	0
Lahmajun	590	13	4.5	30	1310	94	2	4	0	21
Cucumber-Tomato Salad	110	9	1	0	530	6	2	3	0	1
Focaccia	380	14	2	0	650	53	0	1	1	8
Anchovy and Chive Focaccia	410	16	2.5	10	1020	53	0	1	1	11
Grape, Fennel, and Charred Shallot Focaccia	420	15	2	0	660	61	1	7	1	8
Pear and Bacon Flatbread	730	41	15	55	1680	64	3	10	0	22
Mushroom-Miso Flatbread	710	35	8	30	1580	70	3	7	1	26
Easy Skillet Cheese Pizza	680	39	13	45	1480	60	1	11	0	24
Cast-Iron Pan Pizza	740	42	17	75	1310	61	2	2	0	30
Cast-Iron Pan Pizza with Pepperoni, Pickled Peppers, and Honey	830	48	20	95	1700	65	2	4	3	32
Thin-Crust Pizza	370	11	5	25	1120	50	2	6	3	16
Fontina, Arugula, and Prosciutto Pizza	440	16	7	45	1470	51	2	6	3	20
Goat Cheese, Olive, and Garlic Pizza	450	19	7	25	1060	50	2	6	3	16
Ricotta, Bacon, and Scallion Pizza	390	12	6	30	1130	51	2	6	3	17
Basic Pizza Dough	320	3.5	0.5	0	580	58	2	0	0	11
Basic Whole-Wheat Pizza Dough	250	4.5	0.5	0	580	44	4	0	0	9
Pizza Sauce	20	1	0	0	290	2	0	1	0	0
Perfect Pesto	80	8	1	0	85	0	0	0	0	1
Garlic Oil	130	14	1	0	0	0	0	0	0	0
Pepperoni Sheet-Pan Pizza	830	46	20	105	2340	69	2	13	1	39
Caprese Sheet-Pan Pizza	800	48	17	60	2380	56	2	4	1	29
Breakfast Pizza	960	60	19	510	1890	59	0	9	0	47

conversions and equivalents

Some say baking is a science and an art. We would say that geography has a hand in it, too. Flours and sugars manufactured in the United Kingdom and elsewhere will feel and taste different from those manufactured in the United States. So we cannot promise that the loaf of bread you bake in Canada or England will taste the same as a loaf baked in the States, but we can offer guidelines for converting weights and measures. We also recommend that you rely on your instincts when making our recipes. Refer to the visual cues provided. If the dough hasn't "come together in a ball" as described, you may need to add more flour—even if the recipe doesn't tell you to. You be the judge.

The recipes in this book were developed using standard U.S. measures following U.S. government guidelines. The charts below offer equivalents for U.S. and metric measures. All conversions are approximate and have been rounded up or down to the nearest whole number.

example:
1 teaspoon = 4.9292 milliliters, rounded up to 5 milliliters
1 ounce = 28.3495 grams, rounded down to 28 grams

volume conversions

u.s.	metric
1 teaspoon	5 milliliters
2 teaspoons	10 milliliters
1 tablespoon	15 milliliters
2 tablespoons	30 milliliters
¼ cup	59 milliliters
⅓ cup	79 milliliters
½ cup	118 milliliters
¾ cup	177 milliliters
1 cup	237 milliliters
1¼ cups	296 milliliters
1½ cups	355 milliliters
2 cups (1 pint)	473 milliliters
2½ cups	591 milliliters
3 cups	710 milliliters
4 cups (1 quart)	0.946 liter
1.06 quarts	1 liter
4 quarts (1 gallon)	3.8 liters

weight conversions

ounces	grams
½	14
¾	21
1	28
1½	43
2	57
2½	71
3	85
3½	99
4	113
4½	128
5	142
6	170
7	198
8	227
9	255
10	283
12	340
16 (1 pound)	454

conversions for common baking ingredients

Baking is an exacting science. Because measuring by weight is far more accurate than measuring by volume, and thus more likely to produce reliable results, in our recipes we provide ounce measures in addition to cup measures for many ingredients. Refer to the chart below to convert these measures into grams.

ingredient	ounces	grams
flour		
1 cup all-purpose flour*	5	142
1 cup cake flour	4	113
1 cup whole-wheat flour	5½	156
sugar		
1 cup granulated (white) sugar	7	198
1 cup packed brown sugar (light or dark)	7	198
1 cup confectioners' sugar	4	113
cocoa powder		
1 cup cocoa powder	3	85
butter†		
4 tablespoons (½ stick or ¼ cup)	2	57
8 tablespoons (1 stick or ½ cup)	4	113
16 tablespoons (2 sticks or 1 cup)	8	227

* U.S. all-purpose flour, the most frequently used flour in this book, does not contain leaveners, as some European flours do. These leavened flours are called self-rising or self-raising. If you are using self-rising flour, take this into consideration before adding leaveners to a recipe.

† In the United States, butter is sold both salted and unsalted. We generally recommend unsalted butter. If you are using salted butter, take this into consideration before adding salt to a recipe.

oven temperatures

fahrenheit	celsius	gas mark
225	105	¼
250	120	½
275	135	1
300	150	2
325	165	3
350	180	4
375	190	5
400	200	6
425	220	7
450	230	8
475	245	9

converting temperatures from an instant-read thermometer

We include doneness temperatures in many of the recipes in this book. We recommend an instant-read thermometer for the job. Refer to the table above to convert Fahrenheit degrees to Celsius. Or, for temperatures not represented in the chart, use this simple formula:

Subtract 32 degrees from the Fahrenheit reading, then divide the result by 1.8 to find the Celsius reading.

example:
"Cook caramel until it registers 234 degrees."

to convert:
234°F − 32 = 202°
202° ÷ 1.8 = 112.22°C, rounded down to 112°C

index

note: Page references in *italics* indicate photographs.

O